Only Judgment

Only Judgment

The Limits of Litigation in Social Change

ARYEH NEIER

International Debate Education Association

New York, London & Amsterdam

Published by:
International Debate Education Association
400 West 59th Street
New York, NY 10019

Originally published by Wesleyan University Press

Library of Congress Cataloging-in-Publication Data

Neier, Aryeh, 1937-
  Only judgment : the limits of litigation in social change / Aryeh Neier.
    p. cm.
  Includes bibliographical references and index.
  ISBN 978-1-61770-044-6
  1. Adversary system (Law)--United States. 2. Actions and defenses-
-United States. 3. Courts--United States. 4. Justice, Administration
of--United States. 5. Sociological jurisprudence. 6. Political questions and
judicial power--United States. 7. Law reform--United States. I. Title.
  KF8915.N44 2012
  303.40973--dc23
                    2012007926

Design by Kathleen Hayes
Printed in the USA

 IDEBATE Press

For Yvette

Contents

Foreword

Thirty years have passed since I published *Only Judgment*. Much has changed, with some matters discussed then having been overtaken by events. Yet, I see no real necessity to revise the basic thesis of the book: litigation can be an important means of social change. Such use of litigation derives its legitimacy in substantial part from its efficacy in making the elected branches of government more representative. This is particularly the case when litigation is undertaken on behalf of disadvantaged minorities whose rights and interests may be overlooked or ignored in the political process. By themselves, courts have little power to enforce their decisions—they depend on the legislative and executive branches of government to carry them out. It is by requiring the legislative and executive branches of government to address issues affecting the disadvantaged on which they have pronounced judgment that courts help to make those bodies more representative.

When I published *Only Judgment* in 1982, my sole focus was on the United States. At that point, litigation to promote social change was far more developed in America than elsewhere. Other countries where litigation had been so used included India, the United Kingdom, and South Africa. In South Africa, two organizations, the Legal Resources Center and the Center for Applied Legal Studies, had recently been established and begun an effort to use the courts to mitigate the harshness of the apartheid system.

In the intervening years, public interest litigation—the term that subsequently came into use to describe litigation to promote social change—has spread to many other countries. To some extent, this development has been fostered by the establishment of regional courts, including the European Court of Human Rights, the Inter-American Court of Human Rights, and the ECOWAS Court in West Africa, that have the power to override the decisions of national courts. In addition, the creation of constitutional courts on a national level in a number of countries has contributed to the development of public interest litigation. This means of promoting social change has even spread to countries where recourse to such bodies is not available, and there is little or no prospect that courts will hand down decisions than run counter to established public policies. An example is China, where litigators attempt to address such issues as damage to the environment by industrial polluters; the rights of migrants not considered to be legal residents of cities that depend on their labor to gain access to city services such as public education for their children; and the rights of the disabled. Framing their arguments in legal terms and getting attention for those arguments by placing them before a court are, by themselves, important means for getting state authorities to consider these issues more seriously than they would otherwise. Sometimes the authorities are apparently persuaded to modify their policies.

In addition to describing the way that litigation has succeeded in promoting social change, I also wrote in *Only Judgment* about what I thought were the limits of its utility for such purposes. In the United States, what is more apparent than it was three decades ago is that limits exist on the possibility of bringing about shifts in public policy through litigation on behalf of the disadvantaged. What has become, somewhat bizarrely, relatively common is for those with every advantage in the political process, such as corporations, to use the courts to set aside the actions of the representative branches of government. Clearly, in the United States, public interest litigation can be a double-edged sword. Perhaps the main lesson to be derived from the American experience is that those individuals or organizations in other countries who are pursuing litigation for purposes of social change must simultaneously address concerns about legitimacy. The sole focus should not be on outcomes—the process by which those outcomes are sought is important in its own right.

Aryeh Neier
February 2012

Acknowledgments

The Twentieth Century Fund provided me with a generous grant that permitted me to withdraw for a period from the day-in-day-out struggle for legal rights and to study, think and write about what I had been doing. This book would not have been written without that support and I am very grateful for it. I am also indebted to New York University Law School for permitting me to explore the ideas that went into this book with students in the seminars I conducted on litigation and public policy. Another branch of NYU, the New York Institute for the Humanities, provided me with an extraordinarily pleasant setting in which to do the actual writing of this book and good company to talk to about what I was writing and about everything else under the sun. Most of all, I thank the hundreds of skillful, imaginative, and dedicated litigators I came to know during the more than fifteen years I spent as a member of the staff of the American Civil Liberties Union. My debt to them and, I believe, the country's debt to them, are incalculable.

Introduction

"The power vested in the American courts of justice of pronouncing a statute to be unconstitutional," Alexis de Tocqueville observed, "forms one of the most powerful barriers which has ever been devised against the tyranny of political assemblies."[1]

Such power was exercised sparingly in Tocqueville's time. Today courts pronounce statutes to be unconstitutional far more frequently than they did a century and a half ago. Courts play a much more important role in limiting the powers of political assemblies today, however, by construing laws expansively or narrowly; by delaying, sometimes to death, implementation of the decisions of the representative branches of government; by ordering the parties to litigation to produce documents and testimony sought by their opponents; by helping to define an aggrieved class of citizens; by providing a forum in which litigants publicize their grievances; and, most important, by placing grievances on the agendas of the legislative and executive branches of government.

The role played by the courts in determining public policy seems so great that some complain that, far from providing relief from tyranny, the courts themselves are tyrannical. There is talk of an "imperial judiciary" overriding majorities that prevail in political assemblies to advance the cause of favored minorities. "The justices are become a law unto themselves,"[2] complains legal historian Raoul Berger. Attorney General William French Smith accuses the federal courts of an "erosion of restraint in considerations of "justiciability"; of "the extravagant use of mandatory injunctions and remedial decrees"; of "a weakening of resolve to abide by the case or controversy requirement"; and of "forc[ing] major reallocations of governmental resources often with no concern for budgetary limits and the dislocations that inevitably result from the limited judicial perspective."[3] Harvard Law School professor Charles Fried writes that judges are guilty of "usurpation" of power.[4] Even Anthony Lewis of the *New York Times*, an admirer of Earl Warren's leadership in public policy making during his sixteen years as chief justice, has written that "Warren was the closest thing the United States has had to a Platonic Guardian, dispensing law from a throne without any sensed limits of power except what was seen as the good of society."[5] Lewis's comment deliberately invokes Learned Hand's famous statement, "For myself it would be most irksome to be ruled by a bevy of Platonic Guardians, even if I knew how to choose them, which I assuredly do not."[6]

If judicial policy making seems vulnerable to such criticism, it is frequently more consonant with principles of representative government than is generally recognized. Litigation designed to elicit policy making differs fundamentally from traditional litigation, of course, in that it is designed primarily to promote the interests of a class of persons rather than to correct the wrongs done to a particular litigant. The effectiveness of such litigation in promoting changes in public policy, whether through constitutional adjudication or other means, influences many interest groups to turn first to lawyers to help them pursue their goals. They bring the issues to the courts that keep judges in the forefront of public policy development. Despite the transition in the United States Supreme Court from the era of Earl Warren, in which public policy litigation was reputed to be favored, to the era of Warren Burger, in which it is reputedly disfavored, there is no evidence that interest groups have reduced their reliance on litigation to advance their causes.

Professional staffs of lawyers are now employed by specialized organizations seeking to further the interests of such diverse groups as blacks, Chicanos, Puerto Ricans, native Americans, Asian Americans, Jews, women, homosexuals, food stamp users, animal lovers, abortion proponents, abortion opponents, the physically handicapped, the mentally ill, the mentally retarded, taxpayers, government employees, labor union members, labor union dissidents, opponents of labor unions, the deaf, hospital patients, migrant workers, prisoners, former prisoners, veterans, nonsmokers, smokers, marijuana users, television audiences, children, old people, critics of national security practices, victims of crime, advocates of tougher law enforcement, opponents of the draft and draft registration, the poor, consumers, and citizens concerned about the environment. They are met in court by attorneys employed by such business-sponsored groups as the Pacific Legal Foundation, the Washington Legal Foundation, the Mid-American Legal Foundation, the Mid-Atlantic Legal Foundation, the Capital Legal Foundation, the National Legal Center for the Public Interest, and the National Chamber Litigation Center, all adept at advancing their own causes through litigation, as when they sponsor lawsuits challenging pollution control legislation.

The emergence of this "public interest" bar is recent. Two decades ago, it would have been possible to assemble in one small living room all the lawyers in the United States professionally engaged in advancing causes through litigation. Today they would overflow the grand ballroom of a giant hotel. Virtually alone of the innovations of the 1960s, public interest litigation thrives. Massive civil rights demonstrations seem to belong to a bygone era; the Peace Corps long ago lost its luster; there are no more "hippies" and few communes. The antipoverty program has collapsed except for its legal services component—financially weakened by President Ronald Reagan, but surviving nevertheless. Organizations hiring lawyers to sue power companies or challenge sex discrimination, on the other hand, are deluged with applications from outstanding graduates of the best law schools. Public interest lawyers have become stock figures in popular novels and in television melodramas. They symbolize a convergence of idealism and professional skill.

Respect for public policy decisions reached through litigation exists side by side with widespread criticism of judicial power. The respect is evident in the rarity of overt and open defiance of the results of litigation by the other branches of government or by individual citizens. When the United States Supreme Court orders a president to turn over to a special prosecutor tapes of his conversations in the White House because "the legitimate needs of the judicial process outweigh presidential privilege,"[7] the president is compelled to comply. When the Court orders Congress to seat a man it has expelled, the Congress is compelled to comply.[8] When the Court deals with so emotionally charged a public issue as abortion or orders an end to criminal sanctions,[9] or stays implementation of a law terminating federal funding,[10] or upholds the law terminating federal funding,[11] public officials throughout the country comply. If they did not courts would be powerless to enforce their orders. Only widespread acceptance of the legitimacy of judicial authority brings about such compliance.

A 1979 lawsuit challenged President Jimmy Carter's unilateral abrogation of the Mutual Defense Treaty between the United States and Taiwan without the consent of Congress. The suit was brought by Senator Barry Goldwater, Republican of Arizona, and seven other senators, sixteen representatives, and one former senator, all described as political conservatives. They contended that just as the president must submit treaties to Congress for ratification, so he must ask Congress to ratify abrogation of treaties. The Supreme Court dismissed the suit—after a federal district court sided with Goldwater and a court of appeals reversed on the merits—as "nonjusticiable" because it involves the "authority of the President in the conduct of our country's foreign relations and the extent to which the Senate or the Congress is authorized to negate the action of the President."[12] To most students of judicial power, the result seemed inevitable. Yet the bringing of the lawsuit was a remarkable tribute to the legitimacy of litigation and to the prestige of the courts in settling political disputes. By joining as plaintiffs in the suit, twenty-four conservative members of Congress said, in effect, that they believe that the proper forum in which to resolve a conflict between Congress and the president over a crucial question of foreign policy is a court of law. It probably could not have happened anywhere else or in any earlier era of American history.

Some cause litigation detracts from the legitimacy of judicial decision making, as when the courts are employed by interest groups to secure unfair advantages. There is no consensus, of course, as to what constitutes unfair advantage. Is it when blacks persuade a judge to go beyond removal of legal barriers to school desegregation and order affirmative measures, like busing, to bring about integration? Or when a judge orders an employer to eliminate a criterion that job applicants must be high school graduates because it has a disparate impact on racial minorities and does not measure qualification? Or when an employer with a past record of discrimination is ordered to fill a certain percentage of job openings with minority applicants? Is it possible that a judicial decision reserving a certain percentage of job openings for women is less legitimate than a similar decision affecting blacks? What about the legitimacy of a judicial decision advancing the cause of environmentalists?

Cause litigation may be ranged along a spectrum. At one extreme is litigation on behalf of so disadvantaged a group as the mentally retarded. At the other extreme is litigation to advance the causes of groups suffering no special disadvantage in competing through the political processes favored by the civics texts, such as opponents of the Vietnam war or environmentalists. The most troublesome judgments involve locating the place on the spectrum that should be assigned to those neither clearly at one end nor the other end of the spectrum, such as the poor, or women, or women seeking abortions.

What criteria are employed to discriminate among causes and is there a sound basis in law for such discrimination? In addition to grappling with such questions by examining litigation to advance various causes, this book examines how the role of litigation has changed, the impact of litigation in advancing causes, and the impact of litigation on the movements espousing those causes. It explores the historical roots of the transformation that has taken place in the role of litigation, the interplay of litigation to advance causes and legislative and executive action, and the limits of litigation as a means of advancing the interests of causes. This last is especially important because activists in causes, litigators, and judges not sensitive to the limits of litigation often set back causes they mean to advance and the use of litigation to advance causes.

This book will serve its purpose if it contributes to thinking about whether litigation is an appropriate way to advance causes generally; if so, what causes; the manner in which litigation shapes public policy; and what is actually accomplished by litigation. Although these are matters of great importance and the subjects of considerable controversy, they are usually discussed as though the special role of litigation in American public life derived exclusively, as in

Tocqueville's time, from the power of the judiciary to pronounce statutes to be unconstitutional; as though litigation were exclusively a check on representative government and had not evolved into a means of enhancing its representativeness; as though all that matters about litigation is the final decision rendered by a judge; and as though implementation of judicial decisions affecting public policy could take place without representative ratification. The transformation that has taken place in the past three decades in the role of litigation is not directly considered in the typical law school curriculum, much less in graduate school, college, or high school political science courses. Editorial comments about the wisdom of particular judicial decisions appear regularly in the press and often deal with the appropriateness of resolving public policy questions through litigation, but such editorials rarely betray an awareness of the place that litigation has come to occupy in making representative government more representative. Some of the lawyers and judges taking part in the process certainly understand it and have coherent philosophies that guide them. Yet little of their thinking is communicated to the broad public that has a stake in the consequences.

1

Making Pluralism Work

It is a thesis of this book that litigation has earned the acceptance it now enjoys of its place in resolving public policy questions. Its role during the past three decades, starting with its great achievement in bringing about the United States Supreme Court's decision in *Brown* v. *Board of Education,*[1] warrants the deference paid by the other branches of government and by the American public to such policy decisions. Since the early 1950s, the courts have been the most accessible and, often, the most effective instrument of government for bringing about the changes in public policy sought by social protest movements. The causes espoused by these movements ought not to have equal claims on the attention and on the power of courts. Judicial intervention in some causes, I contend, is unwarranted whereas intervention in others should be greater. The resolution of other public policy questions detracts from the prestige and the aura of legitimacy of the courts.

The legitimacy of public policy litigation and of judicial authority to deal with a broad range of issues on balance seems more firmly established, and deservedly so, than ever before. Litigation and the exercise of judicial power in

America today do more than limit the tyranny of political assemblies. Although cause litigation sometimes produces results that validate the charge of judicial exercise of tyrannical powers, in our exceptionally diverse society cause litigation compels the other branches of government to become more representative.

Belief in the emergence of a new homogeneous nation, in which newcomers are assimilated in a generation or two, remained a central theme of the American dream for a century and a half, its most famous expression a line in Israel Zangwill's 1908 play, *The Melting Pot:* "America is God's Crucible, the Great Melting Pot."[2] The differences in American society that seemed ineradicable in the relatively short term during the melting pot era were racial and, more troublesome in the opinion of many, sectional, as between the North and the South and as between the East and the West. To deal with conflict stemming from such differences, the power of the central government in Washington had to grow relative to the power of the state governments. The Supreme Court's decisions generally enhanced the strength of the central government (*Dred Scott* v. *Sandford,*[3] of course, a disastrous exception), and judicial prestige grew accordingly.

The great depression of the 1930s shattered the melting pot image. It made Americans conscious of their diversity. WPA photographs, photographs in the new picture magazines, and the works of socially conscious moviemakers showed Americans pictures of themselves: poor rural whites in Appalachia; poor rural blacks in Alabama; Italian, Jewish, and Slavic immigrants on the lower East Side of New York City; farmers of Scandinavian stock in Minnesota; industrial workers in Detroit and Pittsburgh; the rich on New York's Park Avenue and on San Francisco's Nob Hill; and so on. The American dream was transformed. Heterogeneity began to be celebrated in place of homogeneity. And a new theory of American democracy emerged: pluralism.

In the civics text model of pluralist American democracy, citizens of similar origins and with similar interests join with each other in voluntary associations. Even though individual citizens have little prospect of making their voices heard by giant institutions of government, they may get attention within their own labor union, business association, or ethnic organization. Through these associations, citizens work out positions and programs designed to advance their common interests, which they press on elected officials and candidates for election, forcing them to pay attention because of the size and influence of their constituencies. When the interests of various constituencies conflict, elected officials work out accommodations and compromises. In effect, government acts as a referee. From the 1930s until the 1960s, this pluralist model of democracy was celebrated as making it possible for every citizen to participate in democratic self-government. It is still celebrated by many Americans.

In the 1960s, however, Americans began to discover that they were even more diverse than they had previously realized. Quite suddenly, it seemed, interest groups were springing up they could hardly have imagined previously. Who would have thought that the physically handicapped, or welfare recipients, or homosexuals, or women seeking abortions would assert a right to take part in working out political accommodations and compromises? When proponents of such causes made claims, elected officials turned a deaf ear. They had fixed views about which groups had legitimate claims on their attention. Labor unions, business associations, certain ethnic groups, churches, and political parties were legitimate and important.

Reverting to the civics text model, the new aspirants for political influence should have tried to make their presence felt at the polls. To do so effectively, however, required that they mobilize their own constituencies and persuade those constituencies of the legitimacy of identifying with those movements. They required recognition by mass media, no easy task because the media have the same criteria for determining which interest groups are legitimate and important as do elected officials.

Writing in the 1960s, Robert Paul Wolff pointed out:

> According to pluralist theory, every genuine social group has a right to a voice in the making of policy and a share in the benefits. Any policy urged by a group in the system must be given respectful attention, no matter now bizarre. By the same token, a policy or principle which lacks legitimate representation has no place in the society, no matter how reasonable or right it may be. Consequently, the line between acceptable and unacceptable alternatives is very sharp, so that the territory of American politics is like a plateau with steep cliffs on all sides rather than like a pyramid. On the plateau are all the interest groups which one recognized as legitimate; in the deep valley all around lie the outsiders, the fringe groups which are scorned as "extremist." The most important battle waged by any group in American politics is the struggle to climb onto the plateau.[4]

In a crucial accident of American history, blacks climbed out of the deep valley partway onto the plateau through their victory in the United States Supreme Court in *Brown v. Board of Education*. Historical events converged, requiring some branch of government to end school segregation; the branches other than the judiciary could not act. Before *Brown,* despite their great historical and numerical significance, blacks were, in Ralph Ellison's word, "invisible." White Americans discovered black Americans through

Brown. Having secured the nation's attention blacks did not rely solely on litigation to make known their grievances. They employed another attention-getting device: demonstrations—"body rhetoric," in free speech scholar Franklyn Haiman's term. To hold the interest of the news media, and thereby the interest of the nation, demonstrations must get ever larger and ever more dramatic. At the outset, a handful of blacks and whites could obtain attention by demonstrating peacefully against racial segregation. To maintain public interest, mass demonstrations were required. In August 1963, two hundred thousand demonstrators marched on Washington to listen to the Reverend Martin Luther King, Jr., deliver his "I have a dream" speech and, because of their number, they dominated the headlines for days. Subsequent smaller demonstrations seemed puny by comparison to the march on Washington and usually secured news coverage only if they turned violent. Within less than a decade, civil rights demonstrations came and went, followed by a few years of antiwar demonstrations and demonstrations for other causes. Litigation proved a more durable method of publicizing such grievances. It also proved more palatable to other Americans who wearied of demonstrations and turned antagonistic when they became violent.

The civil rights movement discovered that it could sustain attention to its cause more effectively by litigating than by demonstrating. Victories won in court did not always stay won, of course, when it came time for the executive and legislative branches of government to implement judicial decisions. Court orders to desegregate schools, for example, frequently did not produce desegregation because they were sabotaged in practice. On the other hand, some important achievements of litigation were ratified and extended by the other branches of government. An important example is the federal Voting Rights Act of 1965, which suspended procedures across the South that states had employed to exclude blacks from registering to vote and that previously had been challenged piecemeal by litigators. Litigation, the civil rights movement also discovered, is an effective way of informing the nation about a cause.

Many other previously invisible interest groups have attempted to follow the same path onto the plateau of American politics. *Brown* was a spectacular demonstration that a depressed minority might prevail in the courts, that the usual trappings of power did not predetermine the results of litigation. Any interest group that believed strongly in the righteousness of its cause, the decision suggested, might look to the courts for redress of its grievances. A cause might lack the strength to prevail in the legislatures or to make officials in the executive branch listen to it seriously, but the courts—so the word went out with *Brown*—would pay more attention to its justice than to its resources. In conscious and direct imitation of blacks, newly emerged interest groups have sponsored litigation, often seeking the application to them of the self-same constitutional guarantee of "equal protection of the laws" that was decisive in *Brown*. Framing their demands for recognition in accepted legal language has helped to establish their legitimacy. And the willingness of the judiciary to pay attention has helped to establish their importance.

Despite successes in litigation, blacks are far from securing an equal share of the benefits of the society, and the same is true for many of those following in their footsteps. To the extent that government is capable of distributing benefits, the power lies in the hands of the executive and legislative branches. The authority of the judiciary is largely limited to helping previously ignored interest groups enter the competition.

The idea of fair competition implies a view of representative democracy which suggests that it is not sufficient that
the majority prevail. It is equally important that the process
of forming a majority should be fluid and open. A minority should have a chance to make its point of view heard
and evaluated on its merits. To the framers of the Constitution, possessed of a vision of republican society in which
Americans were united by common interests and differed
only on how best to vindicate those interests, fluidity and
openness were to be guaranteed by forbidding government
interference with speech, publication, or assembly. In contemporary mass society, in which Americans do not share
the same interests and, indeed, have interests that conflict,
we require mechanisms to see that interests may not only be
expressed freely but also that they may be heard. Intervention by the judiciary in policy making on behalf of unheard
minorities has proved an essential means of enabling such
minorities to be heard. In the process, the judiciary enhances
the legitimacy of democratic decision making and establishes the legitimacy of its exercise of authority on questions
of public policy.

The legitimacy of claims to authority, Max Weber taught
us, may rest on rational-legal grounds, in which authority is
accepted because the public believes in the legality of rules
and in the legal right of those in authority to enforce the
rules; on traditional grounds, in which authority is accepted
because it has been validated by time, that is, we do things in
a certain way because things have always been done that way;
and on charismatic grounds, in which authority is accepted
because of the exemplary character or heroic qualities of
the individual exercising authority.[5] On the surface, it might
seem that the legitimacy of judicial authority derives from
its rational-legal basis. Its legitimacy is also traditional, resting
on traditions established by judges who have exercised power

over the years in circumstances where the rules are anything but clear. I contend that the courts, particularly the Supreme Court of the United States, won greatest acceptance by assuming a charismatic role, speaking as one individual in ordering an end to school desegregation and demonstrating heroic qualities in steadfastly refusing to be cowed by resistance. Charismatic authority may be routinized over time, Weber argued, and move in the direction of traditionalization or of legalization. As the exercise of judicial authority has become routinized since *Brown,* its legitimacy seems to be accepted on both grounds. What took place less than three decades ago already seems traditional. Legalization has occurred through representative ratification of judicial decisions invalidating the past practices of the representative branches of government.

2

Thoughts on Legitimacy

In a famous passage in the *Federalist Papers,* Alexander Hamilton wrote that "the executive not only dispenses the honors but holds the sword of the community. The legislature not only commands the purse, but prescribes the rules by which the duties of every citizen are to be regulated. The judiciary, on the contrary, has no influence over either the sword or the purse; no direction either of the strength or of the wealth of the society, and can take no active resolution whatever. It may truly be said to have neither FORCE nor WILL but merely judgment."[1]

The exercise of judgment by the judiciary in a manner that does not take direction of either "the strength or of the wealth of the society" is, borrowing a term from Aristotle, a form of "corrective justice." It is, he said, "the effort of the judge to restore equality by the penalty he inflicts, since the penalty is so much subtracted from the aggressor's profit."[2] A judgment that a criminal should be punished for a crime or that a wrongdoer should compensate a victim or that a citizen should receive redress from government for wrongs done by that government, such as interference with freedom to speak or to worship, intentional discrimination because of race or sex, or improper seizure of property, are examples of corrective justice. In such matters, the role of the judge, in Aristotle's view and the view of this book, is to personify justice.[3] It is not the judge's province to weigh competing interests in the society or to set policy but to invoke known principles so as to restore the order that prevailed or the order that the rules of the society make clear should have prevailed before that injustice was committed. In rendering corrective justice, judges look backward to redress wrongs done in the past according to standards set in the past. It is commonly accepted that it is the province of the judiciary to dispense corrective justice.

The direction of the wealth of the society might be labeled, again borrowing from Aristotle, "distributive justice."[4] Determining fairly how the burden of taxes should be apportioned and determining fairly how scarce resources (like admissions to medical schools) should be allocated, or how public resources should be allocated to provide care in institutions or outside institutions for the retarded, or whether a class of citizens is entitled to welfare assistance, all of these are examples of distributive justice. Unlike corrective justice, distributive justice requires those who dispense it to weigh competing interests. There is no agreed-upon order to restore. Judges must look forward to redress wrongs that would otherwise occur in the future. Rather than simply applying standards set in the past, they often set new standards designed to prevent continuing wrongs. The principles of distributive justice are in dispute. They were in dispute in Aristotle's time, as he noted in explaining that "the cause of strife and complaints is either that people who are equal are given unequal shares or that people who are not equal are given equal shares."[5] They are in dispute now.

Consider the question of welfare assistance. If a citizen complains that he or she was improperly denied welfare assistance that the legislature intended to provide because a welfare worker objected to the exercise of free speech, a judge finding in the citizen's favor would render corrective justice. On the other hand, if the citizen were to complain of improper denial of welfare assistance because the legislature excluded a class of citizens to which he or she belongs made up of new arrivals in a state, a judge finding in the individual's favor and in favor of the members of the class would dispense distributive justice.

Ordinarily, the judiciary is not the proper branch of government to dispense distributive justice or, in Hamilton's words, to exercise direction of the wealth of society. In circumstances where a compelling principle of corrective justice is also involved, however, judicial dispensation of distributive justice may be appropriate, for example, the question of welfare assistance for new arrivals in a state. If the great majority of the new arrivals were members of a particular racial minority, and if the legislation that has excluded new arrivals from welfare assistance was enacted in circumstances that make it plain that its purpose and its effect is to exclude members of that racial minority from welfare assistance, it is commonly accepted that redress may be sought through the judiciary.

A somewhat different situation would arise if the principles of corrective justice underlying a judicial venture into the territory of distributive justice are less compelling or the principles less clearly violated by a legislative or administrative practice. Discrimination against new arrivals in a state in providing welfare may have nothing to do with race. In seeking redress from a court, another principle of corrective justice may be invoked: the right to travel from state to state. The right to travel is an important principle of corrective justice, although perhaps not quite so central in the American constitutional scheme as the right not to be discriminated against because of race. Perhaps more important in this instance, it could be argued that the right to travel is only collaterally violated by exclusion of new arrivals in a state from welfare assistance. Judicial dispensation of distributive justice in such circumstances is controversial because of disagreements about the importance of the right to travel as a principle of corrective justice and because of disagreements about the degree to which it is infringed by the legislation that a court may invalidate.

A third form of justice, involving what Hamilton called the direction of the strength of the society, is political justice. This time, the provenance is not Aristotle but derived from the term courts apply to a class of disputes they believe should be resolved by the other branches of government: "political questions." The best known definition is provided in Justice William J. Brennan's opinion for the Supreme Court in *Baker* v. *Carr,* the landmark decision holding that a state's standards for allocating legislative representation are subject to judicial review under the Fourteenth Amendment's equal protection clause:

> Prominent on the surface of any case held to involve a political question is found a textually demonstrable constitutional commitment of the issue to a coordinate political department, or a lack of judicially discoverable and manageable standards for resolving it; or the impossibility of deciding without an initial policy determination of a kind clearly for non-judicial discretion; or the impossibility of a court's undertaking independent resolution without expressing lack of the respect due coordinate branches of government; or an unusual need for unquestioning adherence to a political decision already made; or the potentiality of embarrassment from multifarious pronouncements by various departments on one question.[6]

Political questions are resolved by formulating policies, not by applying principles. Like questions of distributive justice, their resolution often requires courts to look forward to wrongs that will continue to be committed in the future and requires setting new standards intended to prevent future wrongs.

An example of a political question might be a controversy over the exercise of the war power or of foreign policy. These matters, involving direction of the strength of the society, are committed to the other branches of government in the text of the Constitution. Judicially enforceable standards for resolving such controversies are difficult or impossible to discover. Even here, however, where a compelling interest of corrective justice is also involved, judicial decision making may be appropriate. When American citizens of Japanese descent were banished from the West Coast during World War II, the Supreme Court ruled that this was a proper exercise of the war power.[7] Yet the decision inspired strong dissents at the time, and if the case had been decided after the war, when passions had cooled, the result might well have been different. Judicial relief for Japanese-Americans from such blatant discrimination during the war would have been proper and might have been accepted by the other branches of government and by the general public. Indeed, judicial failure to intervene is now widely regarded as mistaken. Principles of corrective justice should have led to judicial condemnation and invalidation of the actions of the executive branch even though it would be difficult to find a matter more clearly committed to the other branches of government and less judicially manageable than the war power.

Except in instances when political questions can be resolved in accordance with principles of corrective justice, however, competing interests must be weighed and policies formulated as in matters of distributive justice. The executive and legislative branches are better suited to these tasks than is the judiciary. They are directly representative, permitting majoritarian control of policy making. Because policies require constant reconsideration to take into account new developments and must be susceptible to constant amendment or even reversal, they are properly subject to the control of temporary majorities. Principles, on the other hand, should not be revised each time a new majority forms. So the United States Constitution contemplates by placing obstacles in the way of amendments and, thereby, insulating the principles it embodies against abandonment by passing majorities. Representativeness is not a necessary characteristic, therefore, of those charged with the application of those principles. The task is appropriately left to judges chosen for their capacity to apply constitutional principles fairly without regard to the passions of the moment, that is, because they personify justice.

Litigation to advance causes is the effort by interest groups and the lawyers who serve them to persuade the judiciary to take direction of the wealth or the strength of the society, that is, to formulate policy and to dispense distributive or political justice. The effort usually arises out of an interest group's frustration at its inability to secure the relief it seeks from those branches of government charged with the responsibility for weighing its interests against competing interests. It is an effort that is probably doomed to fail and that should fail unless judges can be persuaded that compelling principles of corrective justice require them to enter territory ordinarily outside their province. Interest groups, their lawyers, and judges who dispense distributive justice or political justice must also persuade the other branches of government and the community at large that compelling principles of corrective justice require judicial dispensation of distributive or political justice. Lacking significant acceptance—as in cases requiring major reforms in prison administration—judges find it difficult to implement decisions that exceed the usual boundaries. And refusal to implement a judicial decision undermines judicial power: it implies rejection of the judge as a personification of justice. When such rejection takes place, even judicial capacity to render corrective justice may be threatened. Accordingly, to preserve their power to render corrective justice, judges usually retreat—as they have done in declining to enforce contempt citations against state officials who do not carry out their orders to reform asylums—in the face of rejection by the other branches of government and the community at large of their ventures in distributive justice or political justice.

Principles of corrective justice remain more or less constant; our understanding of their proper application, however, varies as does our sense of their urgency. The principle that no one should be deprived of property without due process of law or without just compensation, for example, is well established and explicitly guaranteed in the Constitution. But this raises many questions of application, among them what may be fairly described as an individual's property. And, even supposing agreement on the answer, how compelling is application of this principle when it conflicts with the policy interests ascertained by the representative branches of government? What if there is a conflict between one man's right not to be deprived of property without due process of law and another principle of corrective justice, such as another man's right not to be deprived of liberty without due process of law? Necessarily, the answers will vary in accordance with the views of the judges and the times in which the answers must be provided.

Chief Justice Roger Taney's decision in *Dred Scott* v. *Sand-ford*[8] in 1857 was an attempt to enter the realm of policy, dispensing what its author apparently believed to be political justice. Taney grounded his holding that the Missouri Compromise was invalid on a principle of corrective justice: the right of the slaveholder not to be deprived of his property without due process of law. The decision did not win acceptance because it undermined the power of the central government vis-à-vis the states; because of the importance of the legislative act it invalidated in diminishing sectional conflict; and because, by 1857, it was no longer generally accepted that Negroes could be considered property. To some, rendering corrective justice to the slaveholder did not appear compelling when weighed against the legislature's policy decision that slavery was impermissible in certain parts of the country. To others, Taney misapplied the principle because he asserted a property right where none could exist; principles of corrective justice dictated a contrary result. Not only was the *Dred Scott* decision condemned and ignored by President Abraham Lincoln and the Civil War Congress, but it also injured Taney's capacity to render corrective justice in a case where the principles and their applications were clearer. No longer the personification of justice, Taney could not obtain the executive branch's cooperation in enforcing the writ of habeas corpus he issued during the Civil War in *Ex Parte Merryman*,[9] a case involving a Confederate sympathizer in Baltimore who was improperly imprisoned. The Supreme Court had greater success in securing compliance in comparable cases in subsequent years, perhaps because the war was over and perhaps because it again came to personify justice when Taney departed from the scene.

During the more than a half century up to 1937 when Supreme Court decision making was guided by laissez-faire economic theories, the Court dispensed what it apparently believed to be distributive justice. Its decisions were grounded on what it held to be a principle of corrective justice: the right of free contract, as in a baker's right to contract to work longer hours than permitted by law. The Court held that this right was part of the principle of liberty guaranteed by the Constitution. As long as unregulated free enterprise appeared to serve the society well, this application of the principle seemed reasonable and the Court's decisions were widely accepted. The great depression of the 1930s changed public perceptions. The Court's decisions frustrated efforts by the other branches of government—executive and legislative—to exercise their power to dispense distributive justice and, thereby, to extricate the nation from its grave difficulties. In the process, the Court's application of the principle of corrective justice embodied in the Constitution's guarantee of liberty was widely rejected and the Court itself so far lost its capacity to personify justice that its independence was threatened by President Franklin D. Roosevelt. Only a hasty retreat from the realm of distributive justice, the famous "switch in time that saved nine," saved the Court from the court-packing plan.

One of several decisions by the Supreme Court announcing its withdrawal from efforts to impose its economic theories on legislation was *United States* v. *Carolene Products*[10] decided in 1938. It is remembered today not for its text but for a footnote by Justice Harlan Fiske Stone that set down the foundations for the next era of judicial activism.

In footnote 4, Stone wrote that although the Court would uphold economic legislation when it had "some rational basis," it was not then necessary to consider whether "more exacting judicial scrutiny" should be given to "legislation which restricts those political processes which can ordinarily be expected to bring about repeal of undesirable legislation." Continuing in a backhand style, he wrote that there was no need then to decide the standard of review for laws directed at "particular religious, or racial minorities; whether prejudice against discrete and insular minorities may be a special condition, which tends seriously to curtail the operation of those political processes ordinarily to be relied upon to protect minorities, and which may call for a correspondingly more searching judicial inquiry."

The significance and the applications of Stone's footnote have been extensively debated. Critics of the approach have suggested that it imposes a hierarchy of values on the Constitution not intended by the framers. Others echo the comment of Justice Felix Frankfurter, who joined the Supreme Court the following year, that "a footnote hardly seems to be an appropriate way of announcing a new constitutional doctrine and the Carolene footnote did not purport to announce any new doctrine; incidentally it did not have the concurrence of a majority of the Court."[11] Even so, the approach has roots in the view expressed by Hamilton in the *Federalist Papers* that it is the special duty of the judiciary to safeguard the rights of individuals when "the influence of particular conjuctures, sometimes disseminate themselves, and . . . occasion dangerous innovations in the government and serious oppressions of the minor party in the community."[12] It provides a rationale that is enormously influential in guiding litigators and judges in confronting questions of distributive justice or political justice.

Carolene Products suggests that although political processes should ordinarily be relied upon in a democratic society to weigh competing interests and to set policies, there are circumstances when the courts should interfere. Those circumstances do not arise when the courts merely disagree with the results of political processes. That is what happened when the Taney Court invalidated the Missouri

Compromise and when the pre-1937 Court invalidated economic legislation that conflicted with its laissez-faire philosophy. Circumstances appropriate for judicial intervention do arise, however, when the acts of the other branches of government restrict the political process itself. Limits on free expression, or the right to vote, or the right to run for office restrict the political process. So much is clear. Stone's formulation provides a rationale for judicial intervention to clear away such restrictions. In so doing courts make representative government *more* representative. The other part of Stone's formulation is more controversial even though it is directed to the same end. It suggests that those stuck on the steep cliffs below the plateau of American politics—as blacks have been for centuries—are entitled to special judicial assistance in combating acts of the other branches of government that adversely affect them. It is not sufficient that they should be free to compete in the political forum. Prejudice against a "discrete and insular minority," such as a racial minority, Stone's footnote argues, may make it impossible for that minority to be heard in the political forum, that is, to exercise freedom to compete. Accordingly, a "more searching judicial inquiry" may be required to ensure that representative government takes into account that minority's interests.

No circumstance, of course, warrants judicial creation of rights not provided by the Constitution. But guarantees of rights incorporated in the Constitution, such as "due process of law" or "equal protection of the laws," do not have a reach that can be fixed with precision for all times. When a court tests whether the acts of the other branches of government comply with those guarantees, the outcome may vary according to the standard of review. For example, a black man seeking a job as a fire fighter might challenge a requirement that all fire fighters must be high school graduates on the ground that it denies blacks equal protection of the laws. If he were unable to prove that this criterion for employment had a discriminatory purpose and a court were to limit itself to determining whether it had a rational basis, almost certainly the suit would be dismissed. In general, high school graduates probably could be shown to be better fire fighters than those who do not graduate from high school, providing the requisite rational basis for the criterion. On the other hand, if a court engaged in a more searching inquiry, it might rule in favor of the applicant for a position as a fire fighter. The requirement of a high school diploma could not be shown to demonstrate fire-fighting capacity; tests devised directly for this purpose would correlate much better. And eliminating the diploma requirement would permit a proportionately larger number of blacks to become fire fighters because fewer blacks graduate from high school than whites.

Litigators' briefs, judicial decisions, and law review articles engage in an ongoing debate as to which rights directly affect the political process and, therefore, hold a "preferred position"[13] and which groups are discrete and insular minorities and, therefore, are entitled to more exacting judicial scrutiny, or "strict scrutiny" of laws and practices affecting them. These are questions of immense significance because Justice Stone's footnote in *Carolene Products* provides a basis for reconciling judicial policy making through dispensation of distributive justice or political justice with principles of representative government. In circumstances where political processes are restricted, judicial intervention is not a limitation on representative government; rather, it makes it work. Similarly, when judges dispense distributive justice or political justice in order to provide corrective justice to discrete and insular minorities, they serve democratic ends. Without a way to deal with the interests of minorities effectively excluded from the political process by prejudice, the government does not enjoy the consent of the governed, the essential ingredient of democracy.

Some who agree that the courts should unclog political processes when obstacles bar the full participation in government of any segment of society point out that the assumption of this responsibility does not necessarily justify judicial dispensation of distributive justice or political justice. John Hart Ely, of Harvard Law School, for example, has written that "a representation-reinforcing approach to judicial review, unlike its rival value-protecting approach, is not inconsistent with, but on the contrary (and quite by design) entirely supportive of, the underlying premises of representative democracy."[14] In Ely's view, however, the role of the judiciary should be restricted to removing barriers to full participation and should not extend to providing benefits that a group might not have obtained because it was denied the right to participate fully. It has a fair opportunity to obtain those benefits for itself once the political processes are opened to it. The practical consequence of adopting this view could include, for example, support for judicial invalidation of legally enforced racial segregation but opposition to judicial requirement that school systems adopt such devices as busing to bring about integration; support for judicial invalidation of employment discrimination but opposition to judicially required "affirmative action"; support for judicial intervention to free mental patients wrongfully confined but opposition to judicial requirements that community services be provided to former patients; support for judicial intervention to end criminal sanctions against women obtaining abortions (though Ely is among those disputing the propriety of this judicial action) but opposition to judicial requirements that the government pay the costs of abortions for poor women; support for judicial intervention to provide that one citizen casts one vote but opposition to judicial invalidation of electoral schemes that make it difficult or impossible for minorities to win elections, such as at-large representation; support for judicial requirements of fair proceedings to determine which persons belong in the class to which the legislature provides welfare payments but opposition to judicial review of the choices made by the legislature in determining the contours of the class.

The difficulty with such an approach is that it assumes that the civics text model of pluralist democracy works. It is oblivious to the difficulties faced by interest groups outside the system and not yet accepted as legitimate—"discrete and insular minorities" suffering from prejudice—in climbing onto the plateau and competing fairly. It ignores the critical role that has been played by the judiciary during the past three decades in making pluralist democracy actually work, even though not in conformance to the civics text model.

In greater or lesser degree, courts have helped minorities of varying discreteness and insularity secure some measure of distributive or political justice. But the extent of success has depended substantially on the capacity of the litigants to demonstrate to the judiciary, and of the judiciary and the litigants to demonstrate to others, that judicial policy making is required by principles of corrective justice. To win acceptance of judicially mandated school integration plans they must show that de facto segregation is rooted in de jure segregation and in public policies on housing, transportation, and employment. To win acceptance of judicially mandated affirmative action, they must show that continuing inequalities in getting jobs or in getting into schools are rooted in discriminatory practices. To win acceptance of judicially mandated community services to mental patients, they must show that such services are required to undo the damage done to mental patients debilitated in confinement. To win acceptance of government payment for the costs of abortions for poor women, they must demonstrate that abortion has been unfairly excluded from the government's program of medical assistance to the poor for the same reasons that it was previously made criminal. To win acceptance of judicial invalidation of at-large voting, they must demonstrate that it is designed to cancel or minimize the votes minorities obtained when they were permitted to register and when districts were reapportioned to make possible one-person one-vote. To win acceptance of judicial review of legislative decisions about those eligible for welfare they must demonstrate invidious discrimination.

The great hurdle that must be overcome by minorities who attempt to persuade the courts to make policies that favor them is to show that mistreatment they suffered in the past must be redressed by setting new standards that will govern in the future. In attempting to surmount this hurdle, they are hampered by the judicial tradition, derived from the judiciary's traditional role of dispensing corrective justice, of looking backward. Litigants succeed in persuading judges to look forward only to the extent that they can demonstrate that wrongs inflicted on them in the past will continue to injure them in the future. For example, blacks seeking judicially required affirmative action must demonstrate that past racial discrimination cannot be redressed solely by compensating them for what took place in the past. Judges, they must demonstrate, should also take into account the extent to which blacks are hampered in competing for jobs and other benefits in the future by what took place in the past. Accordingly, the argument goes, judges must set standards that look forward in order to correct injustices that took place in the past. Mental patients seeking judicially required community services must bear a similar burden. It is not sufficient to show that they suffered from mistreatment when they were confined in institutions. They must also show that the effects of that mistreatment are long-lasting, requiring courts to provide services in the future that will help to correct the injustices done in the past. And so on.

As difficult as it may be to surmount that hurdle, an even higher one must also be overcome if judicial policy making is actually to benefit the minorities attempting to secure it through litigation. The public at large and the other branches of government must also be persuaded. From the standpoint of such minorities, it is most desirable that the public should be persuaded of the merits of the arguments that are presented to the courts. If that is not possible, however, the public must at least be persuaded that the injustices suffered by the minority bringing litigation that seeks judicial policy making were such that it is appropriate for the courts to devise methods of providing redress. Questions involving the extent to which injuries done in the past require redress through the establishment of standards to regulate the future may be too subtle to communicate effectively outside the courts. But if the injuries themselves were severe, it ought to be possible to communicate that information through litigation and through the publicity it generates. Courts engaging in policy making must attend to their need to persuade others that regulating what takes place in the future is warranted by the past injuries suffered by the litigants in whose interests they act. Failing, courts risk not only rejection of their decisions but also rejection of themselves.

There is a school of thought that contends that the checks on judicial exercise of power are more fancied than real. Eugene Rostow, for example, has written that "judicial emasculation by way of popular reaction against constitutional review by the courts has not in fact materialized in more than a century and a half of American experience."[15]

But this takes too narrow a view. Emasculation, or whole-sale destruction of judicial authority, has never occurred. But judges have had enormous difficulty in securing compliance with decisions dealing with racial segregation in the schools, conditions in asylums, police practices, and many other matters. Extrinsic factors surely play a part, but so does judicial success or failure in grounding policy-making decisions on principles of corrective justice.

Political climate is, of course, also an important influence on judicial policy making. It shapes social protest movements and helps to determine what they attempt to get from the courts. It also shapes judicial response and helps to determine whether courts are able to secure compliance with their decisions. Sometimes the political climate for litigation shifts drastically between the commencement of a litigation campaign and judicial disposition of major cases. Adventitious factors may be crucial, as I will attempt to show in discussing the onset of the cold war and the urgency it provided to ending legally enforced segregation of the races in the schools. The emergence of the contemporary feminist movement had a roughly comparable effect on judicial willingness to end criminal sanctions on medical abortions.

At other times, the outcome of a litigation campaign is shaped by a political climate that the litigation itself helps to create. For example, some cases challenging legislative choices about who should get welfare payments and how much were initiated during the early days of Lyndon Johnson's war against poverty. To prevail, litigators attempting to advance the cause of welfare recipients asked courts to take large steps into the territory of distributive justice. Geoffrey Hazard, then of the University of Chicago Law School and now of Yale Law School, suggested, in an influential law review article published in 1969, how far the courts would have to reach:

Income redistribution requires not only a giving
to those who lack but also a taking from those
who have. Since the taking cannot be justified
by reference to ownership rights, it reduces itself
to expropriation (if done by one to another) or
self-denial (if done by one to himself). The legislature being representative can engage in self-denial,
vicariously but genuinely, knowing that it will be
reminded when its generosity becomes excessive.
A court being unrepresentative can only engage in
expropriation if it does not follow the law.[16]

At about the time that Hazard's article appeared, the
United States Supreme Court decided *Shapiro v. Thompson*,[17]
which required that the states not discriminate against new
residents in making welfare payments. The decision was susceptible to Hazard's charge of "expropriation" because new
residents could be given such payments only at the expense
of other welfare recipients, or at the expense of other public
programs, or through levies of increased taxes. In any circumstance, taxpayers would have to pay for that which they
(through their representatives) had not chosen to tax themselves. A year later, in a case involving comparable principles
of corrective justice, *Dandridge v. Williams*,[18] the Supreme
Court reversed field. The war against poverty was proving
ineffectual and looking more tarnished every year. Popular
feeling against "welfare cheats" was running high. It seems
difficult to explain the about-face except by attributing it
to the changes in the political weather.

From the standpoint of litigators hoping to persuade
judges to reach beyond corrective justice in their decisions,
it is frequently important to try to shape the political climate to enhance sympathy for their clients. In attempting to
persuade courts to require the states to provide community
services for the retarded, for example, a litigator's best opportunity to create a sympathetic political climate is to expose

publicly the circumstances of institutional confinement. The litigation itself is often the best method of attracting public attention to institutional conditions and of publicly documenting abuses. If public sympathy is to be enlisted, plans for its arousal must enter into litigation strategy. Effective exploitation of the opportunities for creating a favorable political climate helped make the litigation challenging confinement at Willowbrook asylum for the retarded in New York City,[19] for example, a spectacular success in obtaining distributive justice.

Judicial prestige is another critical factor in judicial policy making. It is all-important in determining whether the courts are able to persuade the public and the other branches of government to go along with judicial policy making in the interest of disadvantaged minorities. Some minorities are so widely disliked, or held in contempt, at various times in history, of course, that they have little hope of persuading the public at large that wrongs they may suffer warrant redress. When courts act on their behalf, only the prestige of the judiciary is likely to persuade the representative branches of government to go along. Judges intent on shaping public policy, therefore, must attend both to the manner in which they decide cases and to the substance of their decisions to make certain that they enjoy the respect of the public.

This is not to say, of course, that judges should avoid acting in the interest of minorities suffering from prejudice for fear of diminishing their own prestige. To the extent that the judiciary has played a part in making representative government more representative, it has no higher duty than intervention on behalf of such minorities. Judicial prestige reached its zenith following the most famous decision on behalf of a minority victimized by prejudice. The year 1954, when *Brown* v. *Board of Education* was decided, was not a time when white prejudice against blacks was especially low.

A contrary impression might be created, of course, by the visibility of those whites who played an active part in the civil rights movement. But civil rights activists were never more than a tiny minority of the white population. And whites in any significant numbers did not become active in the civil rights struggle until several years after *Brown* and probably would not have taken part in that struggle were it not for *Brown*. White prejudice against blacks cannot be measured reliably but it was probably not appreciably different in the 1950s than in the previous decade or two or than in the subsequent decade or two. Yet it was in the aftermath of *Brown* that the Supreme Court of the United States achieved prestige so great that the Court exercised charismatic authority. Prejudice against blacks was not dissipated by the decision but existed side by side with unprecedented reverence for the courts for acting against segregation, the dominant form of institutionalized prejudice against blacks. One of the many lessons of *Brown,* accordingly, is that judicial prestige is not necessarily diminished by judicial policy making on behalf of minorities suffering from prejudice. On the contrary, the prestige the Supreme Court acquired through *Brown* is the main source of the unprecedented authority the courts have enjoyed ever since. The vitality of cause litigation in obtaining political justice and distributive justice for disadvantaged minorities is part of the legacy of judicial prestige created by *Brown*.

3

Racial Equality: Assuming Leadership

Outside the deep South, most newspapers endorsed the Supreme Court's decision in 1954 in *Brown v. Board of Education*[1] declaring enforced racial segregation in the public schools unconstitutional. In their editorials, one theme dominated: ending segregation was essential in fighting world communism, the preeminent concern of the nation in the early 1950s. The *New York Times* editorial was typical: "When some hostile propagandist rises in Moscow or Peiping to accuse us of being a class society, we can if we wish recite the courageous words of yesterday's opinion."[2] The *Washington Post and Times-Herald* added, "It will help us to refurbish American prestige in a world which looks to this land for moral inspiration."[3] The *San Francisco Chronicle* said, "Great as the impact will be upon the states of the South still greater, we believe, will be its impact in South America, Africa and Asia, to this country's lasting honor and benefit."[4] The *Minneapolis Tribune* said, "The words of Chief Justice Warren will echo far beyond our borders and may greatly influence our relations with dark-skinned peoples,"[5] and the *St. Louis*

Post-Dispatch said, "The greater significance is the affirmation in the eyes of millions of people in India, Pakistan and Africa, in China, Japan and Burma, in Indo-China, Thailand and Indonesia that the pledge in the United States of the worth and dignity of the humblest individual means exactly what it says. Had this decision gone the other way the loss to the free world in its struggle against Communist encroachment would have been incalculable."[6] The *Hartford Courant* urged its readers not to forget that the Supreme Court decision "may have an even deeper and more encouraging impact outside our borders."[7] A border state newspaper, the *Chattanooga Times,* said, "Internationally, opinion will benefit this nation in a time of great crisis countering one of the most effective talking points of propaganda."[8]

Newspapers serving black communities echoed the same theme. "This clarion announcement," the *Pittsburgh Courier* commented, "will stun and silence America's Communist traducers behind the Iron Curtain. It will effectively impress upon millions of colored people in Asia and Africa the fact that idealism and social morality can and do prevail in the United States."[9] The *Chicago Defender* added, "Neither the atom bomb nor the hydrogen bomb will ever be as meaningful to our democracy,"[10] and the *Atlanta Daily World* said, "It will strengthen the position of our nation in carrying out the imposed duties of world leadership."[11] This sentiment was repeated in the *Boston Chronicle,* which said, "It strengthens incalculably the diplomatic efficiency of our government."[12] Black leaders agreed. The decision was "communism's worst defeat," according to Representative Adam Clayton Powell, Jr., and "democracy's shining hour."[13] Lester Granger, executive director of the National Urban League, said, "The world will be watching to see how this decision is implemented."[14]

The *New York Times* reported reactions from around the world to the decision, stressing its impact on the cold war struggle. Under the headline, "British Applaud Segregation Ban," the *Times* noted that *"The Daily Worker,* a Communist paper, ignored the ruling entirely."[15] A typical report from a nonwhite country was this item, quoted here in its entirety, with a Karachi, Pakistan, dateline: "Color-conscious Pakistanis were impressed by the decision of the United States Supreme Court. The announcement, which was prominently displayed in several leading dailies, also helped minimize the effectiveness of Communist propaganda against Negro discrimination in the United States."[16]

Brown was decided by the United States Supreme Court several years after the executive branch of the federal government ended enforced racial segregation in those institutions it controlled directly. Racial segregation could hardly be maintained in the post–World War II era. Nazism had given racism a worse name than it ever had previously, and the war had set in motion forces that speedily brought about independence for many nations of nonwhites that had been colonized by whites. President Harry Truman ordered desegregation of the armed forces in 1948[17] but could do nothing directly to end segregation of the schools. Congress almost certainly was empowered by the Fourteenth Amendment to end segregation nationally, but in the postwar era it was dominated by southerners who made such an action unthinkable. And, although the federal government could in subsequent years prod the states by conditioning aid to education on local compliance with desegregation requirements, in the early 1950s little money for schools was provided by the federal government. The schools were controlled by the states and financed by state and local tax revenues. If the national interest, as perceived by the executive branch of the federal government and by most of the nation's opinion leaders, required an end to enforced segregation of the schools, the only body that could act effectively was the Supreme Court of the United States. The executive branch turned to the Supreme Court for assistance and the court accepted the challenge, risking its own authority by ordering social change on a grander scale than ever before in judicial history. Although the Court was asked to do no more in *Brown* than to provide corrective justice by invalidating state-required segregation, the profound impact the decision would have on the nation's way of life was plain for all to see.

The Truman administration was explicit in advising the Supreme Court of its foreign policy interests in the amicus curiae brief it filed with the Court in December 1952 in *Brown* urging the result that the Court announced seventeen months later. It is customary for those filing amicus curiae briefs to explain the interests they are trying to promote. Seven pages of the Truman administration's brief were given over to stating "the interest of the United States"; five pages were devoted to an account of the way school segregation handicapped the United States in its competition with the Soviet Union for the loyalty and friendship of newly independent nations with dark-skinned populations. "It is in the context of the present world struggle between freedom and tyranny that the problem of racial discrimination must be viewed," the Justice Department said in the brief submitted by Attorney General James P. McGranery. "The United States is trying to prove to the people of the world of every nationality, race, and color, that a free democracy is the most civilized and most secure form of government yet devised by man. . . . The existence of discrimination against minority groups in the United States has an adverse effect upon our relations with other countries. Racial discrimination furnishes grist for the Communist propaganda mills."[18] This was followed by a long excerpt from a letter by the secretary of state described in the brief as "an authoritative statement of the effects of racial discrimination in the United States upon the conduct of foreign relations."[19]

The Truman administration brief focused also on the urgent foreign policy reasons for requiring desegregation in Washington, D.C. The Supreme Court had already made it clear that it understood the symbolic significance. When the Court agreed to consider *Brown* and three other cases challenging state-enforced segregation, a case challenging segregation in Washington, D.C., was pending in the lower courts but had not yet been decided by the Circuit Court of Appeals. In an extraordinary move, the Supreme Court reached down on its own initiative and placed the case on its own docket so that the Washington, D.C., case could be argued and decided in conjunction with the challenge to segregation in schools operated by the states. "This city," the attorney general told the Court in the government's brief, "is the window through which the world looks at our house. The embassies, legations, and representatives of all nations are here."[20] James M. Nabrit, Jr., the attorney who represented the black schoolchildren of Washington, D.C., stressed the same point in his oral argument. "Here," he said, "we are dealing with the capital of the free world."[21]

The attorney for the District of Columbia Board of Education, Milton Korman, attempted to counter these arguments. "It has been said by our distinguished opponents," Korman argued orally, "indeed it has been said by the Attorney General of the United States that Washington D.C.'s District of Columbia in which we live, is the window through which the world looks upon us. It does not seem to me that is a constitutional argument, and I should like to read something to the Court."[22] Korman proceeded to read a passage that began: "No one, we presume, supposes that any change in public opinion or feeling, in relation to this unfortunate race, in the civilized nations of Europe or in this country, should induce the court to give to the words of the Constitution a more liberal construction in their favor than they were intended to bear when the instrument was framed and adopted."[23] It was, as many in the audience were quick to realize, a monumental gaffe. The passage Korman read to the Court was from Chief Justice Roger Taney's discredited opinion a century earlier in *Dred Scott* v. *Sandford*.[24] Invoking such authority enhanced the effectiveness of the very arguments about world opinion Korman was trying to rebut.

Segregation in the capital raised a particularly thorny legal problem. In schools operated by the states, the Supreme Court decided in *Brown,* segregation was unconstitutional because "separate educational facilities are inherently unequal" and, therefore, Negro children were "deprived of the equal protection of the laws guaranteed by the Fourteenth Amendment."[25] But as the Court had to acknowledge, "The legal problem in the District of Columbia is somewhat different, however. The Fifth Amendment, which is applicable in the District of Columbia does not contain an equal protection clause as does the Fourteenth Amendment which applies only to the states."[26] This created a serious problem because, as the Court pointed out, "In view of our decision that the Constitution prohibits the states from maintaining racially segregated public schools, it would be unthinkable that the same Constitution would impose a lesser duty on the Federal Government."[27] To avoid the "unthinkable," after reaching down to take the Washington, D.C., case early, the Court held that "segregation in public education is not reasonably related to any governmental objective, and thus it imposes on Negro children a burden that constitutes an arbitrary deprivation of their liberty in violation of the Due Process Clause."[28] School segregation, therefore, violates the

Fifth Amendment, which guarantees due process of law in Washington, D.C.

One reason it was unthinkable to leave the schools of Washington, D.C., segregated is that it would have diluted the moral impact of *Brown*. It would have made desegregation of the races in the public schools in the South appear to depend on the Court's interpretation of the technicalities of the Fourteenth Amendment. This would have prolonged an argument that the Supreme Court viewed as not susceptible to definitive resolution: did the Amendment's framers intend to abolish school segregation? After *Brown* had been argued once during the Court's 1952 term, the last in which Chief Justice Fred Vinson presided, the Court ordered reargument directing the attorneys to discuss particularly in their briefs and oral arguments the historical evidence "that the Congress which submitted and the state legislatures which ratified the Fourteenth Amendment contemplated or did not contemplate, understood or did not understand, that it would abolish segregation in public schools."[29] Reargument took place in the Court's 1953 term, the first in which Earl Warren presided as chief justice. After reading briefs and hearing oral arguments that exhaustively reviewed the history of the adoption of the amendment, the Court was compelled to say, "This discussion and our own investigation convince us that, although these sources cast some light, it is not enough to resolve the problem with which we are faced. At best, they are inconclusive."[30] The inability to resolve the issue was attributable, at least in part, to the fact that free public schools had not taken hold generally, especially in the South, by the time the amendment was adopted in 1868.

Unable to resolve the matter by ascertaining the intentions of the authors of the Fourteenth Amendment, the Supreme Court applied the principle of equal protection of the laws to contemporary circumstances in a manner that it believed comported with the spirit inspiring the incorporation of that principle in the Constitution. Inevitably, the moral outlook of the justices entered into the determination that a particular result, in this instance desegregation of the schools, must follow from application of a general principle. To secure compliance with its decision required the Court to win respect for, if not agreement with, its moral position. Chief Justice Warren followed the precedents of Lord Mansfield in England in the eighteenth century and Chief Justice John Marshall in the United States in the nineteenth century in laboring diligently to achieve unanimous support for a single opinion as a way of enhancing the moral authority of the decision. Reminiscing many years later, Warren said that he departed from the usual practice of taking a poll of the Court the same week as the argument and that, "without committing ourselves one way or another, we continued to discuss *Brown* and the other cases. Week after week, I found time to put them on the agenda for discussion. . . . We took a vote in March [argument took place the previous December]. It was unanimous against the 'separate but equal' doctrine. The fact that we did not polarize ourselves at the beginning gave us more of an opportunity to come out unanimously on it than if we had done otherwise."[31] In reading the decision to those assembled in the Supreme Court chamber on May 17, 1954—and through the journalists present to the entire nation and, indeed, to the world—Warren departed from the printed text to insert one word. "We conclude," the penultimate paragraph of the opinion began, and here Warren interjected "unanimously,"[32] eliciting audible sighs in the hushed court,[33] "that in the field of public education the doctrine of 'separate but equal' has no place. Separate educational facilities are inherently unequal. Therefore, we hold that the plaintiffs and others similarly situated for whom

the actions have been brought are, by reason of the segregation complained of, deprived of the equal protection
of the laws guaranteed by the Fourteenth Amendment."[34]
As Richard Kluger writes in his history of the *Brown* decision, *Simple Justice,* "A unanimous opinion of the Court
inspires a measure of respect and obedience that even a single dissent bespatters. A single opinion says that nine men
have in union apprehended truth and now reveal it; more
than one opinion suggests that truth may be glimpsed from
many angles—or that there is none, only conflicting opinion
among mere mortals, and that another season may bring a
different outcome."[35]

Many commentators note the importance of unanimity;
still, no special attention appears to be taken of the decision's
universality, a principle of at least comparable significance
in establishing its moral authority. Exempting the District
of Columbia—where the Court itself sat—would deny
the desegregation decision universality and, thereby, would
undermine its moral standing at home as well as abroad.
Reading the Fourteenth Amendment's guarantee of equal
protection of the laws into the Fifth Amendment's guarantee of due process of law required a far more expansive
interpretation of constitutional language than discovering
that enforced segregation violates the guarantee of equal
protection of the laws. An obvious objection is that such
an interpretation of the Fifth Amendment makes the language of the Fourteenth Amendment redundant because
the latter prohibits the states from depriving their citizens
of both due process of law and of the equal protection
of the laws. The Court anticipated such an objection and
attempted to answer it: "The 'equal protection of the laws'
is a more explicit safeguard of prohibited unfairness than
'due process of law,' and, therefore, we do not imply that the
two are always interchangeable phrases."[36] Yet without its

novel—some would say strained—interpretation of the Fifth Amendment, the Court would have been left with a result that impaired the moral impact of the decision and that it found unthinkable: segregation prohibited in the states but permitted in the "window," Washington, D.C.

To bolster the apparent morality of *Brown* through the unanimity of the judges and through the universal application of the holding was especially important at that moment. In the early 1950s, many Americans eagerly sought confirmation of the morality of their way of life. At no time before or since has the sense of competition with another way been so strong. Their way, Americans knew, yielded superior material comforts; yet communism was making great strides around the globe, apparently because of the appeal of its egalitarian philosophy. Reassurance of the morality of their way required Americans to reaffirm their own egalitarian commitments. *Brown* seemed to erase the blot that stained the passage in the Declaration of Independence proclaiming that "all men are created equal."

Cold war considerations had determined the position that the executive branch of the federal government took in *Brown*; they created a favorable climate for the Supreme Court to act, shaped the public reception to the decision, and probably influenced the outcome. Nevertheless, cold war concerns played little part in the plaintiffs' presentation of the case to the Court. The petition to the Supreme Court to hear a challenge to enforced segregation of the schools was the culmination of a long litigation campaign to undo the effects of the Supreme Court's 1896 decision in *Plessy* v. *Ferguson* upholding the constitutionality of laws requiring "separate but equal" facilities.[37] It was the good fortune of the litigators who brought *Brown* to have their case heard by the Supreme Court at a moment when the currents of history required an outcome favorable to their cause. It was the misfortune of Albion Winegar Tourgée, the litigator who brought *Plessy* in the 1890s, to have his challenge to racial segregation heard at a moment when historical tides dictated an opposite result.

Tourgée's work in *Plessy* was a prototype for the litigation campaigns that have taken place in the last thirty years. Born in Ohio in 1838, a Civil War veteran and former judge who practiced law in upstate New York in the 1890s, Tourgée had been a prominent "carpetbagger" in the postbellum years and was widely known as the author of several highly regarded popular novels.[38] Tourgée carried on the crusade on behalf of racial equality long after most whites active in the cause during Reconstruction had tired of it. His well-known views prompted an organization of eighteen prominent black men in Louisiana to contact him in 1891 to ask him for help in challenging the constitutionality of a law adopted in their state the previous year requiring that the races be separated when traveling by rail. Similar "Jim Crow" laws had been adopted about the same time by several other southern states. The tide was running strongly in the direction of racial segregation. A challenge was urgently required; at the same time, its chances of success were slender. Despite the apparent difficulty in overturning segregation in the courts, Tourgée accepted the assignment.

Tourgée advised the black men, who called themselves the Citizens' Committee, to test the constitutionality of the separate car law; he said it would be best if a test case were presented on behalf of a Negro who was "nearly white," thus highlighting the absurdity of the racial classifications required by Jim Crow laws. If the litigation succeeded, it would set a valuable precedent for other litigation on behalf of Negroes of darker hue. Railroad officials could be counted on to cooperate by enforcing the law against a passenger who might pass for white because it was to their interest also to overturn the law. Providing separate cars was expensive.

Determining a goal to be pursued through litigation first and then selecting a client is now standard practice in cause litigation but, in Tourgée's time, it probably would have shocked the established bar had the strategy been known. Tourgée's decision to bring a test case on behalf of a nearly white Negro did arouse some dispute at the time among members of the Citizens' Committee. Their leader, Louis A. Martinet, a lawyer and the editor of a New Orleans newspaper for blacks, pointed out in a letter to Tourgée that "people of tolerably fair complexion, even if unmistakably colored, enjoy here a large degree of immunity from the accursed prejudice."[39] Nevertheless, Martinet and his colleagues agreed to cooperate and designated one of their number who could pass for white to be Tourgée's client. The case brought on behalf of this client was mooted, however, because the client held a ticket to Alabama and the state courts held in a separate case brought by the railroad that Louisiana had no right to impose the burden of segregation on interstate commerce.[40] Since most rail travel was intrastate and was not affected by the ruling, another test case was started two weeks after the ruling on interstate travel. Homer Adolph Plessy, "seven-eighths Caucasian and one-eighth African," as he described himself, boarded a train in New Orleans on June 7, 1892, with a ticket to Covington, Louisiana. Apparently by prearrangement with the railroad, Plessy was arrested and charged with violating the segregation law.

Like present-day cause litigators, Tourgée did not confine his efforts to the courthouses. He campaigned against the separate car law through a weekly column, "Bystander," he wrote for a Chicago newspaper, regularly reprinted by newspapers in other cities, and through a National Citizens

Rights Association (NCRA) he had taken the lead in establishing to oppose disenfranchisement of blacks and racial segregation. Within a few months after it was founded, the NCRA claimed more than a hundred thousand members, a far larger number than such twentieth-century groups as the NAACP and the ACLU have ever recruited in so brief a period. (The NCRA lacked a sound structure and disappeared without a trace a few years after it was founded.)

Tourgée, noting the steadily worsening climate, had doubts about proceeding with the litigation even after it was underway. On October 31, 1893, Tourgée wrote a letter to Louis Martinet that demonstrates his grasp of the interplay between cause litigation and representative government:

> My Dear Martinet:
> I have been having some very serious thoughts in regard to Plessy's Case of late, and my preparation for the hearing has extended.
> Shall we press for an early hearing or leave it to come up in its turn or even encourage delay?
> I know you will be surprised to hear this from me, and I will explain the reason of it. When we started the fight there was a fair show of favor with the Justices of the Supreme Court. One, at least, had come to regret the "Civil Rights Cases" who had been most strenuously for them. There are now four men on the court who are not fully committed by participation in those cases. If Hornblower is confirmed there will be five.
> Of the whole number of Justices there is but one who is known to favor the view we must stand upon.
> One is inclined to be with us legally but his political bias is strong the other way.
> There are two who may be brought over by the argument.
> There are five who are against us. Of these one may be reached, I think, if he "hears from the

country" soon enough. The others will probably stay where they are until Gabriel blows his horn.

The court has always been the foe of liberty until forced to move on by public opinion. It moved on up to the level of the "Granger Cases" and the "Intoxicating Liquor Cases," because the general sentiment of the country was so unmistakably expressed as to have an enlightening effect.

It is of the utmost consequence that we should not have a decision against us as it is a matter of boast with the court that it has never reversed itself on a constitutional question.

Now I do not wish to take the responsibility of deciding this matter without the knowledge of the committee.

I wish you would call them or have them called together and lay this letter before them.

My advice is

1—To leave the case to come up when it will and not attempt to advance it.

2—To bend every possible energy to secure the discussion of the principle in such a way as to reach and awaken public sentiment.

Of course, we have nothing to hope for in any change that may be made in the court; but if we can get the ear of the Country, and argue the matter fully before the people first, we may incline the wavering to fall on our side when the matter comes up. . . .

You must unite in making appeal to and in demanding of the American people and of American Christians, *Justice*. Those of us who already believe must join with you and echo this appeal so that it shall be heard by all the world.

It is a case in which in union there is strength, and without it weakness. Without the voice of those white people who believed with you your demand will pass, as it has heretofore, unheeded. Without both united, there is no hope of success.[41]

Tourgée's letter reads much like the correspondence of a present-day cause litigator. Although Plessy was Tourgée's nominal client, the real interest at stake was represented by Martinet and his committee, and Tourgée, therefore, sought their guidance. If the case were lost, Plessy would suffer a criminal conviction, but that was a minor concern. The maximum penalty was a fine of twenty-five dollars (or in lieu thereof, twenty days in a prison—not a real prospect, when a committee sponsored the litigation and was prepared to pay) and a record of conviction. Plessy had accepted those risks in volunteering to take part in a test case. The great concern, valid as it turned out, was that an adverse decision would place the Supreme Court's stamp of approval on segregation.

To improve the chance of success Tourgée urged Martinet and his committee "to bend every possible energy to secure the discussion of the principle." Shifting public opinion outside the courtroom, Tourgée recognized, could have more effect on the decision than citations of precedents in his legal pleadings. Tourgée expected the Court to decide the case in accordance with its political predilections. His aim in trying to affect public opinion was, as he put it, to "incline the wavering" to side with Plessy. He recognized the value of the litigation in stimulating public discussion.

Plessy became as great a disaster as Tourgée feared. With a lone dissent from Justice John Marshall Harlan, the Supreme Court upheld the constitutionality of laws requiring "separate but equal" facilities.[42] The majority neatly side-stepped the question of Plessy's color: "It is true that the question of the proportion of colored blood necessary to constitute a colored person, as distinguished from a white person, is one upon which there is a difference of opinion. . . . But these are questions to be determined under the laws of each state, and are not properly put in issue in this case."[43] The principal issue was whether the Fourteenth Amendment's guarantee of equal protection of the laws prohibited legally enforced segregation. It did not, according to the Court, rejecting Tourgée's argument "that the enforced segregation of two races stamps the colored race with a badge of inferiority. If this be so, it is not by reason of anything found in the act, but solely because the colored race chooses to put that construction on it. . . . If the two races are to meet upon terms of social equality, it must be the result of natural affinities, a mutual appreciation of each other's merits, and a voluntary consent of individuals. . . . Legislation is powerless to eradicate racial instincts, or to abolish distinctions based upon physical differences."[44]

In dissent, Justice Harlan predicted that "the judgment this day rendered will, in time, prove to be quite as pernicious as the decision made by this tribunal in the *Dred Scott* case."[45] Indeed, history has not been kinder to the reasoning of the Court. Anybody looking at the case dispassionately could hardly help noticing that the Court's decision that "voluntary consent of individuals" is necessary "if the two races are to meet upon terms of social equality" is inapposite in validating a law *forbidding* individuals of different races from meeting with each other voluntarily upon terms of social equality. As for the Court's view that segregation only implies inferiority, "because the colored race chooses to put that construction on it," the prevailing judgment today is reflected in Charles Black's famous comment that "the curves of stupidity and callousness intersect at their respective maxima."

In its time, *Plessy* did not arouse anything like the furor that greeted *Dred Scott*. Taney's decision in 1857 overturned an important act of Congress and attempted to reverse a tide running strongly against slavery. *Plessy* was comparably lacking in morality and comparably faulty in its reasoning, but it sustained a state law and went with the tide, its discussion of "natural affinities" perfectly suiting the social Darwinism that was so powerful a force in shaping public thinking. Even "the Great Dissenter," Justice Harlan, wrote in his celebrated opinion that "the white race deems itself to be the dominant race in this country. And so it is, in prestige, in achievements, in education, in wealth, and in power. So, I doubt not, it will continue to be for all time, if it remains true to its great heritage."[46] Little wonder, then, that criticism of *Plessy* was much milder than of *Dred Scott*. The *New York Tribune*, for example, said that *Plessy* "must be accepted as the law. There will, however, be widespread sympathy with the strong dissenting opinion of Justice Harlan, who says there is no more reason for separate cars for whites and negroes than for Catholics and Protestants. It is unfortunate, to say the least, that our highest court has declared itself in opposition to the effort to expunge race lines in State Legislation."[47] This was tame stuff compared to the same paper's editorial comment forty years earlier in response to *Dred Scott* that the decision was entitled to "just so much moral weight . . . as the judgment of a majority of those congregated in any Washington bar-room."[48] Only three of the other eight New York City dailies criticized the decision.[49] The *New York Journal* endorsed *Plessy*: "Colored persons are entitled to all the common rights which pertain to any other persons, but they frequently exaggerate a denial of special privileges, not necessary to them, though hurtful to others, into rights. They are getting their rights; soon they will have their own privileges. They ought to deserve both, then there will be no need to appeal to the courts. In this State colored persons have the same rights in public conveyances, halls and hotels that others have, but they find it produces less friction and promotes their welfare not to use them offensively."[50]

Should Tourgée have proceeded with the litigation despite clear signs that it could not be won at that time? Even with hindsight, it is a difficult question. Cause litigators often bring cases they are almost certain to lose, sometimes because their judgment is poor, sometimes because they delude themselves and their clients about the chances, sometimes because they are seduced by the glory of taking part in a great cause, allowing it to obscure their vision. Sometimes they anticipate defeat in the courts and expect to turn it to advantage because of the publicity it will attract to their cause or because it will galvanize activity that will advance the cause in some other forum.

If Tourgée thought a loss in *Plessy* could be turned to advantage, he was mistaken. Unlike a lawsuit that may expose to public view that which is hidden—a suit dealing with barbaric mental hospital conditions, for example—there was little to be achieved by spreading the word about segregation. Americans were well aware that Jim Crow laws were being adopted in the South. The prospects were better for mobilizing a constituency. A handful of local Negro organizations like the group that sponsored the *Plessy* case already existed, but no national body advocating racial equality had yet been organized. The rapidity with which the National Citizens Rights Association recruited members, even if its claims were inflated, demonstrates that litigation could be used to help launch a popular movement. But it was not a movement with great political clout. The NCRA's membership was biracial, but in the South virtually all its members were black and they had scant chance of reversing the actions of state legislatures without some support from their white neighbors. Simultaneously, it must be recalled, the South was disenfranchising black voters. Deprived of the vote, blacks could not vindicate their rights through the representative branches of government.

Yet because the chances were poor for resisting segregation in other ways, Tourgée, Martinet, and their colleagues may have been justified in pursuing a remedy through litigation. There was an outside possibility that their legal arguments would prevail. If they lost, Supreme Court validation of Jim Crow laws would do little immediate additional damage. Even without such a decision, segregation and disenfranchisement were being speedily adopted all over the South. The precedent of *Plessy* would be difficult to overturn when the climate improved, as Tourgée recognized, but long-term considerations are rarely dispositive to participants in an ongoing struggle.

The decision in *Plessy* so disheartened advocates of racial desegregation that it took nearly a decade and a half before they organized to attempt to overturn it or to mitigate its effects. When such an effort was made in 1909, the organization that emerged was the NAACP, which eventually mounted the struggle that culminated in *Brown*.

Pursuing its goals through litigation could not have seemed an easy way of advancing the NAACP's cause. The association's founders—among them Jane Addams, W.E.B. DuBois, John Dewey, William Lloyd Garrison, Oswald Garrison Villard, Rabbi Stephen Wise, J. G. Phelps Stokes, and Lincoln Steffens—recognized the difficulty of their task as they made plain in the call to the meeting at which it was launched: "The Supreme Court of the United States, supposedly a bulwark of American liberties, had refused every opportunity to pass squarely upon this disenfranchisement of millions. . . . [T]he Supreme Court . . . had laid down the principle that if an individual State chooses, it may make it a crime for white and colored persons to frequent the same market place at the same time, or appear in an assemblage of citizens convened to consider questions of a public or political nature in which all citizens, without regard to race, are equally interested."[51] But because blacks were disenfranchised in the South where most of them resided, vindicating their rights through the representative branches of government seemed even less feasible. Litigation, even before courts infused with the spirit of *Plessy*, must have seemed more promising—or less unpromising. Litigation would draw attention to the cause of racial equality, demonstrate nationally the injustices suffered by blacks in the South, rally support from whites, and, perhaps, ultimately succeed.

The NAACP selected the cases it litigated with care and, thereby, made headway. In its first case, the NAACP attempted to void the death sentence of a Negro sharecropper in South Carolina. He had killed a police officer who had broken into his cabin in the middle of the night to charge him with breach of contract. Other early NAACP litigation challenged mob violence against Kansas City blacks who had purchased homes in a white neighborhood; attempted to overturn Oklahoma's "grandfather clause" disenfranchising that state's black voters; tried to secure the freedom of a black soldier unfairly court-martialed in Hawaii; attempted to win the right of blacks to visit the Palisades Amusement Park across the Hudson River from Harlem; and challenged the firing of black railroad firemen when white unions of railroad workers attempted to displace them. The NAACP's entry into such cases was accomplished by publicity campaigns to win public support.

The first case the NAACP brought to the Supreme Court directly challenging segregation was particularly well chosen. It produced a decision in 1917 that broke a string of decisions over the twenty-year period following *Plessy* that had reaffirmed the Court's sanction of laws requiring the segregation of the races.

Buchanan v. *Warley*[52] involved a white man's sale of a building lot in Louisville to a black man in violation of a city ordinance requiring residential segregation. The circumstances made it even more difficult than in *Plessy* for the Court to suggest that "natural affinities" kept black and white apart because, in the case before it, a black and a white had acted in concert. The ordinance's effort to limit a white man's right to sell his property also offended the Court's prevailing laissez-faire views about commercial transactions. Accordingly, the Court held that the ordinance violated "the fundamental law enacted in the Fourteenth Amendment of the Constitution preventing state interference with property rights except by due process of law."[53] Because the decision was based on the due process clause of the Fourteenth Amendment and not its clause requiring equal protection of the laws, *Buchanan* did not overrule *Plessy*. The decision provided grounds for hope, however, that a well-planned litigation campaign could eventually lead to a reversal of *Plessy*.

If a precise moment can be fixed, the campaign to challenge *Plessy* head-on commenced on May 28, 1930. On that date, the American Fund for Public Service donated $100,000 to the NAACP to finance "a nation-wide legal and educational campaign to secure for the Negroes in this country a fuller and more practical enjoyment of the rights, privileges, and immunities theoretically guaranteed them by the Constitution of the United States."[54]

The fund had been established several years earlier by Charles Garland, an heir to a Boston fortune. During the 1920s and 1930s, it was the most important single source of financial support for organizations advocating civil liberties, racial equality, and the right of labor to organize. A committee comprising Roger Baldwin, Morris Ernst, Lewis Gannett, James Weldon Johnson, James Marshall, Arthur Spingarn, and Walter White—all prominent civil liberties and civil rights activists—was designated to oversee expenditure of the grant. On October 4, 1930, the committee selected

Nathan Margold, a Harvard-trained lawyer and disciple of Felix Frankfurter, who had represented Pueblo Indians in land claims cases, to direct the campaign.

Margold set about on his task by writing a 218-page memorandum outlining a plan. He began by reviewing the proposal that had been submitted to the American Fund for Public Service to obtain the grant. The proposal had noted that "in South Carolina more than ten times as much was expended for the education of white children as for Negro children; that in Florida, Georgia, Mississippi and Alabama, more than five times as much; in North Carolina, Virginia, Texas, Oklahoma and Maryland, more than twice as much."[55] These disparities violated the principle established by *Plessy* that though the states could legally require the separation of the races, they could not provide unequal facilities.[56] "Tax-payer suits," the proposal continued, "should be brought to force *equal* if separate accommodations for Negroes and whites," which would "(a) make the cost of a dual school system so prohibitive as to speed the abolishment of segregated schools; (b) serve as examples and give courage to Negroes to bring similar actions; (c) cases will likely be appealed by city authorities, thus causing higher court decisions to cover wider territory; (d) forces as nothing else will public attention north and south upon the vicious discrimination in the apportionment of school funds."[57]

Margold's memorandum examined this approach in detail and rejected it. The practices of local school boards were little regulated by state laws. Discrimination in expenditures was permitted by the wide discretion vested in local school boards, but it was not required. Courts were unlikely to interfere with the general practice of granting such discretion, according to Margold, only with particular abuses of it that would have to be proved in each instance. Accordingly, a successful challenge to an abuse of discretion in one school district would not eliminate similar abuses in other districts in the same state. Every discrimination in expenditure would have to be litigated afresh to challenge the current practice in that school district. The task, as Margold saw it, was monumental. "It would be a great mistake to fritter away our limited funds," he told the committee that had appointed him, "on sporadic attempts to force the making of equal divisions of school funds in the few instances where such attempts might be expected to succeed. At the most, we could do no more than to eliminate a very minor part of the discrimination during the years our suits commenced. We should not be establishing any new principles, nor bringing any sort of pressure to bear which can reasonably be expected to retain the slightest force beyond that exerted by the specific judgment or order that we might obtain. And we should be leaving wholly untouched the very essence of the evils."[58]

Margold proposed a new approach. "If we boldly challenge the constitutional validity of segregation if and when accompanied irremediably by discrimination," he wrote, "we can strike at the most prolific sources of discrimination. We can transform into an authoritative adjudication the principle of law ... that segregation coupled with discrimination resulting from administrative action permitted but not required by state statute is just as much a denial of equal protection of the laws as is segregation coupled with discrimination required by express statutory enactment."[59]

Charles Houston, William Henry Hastie, and Thurgood Marshall, the three black lawyers who spearheaded the NAACP and NAACP Legal Defense Fund drive against unequal schools over the next three decades, drew heavily on this analysis. But Margold's approach did not arouse universal enthusiasm among civil rights advocates. In 1935, W.E.B. DuBois attacked the strategy espoused by Margold, asserting, "The NAACP and other Negro organizations have spent thousands of dollars to prevent the establishment of segregated Negro schools, but scarcely a single cent to see that the division of funds between white and Negro schools, North and South, is carried out with some faint approximation of justice. There can be no doubt that if the Supreme Court were overwhelmed with cases where the blatant and impudent discrimination against Negro education is openly acknowledged, it would be compelled to hand down decisions which would make this discrimination impossible."[60]

No advocate of segregation, DuBois nevertheless was convinced that it would persist for a very long time. Lacking a crystal ball that might have allowed him to foretell that, in the 1950s, the United States would have urgent foreign policy reasons for ending enforced segregation, DuBois estimated it would last for another two centuries.[61] He wanted to be certain that the education of Negroes was not neglected in the interim. "I know," DuBois wrote, "that this article will forthwith be interpreted by certain illiterate 'nitwits' as a plea for segregated Negro schools and colleges. It is not. It is simply calling a spade a spade. It is saying in plain English: that a separate Negro school, where children are treated like human beings, trained by teachers of their own race, who know what it means to be black in the year of salvation 1935, is infinitely better than making our boys and girls doormats. . . . To sum up this: theoretically, the Negro needs neither segregated schools nor mixed schools. What he needs is Education. . . . Other things being equal, the mixed school is the broader, more natural basis for the education of all youth. It gives wider contacts; it inspires greater self-confidence; and suppresses the inferiority complex. But other things seldom are equal."[62]

DuBois did not persuade the organization he had helped to found to shift course. Attacking "segregation . . .

accompanied irremediably by discrimination," NAACP lawyers persuaded the Maryland Court of Appeals in 1936 that, since there was no law school for blacks in the state, it should order the University of Maryland to admit a black to its law school.[63] In 1938, the NAACP established a nationwide precedent on the same issue when the United States Supreme Court ordered the University of Missouri Law School to admit Lloyd Gaines.[64] The decision invalidated Missouri's requirement that the state pay tuition for blacks who had qualified for admission to law school to attend schools in neighboring states rather than mingle with whites at the University of Missouri. This violated the Fourteenth Amendment's guarantee of equal protection of the laws, the Supreme Court decided in *Gaines,* because "Manifestly, the obligation of the State to give the protection of equal laws can be performed only where its laws operate, that is, within its own jurisdiction."[65] The NAACP did not make significant further headway in its legal campaign against segregated schools during World War II, but in 1948, the NAACP Legal Defense Fund—by this time a separate organization—persuaded the Supreme Court to reject Oklahoma's excuse for maintaining an all-white law school.[66] The successful lawsuit was brought on behalf of Ada Lois Sipuel, who had been denied admission to the University of Oklahoma Law School on the ground that a new law school for Negroes would soon be opened by the state.

Two years after *Sipuel,* in 1950, the NAACP-LDF appeared before the Supreme Court in two cases challenging segregated graduate schools: in a suit on behalf of Heman Marion Sweatt, an applicant for admission to the University of Texas Law School, who had been rejected because a new law school for blacks had just been opened; and in a suit on behalf of George W. McLaurin, a candidate for a doctorate in education at the University of Oklahoma, who had been admitted after a legal struggle. McLaurin, an older man than most of his fellow students, was required to sit in a hallway by himself—participating in classes by listening through an open door—and to keep apart from other students in the library and in the school cafeteria. An important development in the *Sweatt*[67] and *McLaurin*[68] cases was the entry of the Justice Department as a friend of the court, the first time the executive branch of the federal government took part in a case challenging segregated schools.

The 1952 call to the Supreme Court in *Brown* to take into account cold war needs was foreshadowed in the brief the United States filed in *Sweatt* and *McLaurin* in 1950. "The racial discriminations typified by these cases," the Justice Department told the Supreme Court,

> represent a challenge to the sincerity of our profession of the democratic faith. The President has stated: "If we wish to inspire the peoples of the world whose freedom is in jeopardy, if we wish to restore hope to those who have already lost their civil liberties, if we wish to fulfill the promise that is ours, we must correct the remaining imperfection in our democracy." . . . If the imprimatur of constitutionality should be put on such denial of equality, one would expect the foes of democracy to exploit such an action for their own purposes. The ideals embodied in our Bill of Rights would be ridiculed as empty words, devoid of any real substance. The lag between what Americans profess and what we practice would be used to support the charges of hypocrisy and the decadence of democratic society. . . . It is in the context of a world in which freedom and equality must become living realities, if the democratic way of life is to survive, that the issues in these cases should be viewed.[69]

In another brief filed with the Supreme Court at about the same time in a railroad segregation case, the Justice Department devoted four pages to documenting the way domestic discrimination embarrassed the government in the conduct of its foreign policy.[70] Cold war competition for the affections of newly independent nations of nonwhites was in full swing by 1950, and the executive branch of the federal government was starting to turn to the courts to deal with aspects of American racial practice beyond its own control.

With the help of the United States Department of Justice, the NAACP Legal Defense Fund prevailed. The Supreme Court held that the law school to which Texas was willing to admit Heman Sweatt was unequal

> in terms of numbers of the faculty, variety of courses and opportunity for specialization, size of the student body, scope of the library, availability of law review and similar activities. . . . [M]ore important, the University of Texas Law School possesses to far greater degree those qualities which are incapable of objective measurement but which make for greatness in a law school . . . reputation of the faculty, experience of the administration, position and influence of the alumni, standing in the community, traditions and prestige. . . . The law school to which Texas is willing to admit plaintiff [Sweatt] excludes from its student body members of the racial groups which number 85% of the population of the State and include most of the lawyers, witnesses, jurors, judges and other officials with whom the plaintiff will inevitably be dealing when he becomes a member of the Texas Bar.[71]

In *McLaurin,* decided the same day, the Supreme Court held that Oklahoma's rules forcing McLaurin to keep apart from other students "handicapped [him] in his pursuit of effective graduate instruction. Such restrictions impair and inhibit his ability to study, to engage in discussions and exchange views with other students, and, in general to learn his profession."[72]

The two decisions invalidated instances of segregation accompanied irremediably by discrimination. The logical next step was to attack segregation per se as *always* accompanied irremediably by discrimination. After all, the Supreme Court had held in both *Sweatt* and *McLaurin* that restrictions on contacts helped to make segregated education unequal. Such restrictions are inherent in all segregated education. *Sweatt* and *McLaurin* undermined the logic of a system that pretended to offer separate but equal education.

The legal reasoning of the decisions in *Pearson, Gaines, Sipuel, Sweatt,* and *McLaurin* led inexorably to *Brown*. But in terms of social impact, to take the next step required a gigantic leap, even if it was a leap required by world events. The cases prior to *Brown* had enabled a handful of black college graduates to obtain professional training in previously all-white universities in border states. Of itself, this was a meager showing for two decades of effort by a group of extraordinarily talented black lawyers and for the expenditure of many times the sum that had been granted to the NAACP in 1930 by the American Fund for Public Service. Except for their value in opening the path to *Brown,* the results achieved between 1930 and 1950 amply justified W.E.B. DuBois's 1935 complaint.

The Supreme Court controls its own docket. In deciding to consider segregation in the public schools, therefore, the Court's own view that the question was ripe for resolution was at least as important as the strategic planning of the lawyers. The Court's intention to hand down a definitive decision was evident because it selected five cases for review, two from southern states (South Carolina and Virginia), one from a border state (Delaware), one from a midwestern state (Kansas), and the case from the District of Columbia placed on the docket on its own initiative before it was decided by the Circuit Court of Appeals.

The *Brown* decision of May 17, 1954, held that the enforced separation of nine million white children from three million black children in some five thousand school districts was illegal. It was certainly the Court's most momentous decision since *Dred Scott* more than a century earlier, a decision that had helped to produce a civil war. Few suggested that the consequences of *Brown* would be so drastic, though a handful of southern editorial writers did their best to inflame passions in their communities. "Human blood may stain southern soil in many places because of this decision," said the *Jackson* (Mississippi) *Daily News*, "but the dark red stains of that blood will be on the marble steps of the United States Supreme Court building. . . . It means racial strife of the bitterest sort. Mississippi cannot and will not try to abide by such a decision."[73]

Even W.E.B. DuBois was enthusiastic about *Brown* and noted its cold war significance. "One hundred years before Chief Justice Warren declared that racial segregation in public schools 'is a denial of the equal protection of the law,'" DuBois wrote in a leftwing newspaper, "another chief justice declared that Negroes have no rights which a white man must respect. Thus in a century this nation has taken mighty steps along Freedom Road and raised the hopes of mankind, black, yellow and white. . . . We rejoice and tell the world, and by so doing admit freely that heretofore this nation has not been a free democracy and that the criticism of the Communist world has in this respect been entirely justified."[74] As time passed, however, it became increasingly clear that a long period of turmoil would accompany the effort to secure compliance. Although the executive branch of the federal government had urged the Supreme Court to invalidate segregation for urgent foreign policy reasons,

Dwight Eisenhower, who had taken office as president while the case was under consideration by the Supreme Court, refused to endorse the decision. The absence of leadership from the White House was reflected in the turnabout by such southern leaders as Governor Thomas Stanley of Virginia, who had reacted to *Brown* on May 17, 1954, calling for "cool heads, calm study and sound judgment" and promising to consult "leaders of both races." A bare six weeks later, Governor Stanley declared, "I shall use every legal means at my command to continue segregated schools in Virginia."[75] Despite such a hardening of line throughout the South, W.E.B. DuBois expressed guarded optimism in February, 1955: "At best it will be a generation before the segregated Negro public school entirely disappears. But considering the worldwide advertisement that the United States has at last started to become a democracy without a color line, it is going to be difficult for the South and the northern copperheads to treat the separate school decision as they have treated Negro disenfranchisement since 1876."[76]

The battle to secure compliance with *Brown* has not been so bloody as the *Jackson Daily News* anticipated, but it has been more difficult and more protracted than was generally envisioned in 1954. The significance of *Brown*, however, went far beyond the schools. A handful of lawyers acting on behalf of a depressed minority triumphed over the several states and the teams of eminent lawyers from prestigious firms ranged against them. Not only did the highest court in the land declare itself for equality, it demonstrated that courtrooms were a forum in which the usual trappings of power did not predetermine the results. If anything the apparent morality of the Supreme Court's decision and the Court's prestige were enhanced by the defiant responses of southern political leaders, such as the seventeen senators and seventy-seven representatives who signed the "Southern Manifesto" in 1956, denouncing the "stab-in-the-back" decision. The Manifesto signers became the rebels. Blacks, *Brown* proclaimed, could prevail by working within the system. A branch of the government had responded to their claim for justice, and most of the white establishment outside the South, for its own reasons, welcomed the decision. It was worthwhile, it appeared, for blacks to organize and to work within the system to change it by making additional demands for their rights. As Martin Luther King, Jr., wrote a few years later, "For all men of good will May 17, 1954, marked a joyous end to the long night of enforced segregation. . . . This decision brought hope to millions of disinherited Negroes who had formerly dared only to dream of freedom. It further enhanced the Negro's sense of dignity and gave him even greater determination to achieve justice."[77]

When *Brown* was decided, King was an obscure twenty-five-year-old Baptist minister in Alabama. A year later, he achieved national recognition as the leader of the protest that launched the "civil rights movement," the Montgomery bus boycott. The first great manifestation of the sense of hope fostered by *Brown,* the boycott started when a middle-aged black seamstress, Rosa Parks, was arrested for refusing to move to the back of the bus. It was a peaceful and dignified protest, and the photographs of blacks walking long distances to work that appeared in newspapers and on television enhanced the aura of moral urgency that *Brown* contributed to the equal rights cause. Inevitably in the wake of *Brown,* the issues raised by the boycott were taken to court. In his memoir of the boycott, King marked this moment with a comment reflecting the impact of *Brown:* "It was a great relief to be in a federal court. Here the atmosphere of justice prevailed . . . the southern Negro goes into the federal court with the feeling that he has an honest chance of justice before the law."[78] Noting that in *Brown,* "the separate but equal doctrine was repudiated,"[79] the federal court vindicated King's faith by invalidating the Alabama laws requiring the segregation of public transportation. The decision was quickly affirmed by the United States Supreme Court.[80]

The Montgomery bus boycott inspired street demonstrations, marches, sit-ins, freedom rides, pray-ins, and other nonviolent protests. King, the boycott leader, became the universally acknowledged leader of the civil rights movement of the 1960s. Wherever the movement went, lawyers accompanied it. Defending the movement became a principal preoccupation of the NAACP Legal Defense Fund, the NAACP, the American Civil Liberties Union, and such organizations especially created for this purpose as the Lawyers Constitutional Defense Committee, the Law Students Civil Rights Research Council, and the Lawyers Committee for Civil Rights Under Law.

Despite lapses—most pronounced in the late 1960s because the pace of change failed to keep up with expectations—the struggle for racial equality in the United States has continued to bear the imprint placed on it by the United States Supreme Court in *Brown*: it has been peaceful and it has been legal. It is only possible to speculate about what might have occurred if the United States Supreme Court had not provided the nation with a peaceful means of ending state-enforced segregation of the races. Almost entirely disenfranchised when *Brown* was decided and for a decade thereafter, and substantially disenfranchised for much longer, southern blacks could not have secured an end to segregation through the ballot box. Indeed, were it not for *Brown,* their disenfranchisement and political powerlessness to secure change would almost certainly have persisted much longer.

Perhaps blacks would have remained quiescent or perhaps some other way would have been found to end enforced segregation peacefully. Looking back more than a quarter of a century after *Brown,* those seem only remote possibilities. More likely, were it not for *Brown* or some comparable decision by the Supreme Court, American blacks would have engaged in violent struggle to end state-enforced segregation. The Supreme Court's assertion of the authority to shape public policy in *Brown* may have had a large part in averting civil strife just as the Court's decision a century earlier in *Dred Scott* played a large part in bringing about a civil war.

The impact of *Brown* on the foreign policy interests that were so important to government brief writers and newspaper editorial writers in the 1950s is difficult to assess. It seems likely that the decision was helpful to the United States in its competition with the Soviet Union for the friendship of dark-skinned people around the world, though not so helpful as was generally asserted in 1954. On the other hand, if the alternative to *Brown* had been violent racial strife, there seems little doubt but that the United States would have suffered greatly in its competition with the Soviet Union. In that sense, it was not so much that the decision bolstered U.S. foreign policy interests as that it may have helped prevent great damage to them.

There is little need to speculate about one part of the legacy of *Brown*. It stimulated blacks and other deprived minorities to seek redress of their grievances through litigation. Three decades after *Brown*, belief that litigation can advance such causes is firmly established. Few Americans any longer doubt that litigation plays an important part in public policy. *Brown* is the cause of the transformation and remains its symbol.

How did *Brown* become so important? The explanation seems to lie in its value to Americans in demonstrating to themselves their own moral worth. At a moment when Americans needed it most, *Brown* proclaimed that their way of life meant liberty and justice for all. Perhaps all those newspaper editorials touting the advantage *Brown* would give the United States in competing with world communism were just a way of selling the decision. If so, they were very effective. *Brown* made Americans—minorities, judges, lawyers, and much of the public—proud, and the way of dealing with a social problem that it symbolized was the beneficiary of that pride. In the process, it endowed the United States Supreme Court, which spoke with one voice to the entire nation, with the charismatic authority that ordinarily can be obtained only by an individual, not by an institution.

"In traditional periods [an apt way of characterizing the 1950s], charisma is the great revolutionary force,"[81] Max Weber pointed out. Certainly, the Supreme Court that decided *Brown* became a revolutionary force. Although it is difficult to think of so tradition-bound an institution as the Court as fostering revolution, that was the effect of *Brown* and the Court's refusal to flinch when the decision was attacked. The *Brown* Court set in motion the civil rights movement, the social activism of the 1960s that grew out of the civil rights movement, and the scramble by previously invisible interest groups to climb onto the plateau of American politics. Not least among its revolutionary accomplishments, it allowed the judiciary to venture deeper into the territory of political justice and distributive justice than ever previously.

4

Racial Equality:
Relinquishing Leadership

After declaring enforced racial segregation in the public schools to be unconstitutional in *Brown* v. *Board of Education,* the Supreme Court considered another aspect of the same case the following year, 1955: how should desegregation take place. *Brown II,*[1] as it is known, is best remembered for the Court's use of the term "with all deliberate speed"[2] to characterize the manner in which black children should be admitted on a racially nondiscriminatory basis to previously all-white public schools. That delphic language was the most precise guidance the Court provided in *Brown II* on the implementation of *Brown I.*

In retrospect, the Court's approach in *Brown II* seems mistaken. Robert Carter, an attorney in *Brown,* subsequently general counsel of the NAACP, and now a federal judge, wrote a decade and a half after *Brown* that the Court "apparently believed that its show of compassion and understanding of the problem facing the South would develop a willingness to comply. Instead the 'all deliberate speed' formula aroused the hope that resistance to the constitutional imperative would succeed."[3] Yet, given the Court's lack of experience in ordering massive social change, probably no more specific guidance was then possible. Moreover, the generality of the language reflected the long tradition of judicial deference to administrative officials in the implementation of court decisions. It was assumed that once judges said what was right or wrong, administrators would act in good faith to implement the law of the land. The only overt defiance of its decisions the Court had encountered previously involved small numbers of officials, like those who refused to implement Justice Taney's order in *Merryman* in 1861 calling for release of a secessionist held in a military prison.[4] Defiance by thousands of officials in an entire section of the country was new to the Court if only because it had never previously decided a case requiring so many to alter radically the way they did their jobs.

Some administrators reacted in good faith to *Brown II*, but the rule in much of the South was "massive resistance" against school desegregation. Alexander Bickel was surely exaggerating when he wrote that the turmoil made the South look "like the American Algeria,"[5] but there were many ugly mob scenes, riots, bombings, and even murders. Much of the blame must rest on President Eisenhower. Even though the executive branch of the federal government played a crucial role in the early 1950s in persuading the Supreme Court to decide *Brown,* under Eisenhower it did little in the years immediately following the decision to implement it or to win national support for it.

One of the many places where battle lines were drawn was Little Rock, Arkansas. State officials, led by Governor Orval Faubus, claimed that they were not bound to implement *Brown* because Arkansas was not a party to the Supreme Court case. The Little Rock school board, however, attempted to carry out a lower court decision to desegregate.

On September 2, 1957, Faubus called out the National Guard to prevent a group of black students, "the Little Rock nine," from entering Central High School. This action forced the hand of a reluctant president and, on September 24, he issued an order federalizing the Arkansas National Guard and dispatching five hundred guardsmen of the 101st Airborne Division to Little Rock to make it possible for the black children to attend Central High. Eisenhower had helped to bring on the crisis. As one of Eisenhower's aides, Emmett John Hughes, wrote a few years later, "his limp direction of the struggle in Congress for the Civil Rights Act of 1967 had served almost as a pathetic and inviting prologue to Little Rock."[6] Indeed, three months before sending in the troops, Eisenhower said at a press conference, "I can't imagine any set of circumstances that would ever induce me to send federal troops . . . into any area to enforce the orders of a federal court, because I believe that the common sense of America will never require it. . . . I would never believe that it would be a wise thing to do."[7] Eisenhower's closest associate in the White House, Sherman Adams, subsequently commented that Eisenhower regarded his dispatch of troops to Little Rock as "a constitutional duty which was the most repugnant to him of all his acts in his eight years in the White House."[8]

The Little Rock case, *Cooper* v. *Aaron,* considered by the Supreme Court in 1958, elicited a unanimous opinion. The significance the Court attached to the opinion and the Court's understanding that its authority derived from the charismatic quality of its leadership are reflected in the decision of the justices to speak as one by issuing the opinion in all their names, thereby going beyond the precedents of *Marbury* and *Brown* in which all the justices joined in the opinions of the chief justice. In *Cooper* v. *Aaron* the Court made its boldest assertion of its authority to act as the ultimate interpreter of the Constitution.[9] Quoting Chief Justice Marshall's famous statement in *Marbury* that "it is emphatically the province of the judicial department to say what the law is," the Court declared:

> The federal judiciary is supreme in the exposition of the law of the Constitution, and that principle has ever since been respected by this Court and the Country as a permanent and indispensable feature of our constitutional system. It follows that the interpretation of the Fourteenth Amendment enunciated by this Court in the *Brown* case is the supreme law of the land, and Art. VI of the Constitution makes it of binding effect on the States "any Thing in the Constitution or laws of any State to the Contrary not withstanding." Every state legislator and executive and judicial officer is solemnly committed by oath taken pursuant to Art. VI. ¶3. "to support this Constitution."[10]

Bickel, who regarded this assertion as a dubious claim of authority that went far beyond *Marbury,* argued that its widespread acceptance at the time owed much to the fact that "southern leaders had overplayed their hand, mob action led to the mobilization of northern opinion in support of the Court's decision—not merely because the mob is disorderly, but because it concretized the abstraction of racism, somewhat in the manner in which the cases and controversies in whose context the Court evolves its principles concretize all abstractions."[11] Bickel notwithstanding, the legitimacy of judicial exercise of such authority has not been seriously questioned in the nearly three decades since Little Rock, reflecting the process whereby charismatic authority is routinized and becomes traditional authority.

Cooper v. Aaron broke the back of "massive resistance," but resistance persisted, and in many southern communities dual school systems continued for more than another decade.

Indeed, they persist de facto today in many communities. Yet so much progress was made in the South in ending school segregation that during the past decade a larger proportion of black and white children attended desegregated schools in the South than in the North. By 1976, the United States Commission on Civil Rights reported that 23 percent of black children in the South attended public schools at least 90 percent minority; 58 percent in border states and states in the Northeast; 62 percent in the Midwest; and 50 percent in the West.[12]

Milestones in bringing about desegregation in the South include the United States Department of Justice's assumption of a significant share of responsibility for bringing school desegregation litigation starting when John Kennedy took office as president and Robert Kennedy took office as attorney general in 1961; the passage of the Civil Rights Act of 1964 permitting the federal government (which was becoming a major source of financial support for public schools) to cut off funds of school districts that failed to desegregate; the Supreme Court's 1964 decision in *Griffin v. Prince Edward County Board of Education*,[13] saying that the time for "deliberate speed" had expired; the Court's 1965 decision in *Bradley v. School Board of Richmond*,[14] saying that "delays in desegregating school systems are no longer tolerable"; the Court's 1968 decision in *Green v. County School Board of New Kent County*,[15] holding that a so-called "freedom-of-choice" plan was an unconstitutional evasion of *Brown;* and the Court's 1969 decision in *Alexander v. Holmes County Board of Education*,[16] ordering Mississippi schools to desegregate "at once" even though the new Nixon administration had urged delay.

In 1971, with Warren Burger as chief justice of the United States, school desegregation litigation entered a new phase. In *Swann v. Charlotte-Mecklenburg Board of Education,* the

Supreme Court held for the first time that the redrawing of attendance zones, busing, and assignment of students on the basis of race were appropriate remedial measures in school districts that had been "deliberately constructed and maintained to enforce racial segregation. The remedy for such segregation may be administratively awkward, inconvenient, and even bizarre in some situations and may impose burdens on some; but all awkwardness and inconvenience cannot be avoided in the interim period when remedial adjustments are being made to eliminate the dual school systems."[17]

In giving its blessings to a desegregation plan involving busing—or "forced busing," as its enemies usually call it—the Supreme Court entered an area of great public controversy. In *Swann,* the Court had made it plain that the busing it approved was remedial in circumstances where a voluminous record demonstrated that segregation was state-imposed. It was a venture in distributive justice clearly required to correct the injustice of enforced segregation. The Court explicitly disavowed any interest in requiring racial balance per se. "The constitutional command to desegregate schools," Chief Justice Burger wrote for an unanimous Court, "does not mean that every school in every community must always reflect the racial composition of the school system as a whole."[18] Such language in the opinion warranted the puzzlement with which Burger is reported to have reacted to the headlines announcing the opinion. "Burger couldn't understand it," Bob Woodward and Scott Armstrong reported in *The Brethren.* "He told his friends that he considered his opinion 'antibusing.'"[19]

In appearing to support busing, the Supreme Court frightened many whites in the North. Litigation challenging de facto segregation in their school systems had been under way for a decade, and busing had been required as a remedy by several court decisions. A March 1972 Gallup poll found 69 percent of Americans opposed to busing for desegregation and only 20 percent in favor. Richard Nixon gauged the widespread public antagonism to busing and exploited it in several speeches as a candidate for president in 1968 and 1972 and as president.[20] Even Nixon's denunciations of busing did not satisfy some opponents, permitting George Wallace to build an independent presidential candidacy on fervid antibusing sentiment. Congress and the state legislatures adopted numerous antibusing resolutions and laws.[21] There was even an attempt to adopt a constitutional amendment prohibiting school busing.

How did the antibusing furor affect the prestige and the authority of the Supreme Court and of the courts generally? It certainly produced many vigorous denunciations of judicial intervention in matters that should be decided elsewhere. If the decibels had been measured, those denouncing the courts over busing decisions would have been found to be far more vociferous than those expressing support. At the same time, decisions like *Swann* appeared to reflect the Court's maintenance of a steady course in combating racial segregation. The unanimity of the decision overcame the ambiguity of its language in creating the impression that a united Court was still proceeding along the path charted in *Brown*. And *Brown* had such great prestige that even those who denounced busing—not including George Wallace—generally prefaced their remarks by lauding the Court for its decisions striking down de jure segregation. Americans might dislike busing and might denounce the courts for ordering busing, but they respected an institution that tried to hold them to a higher standard.

Subsequent to *Swann*, the Supreme Court has followed a wavering path. A notable decision supporting desegregation was *Keyes* v. *School District No. 1*[22] in which the Court made it clear that intentional segregation resulting from school board practices required remedial action as in the case of segregation required by law. Analyzing such practices in Denver, the first northern city to become the subject of a school desegregation decision by the high Court, Justice Brennan wrote in his majority opinion:

> First it is obvious that a practice of concentrating Negroes in certain schools by structuring attendance zones or designating "feeder" schools on the basis of race has the reciprocal effect of keeping other nearby schools predominantly white. Similarly, the practice of building a school . . . to a certain size and in a certain location, "with conscious knowledge that it would be a segregated school," has a substantial reciprocal effect on the racial composition of other nearby schools. So also, the use of mobile classrooms, the drafting of student transfer policies, the transportation of students, and the assignment of faculty and staff, on racially identifiable bases, have the clear effect of earmarking schools according to their racial composition, and . . . causing further racial concentration within the schools.[23]

There were several opinions in *Keyes*, but only Justice William H. Rehnquist flatly dissented from the majority decision. In 1974, however, the Court's unity on school desegregation matters was shattered. After twenty years, the era of the Court's charismatic leadership in desegregating the schools came to an end in a 5–4 opinion in *Milliken* v. *Bradley*,[24] reversing a lower court decision requiring metropolitan desegregation of the schools in Detroit, where the schools are predominantly black, and its suburbs, where the schools are predominantly white.

A lower court had found intentional segregation by Michigan and by Detroit of the Detroit city school system. The court's remedy embraced fifty-three suburban school districts, creatures of the state, which was responsible for intentional segregation even though it was not shown that the suburban districts themselves intentionally brought about segregation. Chief Justice Burger wrote the majority opinion reversing this decision on the ground that "absent an interdistrict violation there is no basis for an interdistrict remedy."[25]

Ordering desegregation of schools in suburban districts that are not themselves shown to be intentionally segregated would, in the view of the Court's majority, require the Supreme Court to take a significant step. It differs fundamentally from ending intentional segregation, which involves correcting a past wrong. Established principles of corrective justice guide courts in such circumstances, even when the remedies they devise require them to look forward and involve principles of distributive justice. Devising a plan to end past segregation where a specific past wrong cannot be proved, on the other hand, requires a vision that connects a general set of past wrongs done to blacks to present injustice for which the particular school officials affected by a judicial order have not been found responsible. This vision must also embrace a desirable set of practices which should prevail in the future to correct that general set of past wrongs even though those wrongs cannot be blamed on the public bodies affected. A court attempting to carry out such a vision cannot rely on traditional principles of corrective justice to guide its ventures in distributive justice.

To the lower courts in *Milliken,* this problem did not arise because intentional segregation by Michigan and Detroit were sufficiently specific past wrongs to guide their actions. To the Supreme Court, which insisted that those seeking desegregation prove specific, intentional past wrongs in each school district that might be affected by a desegregation plan, the problem was insuperable.

Yet since desegregation of Detroit schools, 70 percent black when the Supreme Court decided *Milliken,* is impossible without a remedy that embraces suburban schools, the city's schools remain segregated. Indeed the major practical consequence of *Milliken,* and the Supreme Court's refusal to go beyond traditional backward-looking corrective justice, is to encourage whites to flee from cities to suburbs, where, the decision helps to make certain, their children attend virtually all-white schools. One of the places that has happened is Detroit, where the school system is 80 percent black at this writing.

Although the Supreme Court subsequently reaffirmed support for school desegregation within northern cities,[26] the obstacle it placed in the way of metropolitan desegregation in *Milliken* makes it unlikely that more black and white children will attend school together in the North. If anything, segregation is increasing and will continue to increase. Segregation is also increasing in southern cities like Atlanta—where the school system is now 90 percent black—which are coming to resemble northern cities in the development of their suburbs. Ironically, it is in the rural South and in small towns in the South where the greatest proportion of black and white children attend school together nearly three decades after *Brown.*

Public controversy over school desegregation litigation has declined in recent years despite increasing de facto segregation in much of the country. Even the "new right" devoted more attention in the 1980 elections and in the first years of the Reagan administration to such issues as abortion, religion in the schools, the Equal Rights Amendment, and American military might. One reason is the Supreme Court's decision in *Milliken.* It provided most white families with a way to avoid busing their children for purposes of racial segregation. Accordingly, their protests abated. The last great antibusing demonstrations were staged by whites in Boston in the mid-1970s and in Los Angeles in the late 1970s. By demography and geography, a metropolitan solution is not essential for court-ordered desegregation in those cities; accordingly, it was not foreclosed by *Milliken.*

Another factor in the abatement of controversy over school desegregation is increasing acceptance of the views expressed in the 1969 "Coleman Report," suggesting that the schools are a less significant instrument for achieving equality than had been supposed earlier. The report asserted: "Schools bring little influence to bear on a child's achievement that is independent of his background and general social context; this very lack of independent effect means that the inequalities imposed on children by their home, neighborhood, and peer environment are carried along to become the inequalities with which they confront adult life at the end of school. For equality of education opportunity through the schools must imply a strong effect of the schools that is independent and that strong independent effect is not present in American schools."[27] Coleman's conclusions were echoed by many others, among them Christopher Jencks, who wrote, "There is no evidence that school reform can substantially reduce the extent of cognitive inequality, as measured by tests of verbal fluency, reading comprehension, or mathematical skill. Neither school resources nor segregation has an appreciable effect on either test scores or educational attainment."[28]

The predominant view of blacks during the past decade does not dispute the ineffectuality of the schools as they presently operate in bringing about equality, but there is a difference in emphasis. Kenneth B. Clark has written that "American public schools have become significant instruments in the blocking of economic mobility and in the intensification of class distinctions rather than fulfilling their historic function of facilitating such mobility."[29] There is nothing inevitable, in Clark's view, about the failure of the schools to promote social mobility and equality. The fault, as he sees it, lies in the accountability of the school system only to itself and to its professional employees and its lack of accountability to its pupils, their families, and their communities.

The prevalence of the views represented by Coleman and Jencks on the one hand and by Clark on the other has made desegregation of the schools less central than it once was to those concerned about equality, even to those who, like Clark, maintain their commitment to desegregation.

For about the last decade, it has not been clear that a majority of black parents support the desegregation litigation of which their children are presumably intended to be beneficiaries. Whether this attitude results from a sense that desegregation will fail—among other reasons, because whites will take advantage of *Milliken* to move to suburbs that cannot be affected by desegregation plans—or from a sense that desegregation is not important is difficult to assess. Either way, black parents now are more passionately engaged in struggles for accountability than in efforts to secure desegregation.

Disputes over accountability can be as explosive as disputes over desegregation, as strife in New York City over "community control" of the schools made plain in the late 1960s, but proponents of accountability have not found the question susceptible to resolution in the courts. Much litigation about equality in education continues to focus on desegregation, but desegregation no longer occupies center stage. Accordingly, such litigation has declined in significance as a battlefield in the ongoing war about equal educational opportunity.

Public opinion polls indicate that many Americans who oppose busing simultaneously insist that they believe in desegregation. They say they favor waiting until neighborhoods are desegregated, thereby avoiding the transportation of children for purposes of desegregation.[30] "The problem with busing," says T.H. Bell, secretary of education in the Reagan administration, "is that at the end of the bus ride you're still back in that racially isolated neighborhood."[31] The difficulty with this position is that neighborhoods are not becoming less segregated and, in part because of *Milliken,* significant residential desegregation will not take place soon. Though the courts long played an important role in striking down laws and practices fostering residential segregation, in the 1970s the Supreme Court abandoned leadership in this area, paralleling what it did with respect to school segregation.

The Supreme Court acted against residential segregation as early as 1917. In *Buchanan* v. *Warley,*[32] the Court invalidated a Louisville ordinance prohibiting blacks from occupying homes on blocks where the majority of homes were occupied by whites. At first glance, the decision seems out of step for a time when the "separate but equal" doctrines of *Plessy* v. *Ferguson* prevailed. A closer look, however, suggests that the Court was not so much concerned with striking down segregation to promote equality for blacks as with striking down interference with the property rights of whites.

The courts of Kentucky had held that a white's contract to sell property to a black was unenforceable because of the ordinance prohibiting the black from occupying that property. This ordinance violated that provision of the Fourteenth Amendment prohibiting the taking of property without due process of law, the Supreme Court said, because "property is more than the mere thing which a person owns. It is elementary that it includes the right to acquire, use, and dispose of it. The Constitution protects these essential attributes of property."[33] Distinguishing this case from *Plessy*, the Court noted that *Buchanan* "does not deal with an attempt to prohibit the amalgamation of the races. The right which the ordinance annulled was the civil right of a white man to dispose of his property if he saw fit to do so to a person of color."[34] It is difficult to imagine many other circumstances that would have prompted the Supreme Court to strike down a law requiring segregation at that time. But *Buchanan* involved the issue that seemed to matter most to the Supreme Court: property rights.

Whites intent on maintaining residential segregation quickly devised a way to make the judicial concern for property rights work in their favor. They began going to court to enforce racially restrictive covenants in which property owners committed themselves to limit the future uses of property by barring their sale to blacks. In the aftermath of *Buchanan*, the leading case involving racially restrictive covenants was *Corrigan v. Buckley*,[35] considered by the Supreme Court in 1926. The Constitution limits only "the powers of the general government and is not directed against the action of individuals,"[36] the Supreme Court said in dismissing an appeal from a lower court decision. Laws enforcing racially restrictive covenants were held to be valid because they "do not in any manner prohibit or invalidate contracts entered into by private individuals in respect to the control and disposition of their own property."[37]

Black ghettos like "Nigger Hill" and "New Guinea" in Boston and "Little Africa" in Cincinnati[38] had existed for many years before the Supreme Court gave its blessings to racially restrictive covenants. But the Supreme Court's action in *Corrigan* and similar decisions by several state courts played important roles in making certain that the rural blacks who migrated to industrial cities in great numbers between the two wars were restricted to residing in such ghettos, which grew far larger than those that had existed previously. Because the ghettos were larger, the residential segregation of whites from blacks became more pronounced.

In 1948, in *Shelley* v. *Kraemer*,[39] the Supreme Court again considered racially restrictive covenants. Without explicitly overruling *Corrigan*, the Court effectively nullified all such covenants. The distinguishing factor, according to Chief Justice Vinson's opinion for the Court, was that *Corrigan* questioned only the validity of the covenants, whereas the question in *Shelley* was enforcement of such agreements in state courts. Enforcement violated the Fourteenth Amendment, Vinson wrote, because "the action of the States to which the Amendment has reference, includes action of state courts and state judicial officials."[40] No longer enforceable, the covenants became meaningless.

A black newspaper, the *Pittsburgh Courier*, reported its story on *Shelley* v. *Kraemer* under the headline, "Live Anywhere You Can Buy."[41] The headline over the *Chicago Defender's* story was "Let Freedom Ring," and, after describing racially restrictive covenants as "responsible for more human misery, more crime, more disease and violence than any other factor in our society," the paper lauded the Supreme Court for bringing "to a dramatic close one of the ugliest developments in American history."[42]

In retrospect, these responses exaggerate the decision's practical significance, though not its symbolic importance in ending judicial participation in an unsavory practice. Ghettos did not disappear; indeed, they continued to grow, even though "fair housing" laws were enacted in many industrial states in the decade and a half following the decision. Attempts by blacks to move into previously all-white neighborhoods met resistance almost everywhere, sometimes violent. And, in the mid-1960s, several communities repealed fair housing laws by referendum.

In California, the referendum in 1964 to repeal the state's fair housing law took the form of an amendment to the state constitution adopted by a wide margin after a bitterly fought campaign. It provided that "neither the State nor any subdivision or agency thereof shall deny, limit or abridge, directly or indirectly, the right of any person, who is willing or desires to sell, lease or rent any part or all of his real property, to decline to sell, lease or rent such property to such person or persons as he, in his absolute discretion chooses."[43] In 1967, the United States Supreme Court held that this amendment to the California Constitution violated the Fourteenth Amendment to the United States Constitution because it involved the state in racial discrimination.[44] And, in 1968, the Supreme Court held that a post-Civil War federal law providing that all citizens have the same rights as whites to hold or purchase real property[45] prohibits a private citizen from refusing to sell a home to a black.[46]

Despite such decisions, little housing desegregation took place. By the end of the 1960s it was plain that more would be required than legal protection of the right of an individual black to purchase a home in a white neighborhood. The economic gap between blacks and whites made it impossible for most blacks to live in relatively affluent white neighborhoods. Blacks who could afford such housing were often reluctant to live in areas where there were no other blacks, or hardly any other blacks, and where they were made unwelcome. Housing desegregation could take place, it became plain, only on a large scale. Low-cost public housing would have to be provided in white areas, and zoning restrictions in the suburbs would have to be modified.

Just as the referendum was used by whites opposed to housing desegregation in an effort to repeal fair housing laws, so it was used in an attempt to bar public housing that would bring blacks into white areas. Four years after the Supreme

Court struck down the results of a referendum in California that would have allowed whites to refuse to sell or rent homes to blacks, the Court shocked advocates of residential desegregation by upholding the results of referendums in California that barred low-cost public housing from being constructed in San Jose and in San Mateo County. In an opinion by Justice Hugo L. Black in *James* v. *Valtierra*,[47] the Court noted that the referendums did not make "distinctions based on race."[48] The Court refused to consider economic discrimination as a justification for exacting scrutiny, and it refused to assume that the purpose of economic discrimination was racial discrimination. Since the Court's majority found that racial discrimination had not been proved, no compelling principles of corrective justice seemed to be at stake. Accordingly, the Court refused to render distributive justice.

The attempt to bring about housing desegregation on a significant scale was set back further in 1975 in *Warth* v. *Seldin*.[49] In an opinion by Justice Lewis F. Powell, Jr., the Supreme Court held that a group of plaintiffs who challenged exclusionary zoning practices in Penfield, a suburb of Rochester, New York, lacked standing to sue. The plaintiffs included low- and moderate-income residents of Rochester who were members of racial minorities. They lacked standing, the Court said, because they could not point to housing in Penfield in which they could afford to live but had been denied the right to live. Other plaintiffs also held to lack standing included builders who had been denied the right to construct low-income or moderate-income housing in Penfield. The Court said that they could not point to specific projects that had been barred so their claim of exclusion was too speculative to confer standing. As Justice Brennan complained in dissent, "The Court turns the very success of the allegedly unconstitutional scheme into a barrier to a lawsuit seeking its invalidation."[50]

The obstacles in the way of significant housing desegregation established in such decisions as *James* v. *Valtierra* and *Warth* v. *Seldin* are occasionally surmounted. In *Hills* v. *Gautreaux*,[51] the Supreme Court upheld a lower court's order requiring metropolitan desegregation of public housing in Chicago, where such housing had previously been located in a fashion designed to reinforce residential segregation. Similarly, a few state court cases have invalidated racially exclusionary zoning. But these cases required such massive efforts—eleven years of litigation in *Gautreaux* before the Supreme Court decision in 1976 and continuing litigation seeking implementation thereafter—that there is no chance that they will be replicated in many places. Thanks to decisions like *Valtierra* and *Warth*, litigation challenging housing segregation has declined in significance.

With litigation rendered largely ineffectual, residential desegregation proceeds at a snail's pace. In 1977, 77.2 million whites, or 41.9 percent of the white population, lived in suburban areas; only 4.6 million blacks, or 18.8 percent of the black population, lived in suburban areas. The percentage of blacks in the suburbs had risen by just over 4 percent since 1960, a rate that would require a century to pass before the proportion was the same as for whites if their residential distribution remained constant. Even these figures suggest more desegregation than is actually taking place because most blacks living in suburbs are residents of suburban ghettos.[52] Residential segregation is now more or less accepted as a permanent way of life, and litigation challenging it could not possibly elicit comments like those that the *Pittsburgh Courier* and the *Chicago Defender* made about *Shelley* v. *Kraemer*.

Just as some opponents of busing profess support for desegregating the schools by desegregating housing, so some opponents of locating public housing in white neighborhoods and of challenges to exclusionary zoning profess support for residential desegregation. They say that residential desegregation should take place naturally by the desegregation of employment. If blacks and whites hold the same jobs and earn the same incomes, their reasoning goes, there would be no need to desegregate neighborhoods artificially by building public housing projects in affluent neighborhoods or by changing zoning laws. This argument may be accepted by some litigators on behalf of racial equality, at least *sub silentio*, because their efforts are now overwhelmingly focused on getting jobs for members of minorities. Yet the methods they use in challenging the underrepresentation of minorities in certain jobs often arouse sentiments similar to those expressed in opposition to school busing and efforts to locate public housing in white neighborhoods.

Although challenges to employment discrimination now make up the bulk of litigation on behalf of racial equality, such litigation got under way relatively recently. Indeed, no significant volume of litigation on behalf of equality in employment was undertaken until after Congress enacted the Omnibus Civil Rights Act of 1964. Title VII of the act (amended in 1966 and again in 1972) established administrative procedures and rules governing litigation to challenge discrimination by virtually every public and private employer engaged in interstate commerce with at least fifteen employees.[53]

Initially, Title VII served primarily to redress grievances by individuals claiming they were victims of job discrimination. This proved almost as slow and tortuous a process of securing equality as desegregating residential neighborhoods by enforcing fair housing laws against owners of property discriminating in sales and rentals. Then, in 1971, in *Griggs* v. *Duke Power Company*,[54] in a unanimous decision, the Supreme Court provided litigators with a powerful weapon against employment discrimination.

Griggs involved a claim by black employees at the Dan River power plant in Draper, North Carolina, that they were restricted to low-paying jobs by Duke Power Company's policy that employee transfers to higher paying jobs would be permitted only for high school graduates who performed satisfactorily on two tests. According to the 1960 census, only 12 percent of black males in North Carolina had graduated from high school, compared to 34 percent of white males. In addition, whites scored much better than blacks on the tests, in part reflecting the effects of more and better schooling. The black employees claimed, however, that neither the high school completion requirement nor performance on the tests could be shown to bear a relationship to successful job performance. Evidence presented to the trial court that considered *Griggs* supported the claim that the requirements were not relevant to performance.

In the opinion for the Supreme Court, Chief Justice Burger acknowledged that the record showed that Duke Power "had adopted the diploma and test requirements without any 'intention to discriminate against Negro employees.'" Yet this did not mean that the company's practices were legal under Title VII, Burger wrote, because "good intent or absence of discriminatory intent does not redeem employment procedures or testing mechanisms that operate as 'built-in headwinds' for minority groups and are unrelated to measuring job capability."[55] In an especially noteworthy passage, Burger wrote, "If an employment practice which operates to exclude Negroes cannot be shown to be related to job performance, the practice is prohibited."[56]

In *The Brethren*, in one of many passages in which Woodward and Armstrong purport to know what was in the mind of a Supreme Court justice, Potter Stewart is reported to have been "staggered ... by the sweeping language of the opinion."[57] Whether or not Stewart was staggered, the decision stands out in bold relief against decisions like *Milliken* and *Valtierra*. In *Griggs*, the Supreme Court looked to discriminatory effect regardless of the lack of discriminatory intent, whereas in *Milliken* and *Valtierra*, the Court looked to the lack of discriminatory intent regardless of discriminatory effect. Effect is susceptible to documentary proof, whereas intent can be readily inferred but only rarely proved. Accordingly, *Griggs* made the likelihood of success in challenges to employment discrimination far greater than in challenges to school segregation and housing segregation, where intent had become the test.

Five years after *Griggs*, the Supreme Court decided *Washington v. Davis*[58] and reached an opposite result. The Supreme Court denied a claim by two unsuccessful black candidates for positions as police officers in the District of Columbia that their constitutional rights had been violated by the use of a test that had a discriminatory effect. They did not allege that it had discriminatory intent. The result in *Davis* was distinguished from that in *Griggs* because the suit had not been brought under Title VII but under the Civil Rights Law of 1866 implementing the Fourteenth Amendment's guarantee of equal protection of the laws.[59] According to Justice Byron A. White's opinion for the Court, "Under Title VII, Congress provided that when hiring and promotion practices disqualifying substantially disproportionate numbers of blacks are challenged, discriminatory purpose need not be proved," but the Court was "not disposed to adopt this more rigorous standard for the purposes of applying the Fifth and the Fourteenth Amendments."[60]

Most cases challenging employment discrimination brought under the 1866 Civil Rights Law to implement the Fourteenth Amendment may also be brought under Title VII. The procedures and remedies differ, but, as the Supreme Court was aware, *Washington* v. *Davis* does not critically affect litigation challenging employment discrimination. Its significance lies elsewhere. If the Court had held that the Fourteenth Amendment prohibits government practices that have a racially discriminatory effect on employment, consistency would require it to hold that the Fourteenth Amendment also prohibits government practices that have a racially discriminatory effect on housing and education. Yet, as cases like *Milliken* and *Valtierra* make clear, the present Supreme Court is not prepared to prohibit discrimination in housing and education except when it is shown that the discrimination is intentional. By insisting that the holding in *Griggs* is mandated solely by Title VII, the Court established a rationale for subjecting employment discrimination to more exacting scrutiny.

Title VII does not explicitly provide that discriminatory effect is sufficient to invalidate employment criteria that are not demonstrably and directly valuable in predicting performance. The Supreme Court's holding prohibiting reliance on such criteria, therefore, represents its gloss on the law. The Court could validly put a similar gloss on the Fourteenth Amendment. Judicial tradition looks at least as kindly— usually more kindly—on construing a constitutional provision expansively as on construing a statute expansively. Yet despite frequent insistence by the justices that questions of race discrimination warrant the most exacting scrutiny by the courts because they involve the rights of a discrete and insular minority that is the intended beneficiary of the Fourteenth Amendment, the Court, in Justice White's words, is presently "not disposed to adopt this more rigorous standard."

Under the circumstances, the conclusion seems warranted that the present Supreme Court sees more compelling principles of corrective justice at stake when minorities are denied the right to hold the same jobs as whites than when they are denied the right to receive the same education or live in the same neighborhoods. Accordingly, the Supreme Court will provide distributive justice to minorities to help them overcome inequality in access to jobs but will not provide them with distributive justice to help them overcome inequality in access to housing or to education.

This conclusion seems borne out by the Supreme Court's approach to cases involving affirmative action. To date, the cases the Court has considered have involved education and employment. In the 1978 case of *Regents of the University of California* v. *Bakke*,[61] five justices voted to invalidate a plan in which a medical school set aside sixteen places out of a hundred for disadvantaged minority students to be admitted according to separate criteria. Justice Powell, who cast the swing vote to make up the majority, indicated that he would uphold a race-conscious admissions program in which race is one factor to be considered in securing a diverse student body. In his view, the University of California program at issue in *Bakke* was too rigid to be sustained, however, because race was an exclusive criterion.[62] The following year, 1979, Justice Powell again cast the swing vote in an affirmative action case, this time involving employment. In *United States Steelworkers of America* v. *Weber*,[63] five members of the Supreme Court voted to uphold a plan providing that 50 percent of all openings must be set aside for minorities in a training program for employees seeking better jobs at a Kaiser Aluminum plant in Louisiana. Although it is possible to distinguish *Bakke* and *Weber* on a number of grounds, ultimately the fact that the one case involved education and the other involved employment seems controlling. As in *Griggs*, the Supreme Court cited Title VII as grounds for distinguishing employment. A 1980 affirmative action case dealing with the distribution of jobs, *Fullilove v. Kreps*,[64] did not involve Title VII, but another federal statute. As in *Weber*, the Supreme Court upheld affirmative action even though the case involved just the sort of rigid numerical criteria—a requirement that 10 percent of all federal funds spent on public works projects go to businesses at least 50 percent owned by minorities—the Court had found unconstitutional in *Bakke*.

That the circumstance in which discrimination takes place determines whether the Supreme Court looks to discriminatory intent or discriminatory effect is also indicated by a case involving grand jury selection in Texas, *Castaneda v. Partida*,[65] decided in 1977, the year after *Washington v. Davis*. In *Castaneda*, the Supreme Court noted that only about half as many Mexican-Americans were summoned for grand jury service during a decade as their proportion of the population would warrant. In the Court's view, this disparity made chance or accident a highly unlikely explanation. Accordingly, the Court inferred intent from effect even though intent was not separately demonstrated. During the same term, the Supreme Court decided a housing case, *Arlington Heights v. Metropolitan Housing Development Corp*,[66] involving a builder who had acquired land with the intent of building racially integrated low- and middle-income housing. These plans were frustrated when public officials refused to grant a zoning variance to permit the construction of multifamily dwellings. Discriminatory intent was not shown, and the Court refused to invalidate the zoning decision despite its clear discriminatory effect. Once again, the Supreme Court seems to have decided—though it did not say so—that desegregating housing does not involve compelling principles of corrective justice. Ensuring proportionate racial representation on grand juries, seems more comparable to ensuring proportionate racial representation in employment in getting the Supreme Court to provide distributive justice.

Many Americans, including members of minorities, may share the view that it is more important that minorities hold the same jobs as whites than that they attend the same schools or live in the same neighborhoods. There are at least two difficulties with this approach, however. First, despite the Court's purported reliance in *Griggs* and *Weber* on the greater protection afforded by Title VII, it is not clear that there is a sound basis in law or principle for less exacting scrutiny of housing segregation and school segregation than of employment discrimination. *Castaneda* makes clear that in the absence of statutory guidance the Court is willing to apply the Fourteenth Amendment to invalidate discriminatory effect in certain circumstances by using statistical evidence to infer discriminatory intent. It could do the same with respect to housing and school segregation if, in Justice White's word, it were "disposed" to do so. That it is not disposed to do so with respect to some aspects of discrimination but is disposed to with respect to other aspects of discrimination betrays the Court's unarticulated values; jobs and jury service matter more than housing and education. Second, the Court's approach is self-defeating because employment discrimination cannot be isolated from school segregation and housing segregation. Ensuring that minorities hold the same jobs as whites enables them to live in the same neighborhoods and attend the same schools, but it also works the other way around. Unless minorities get the same education as whites—which includes, as the Supreme Court recognized in 1950 in *Sweatt* and *McLaurin*, forming the same contacts as whites—they will not get the same jobs. Unless minorities reside in the same proximity to jobs—which, in much of the country, have moved out of the city centers to almost exclusively white suburbs and satellite towns poorly served by public transportation—they will not get the same jobs. If compelling principles of corrective justice demand that the Supreme Court dispense distributive justice to desegregate employment, those same principles also require it to dispense distributive justice to desegregate schools and housing.

The failure of the courts in the 1970s to provide leadership in bringing about racial equality as they did in the 1950s and in the 1960s has diminished the prestige of the judiciary. Though still high, judicial prestige is not as high as it was a decade ago. From the standpoint of most blacks, it would be a cause for surprise if some present-day counterpart of Martin Luther King were to echo his words at the time of the Montgomery bus boycott—"It was a great relief to be in a federal court. Here the atmosphere of justice prevailed." Much of the litigation on behalf of racial equality that is under way today seems almost clientless. One does not have the sense that any substantial portion of the black community eagerly anticipates its outcome. Even if a court decision should purport to advance the cause of racial equality, there is a pervasive sense that the whites affected by it will discover a way to resist it or to circumvent it and that the courts will ultimately ratify that resistance or circumvention.

From the standpoint of most whites, the courts still seem to regard blacks as special favorites, ordering busing for purposes of school desegregation and ordering affirmative action programs to regulate employment and admissions to educational programs. Such court decisions are widely resented even though most whites are aware, as blacks are aware, that they can be resisted or circumvented successfully. Far from mitigating resentment of the judiciary, awareness that resistance and circumvention work may exacerbate it. The implacability of the courts in the 1950s and 1960s in striking down a multitude of schemes designed to resist or circumvent their desegregation orders inspired respect. The willingness of the courts in the 1970s and the 1980s to ratify resistance and circumvention inspires cynicism.

It would be extraordinarily difficult for the courts in the 1980s to resume providing national leadership in bringing about racial equality. Racial polarization, of which judicial failure to provide leadership in the 1970s may be one of the important causes, seems so great today that it is difficult to imagine any public body providing leadership. Perhaps, someday, the courts will again try to lead the nation in bringing about racial equality. If so, one guesses that it will be because extraneous considerations—unanticipatable at this writing—will again impose a duty of leadership upon the courts, just as cold war considerations in the 1950s imposed on them the duty to end legally enforced racial segregation.

5

Political Equality: A Lustrous Achievement

"Creatures of the same species and rank, promiscuously born to all the same advantages of Nature and the use of the same faculties," wrote John Locke, "should also be equal one amongst another without subordination or subjection."[1]

Such views linking political equality with natural law strongly influenced the framers of the United States Constitution. Nevertheless, several of that document's provisions indicate that they did not regard exact numerical representativeness as an essential feature of democratic government. The Constitution provides that two senators shall be elected from each state regardless of population;[2] that the president and vice-president shall be chosen by an electoral college rather than by popular vote;[3] that the number of electors from each state shall equal the number of representatives and senators, thereby enhancing the voting strength of citizens of small states;[4] and that extraordinary majorities are required to remove federal officers,[5] amend the Constitution,[6] overturn vetoes,[7] or ratify treaties.[8] Some of these provisions reflect political compromises needed to secure ratification of the Constitution. Others reflect a fear of the tyrannical consequences of simple majoritarianism. The only provision of the Constitution explicitly concerned with numerical representativeness governs the election of the members of the House of Representatives, providing that "Representatives shall be apportioned among the several States according to respective numbers counting the whole number of persons in each State, excluding Indians not taxed."[9]

In the century following the adoption of the Constitution, the national commitment to political equality grew stronger, and "no state was admitted to the Union in which the original constitution did not provide for representation principally based on population in both houses of the legislature."[10] That view changed in the last decade of the nineteenth century when rural populations started to decline. Fearing the power of rapidly growing cities, a rural-dominated Congress began admitting western states to the Union in which legislators represented counties even though the counties had greatly disparate populations. States already in the union, dominated by rural legislatures, revised their constitutions before power could shift to legislators representing cities, and rural legislators in a few states dispensed with constitutional amendments simply by using their control to block reapportionment that would reflect shifts in population.

The first significant case considered by the United States Supreme Court challenging unrepresentativeness did not involve a state legislature but the United States House of Representatives. No popular movement led to the litigation. Rather, the case had its origins in academic criticism of electoral inequality. The principal plaintiff, Kenneth R. Colegrove, was a political science professor at Northwestern University who led a small group of Chicago and suburban university faculty members in attempting to invalidate inequalities in population districts used for congressional elections in Illinois. Even though the disparities of which Colegrove complained were the most extreme in the nation—the largest congressional district in the state had a population of 914,053 and the smallest had a population of only 112,116—in *Colegrove* v. *Green*,[11] the Court refused to consider the merits. Declining to enforce the explicit constitutional provision that "Representatives shall be apportioned ... according to respective numbers," Justice Felix Frankfurter wrote in the opinion of the Court that the question was "of a peculiarly political nature and therefore not meet for judicial determination."[12] In explanation of this holding, he noted that "to sustain this action would cut very deep into the very being of Congress. Courts ought not to enter this political thicket. The remedy for unfairness in districting is to secure State legislatures that will apportion properly, or to invoke the ample powers of Congress."[13]

The remedy Frankfurter proposed was preposterous. Malapportioned legislative bodies concentrated power in the hands of legislators who would be voting themselves out of office and denying their own constituents disproportionate power if they acceded to demands for equal political representation. It would require an altruism not common in political bodies, as was plain from the history of schemes devised by rural legislators to retain power despite demographic changes. If ever there was a case for judicial intervention to enhance the representativeness of representative government in accordance with the principles of Justice Stone's footnote in *Carolene Products*, this was it. Here was a textbook example of "legislation which restricts those political processes which can ordinarily be expected to bring about the repeal of undesirable legislation."[14] But Stone died on the eve of the Court's consideration of *Colegrove*, and Frankfurter's very different judicial philosophy prevailed.

The term "political thicket" entered judicial parlance through Frankfurter's opinion. It was apt in suggesting that the Court would encounter political opposition to any attempt to regulate legislative apportionment. The "very being" of legislative bodies was indeed involved in the sense that the jobs of legislators were at stake. But it was inapposite in suggesting that policies, rather than principles susceptible to judicial determination and management, were at stake. The right of all to be "equal one amongst another" (in Locke's words) in voting strength is a clear and forthright principle, explicitly guaranteed by the language of the Constitution so far as the United States House of Representatives is concerned.

Although the language of the Court's opinion in Colegrove appeared to foreclose relief from malapportionment in the federal courts, it was only a 4–3 plurality decision. This split provided grounds for some optimism that the Supreme Court might be persuaded to reverse itself. World War II had strengthened egalitarian sentiment and had set in motion an accelerated shift of population from rural areas to the cities and, in the years following the war, to the suburbs. Conflicts between rural-dominated state legislatures and big city political leaders over state taxes and expenditures became more intense than ever, and lawsuits were filed in many states attempting to circumvent or overturn the precedent of Colegrove. A breakthrough took place in Hawaii in 1956 when a territorial court—not bound by the same constitutional limits as federal courts considering lawsuits affecting the states—announced that it was prepared to grant relief from malapportionment of the territorial legislature.[15] That decision was mooted by Congress, which itself undertook to redistrict the territorial legislature. Another breakthrough came in 1960 when the Supreme Court, with Justice Frankfurter writing the opinion of the

Court, decided *Gomillion* v. *Lightfoot*,[16] invalidating racial gerrymandering in Alabama. The purpose of the gerrymandering had been to exclude the predominantly black faculty of Tuskegee Institute from taking part in the political life of the town of Tuskegee. Frankfurter avoided the precedent of his own opinion in *Colegrove* by grounding his opinion in *Gomillion* on the Fifteenth Amendment, which prohibits the states from restricting the right to vote on grounds of race. Even so, it was difficult to suggest that the decision steered entirely clear of what Frankfurter had labeled the political thicket.

Colegrove was effectively reversed sixteen years after it was decided by the Supreme Court's historic decision in *Baker* v. *Carr*,[17] a case challenging Tennessee's failure to reapportion its representation in either house of its state legislature for sixty years despite substantial growth and redistribution of population. One area of the state shortchanged by the shifts that had taken place was Shelby County, where Memphis is located. The growth of Memphis and its suburbs during the twentieth century was not matched by allocations of state tax revenues by the Tennessee General Assembly, prompting Charles W. Baker, a Shelby County political leader, to file suit seeking equity in representation. Baker obtained assistance in the litigation from other metropolitan area political leaders whose communities were treated similarly by the state legislature. Intervention in *Baker* v. *Carr* by Nashville Mayor Ben West proved especially helpful to Baker because the Nashville Planning Commission supplied data that documented exhaustively the consequences for city residents of malapportionment of the state legislature. Although the Constitution contains no explicit language guaranteeing equal representation in state legislatures, in Justice Brennan's opinion, the Court held that the case was justiciable because "judicial standards under the Equal Protection

Clause are well developed and familiar, and it has been open to courts since the enactment of the Fourteenth Amendment to determine, if on the particular facts they must, that a discrimination reflects no policy, but simply arbitrary and capricious action."[18]

In dissent Justice Frankfurter questioned whether the equal protection clause was properly invoked. He wrote:

> The notion that representation proportioned to the geographic spread of population is so universally accepted as a necessary element of equality between man and man that it must be taken to be the standard of a political equality preserved by the Fourteenth Amendment—that it is, in appellants' words, "the basic principle of representative government"—is, to put it bluntly, not true. However desirable and however desired by some among the great political thinkers and framers of our government, it has never been generally practiced, today or in the past.[19]

The heart of Frankfurter's objection to the holding, however, did not lie in his reading of history. Restating the thesis of *Colegrove,* he contended that questions of apportionment are not justiciable, that is, manageable by the courts: "Even assuming the indispensable intellectual disinterestedness on the part of judges in such matters, they do not have accepted legal standards or criteria or even reliable analogies to draw upon for making judicial judgments. To charge courts with the task of accommodating the incommensurable factors of policy that underlie these mathematical puzzles is to attribute, however flatteringly, omnicompetence to judges."[20]

Frankfurter's views in *Baker* did not strike as sympathetic a chord as when he wrote the Court's opinion in *Colegrove.* Halfway between the two decisions, the Court had decided *Brown* v. *Board of Education,* radically altering the political context in which Supreme Court decisions were viewed. The prestige and authority the Supreme Court obtained through *Brown* gave it the strength to deal with the "very being" of legislative bodies. In 1962, when the Supreme Court decided *Baker,* it was at the peak of its charismatic authority because in decisions like *Cooper* v. *Aaron* it had held firm and spoken with a single, magisterial voice in resisting challenges to the mandate of *Brown.* And *Brown* established the potency of the equal protection clause as an instrument for bringing about social and political change. Although legislators who saw their offices and their hegemony directly threatened by *Baker* could constitute a formidable opposition, the Supreme Court had acquired the strength to take on formidable opponents in matters where evident principles of corrective justice such as the right to equal political representation were at stake.

There have been substantial attacks on *Baker* by legal scholars. Archibald Cox argues that the Court read into the equal protection clause "notions of wise and fundamental policy which are not even faintly suggested by the words of the Constitution and which lack substantial support in other conventional sources of law."[21] Raoul Berger contends that "the historical records all but incontrovertibly establish that the framers of the Fourteenth Amendment excluded both suffrage and segregation from its reach,"[22] citing the decision as a prime example of subversion of the Constitution, "government by judiciary." But such criticism rests on the theory—not controlling in *Brown*—that the application of a constitutional principle must be limited to matters clearly contemplated by its framers. Even if such critics are right historically—and this is in dispute[23]—they would have the courts ignore the implications of John Marshall's famous dictum that it is "a constitution we are expounding." The equal protection clause, which did not encompass equality of the sexes when the Fourteenth Amendment was drafted, would mean now what it meant then. Similarly, because the Fourteenth Amendment might not have been thought by its authors to apply to equal representation because when it was adopted every state admitted to the union guaranteed equal representation to all except blacks, who were its intended beneficiaries, it would not authorize the result the Supreme Court reached in *Baker.* The Constitution would become a sterile document, stripped of capacity to accommodate evolving public understanding of broad concepts such as equal protection of the laws. In the process the Constitution's fundamental commitment to representativeness could be nullified by the representative branches themselves.

Earl Warren believed that *Baker* was the most important decision of the Court in his sixteen years as chief justice.[24] Although few today would agree that it compares in significance with *Brown* v. *Board of Education,* it was certainly a landmark decision. As a matter of constitutional theory, it provided us with Justice Brennan's famous definition of a "political question" (see Chapter 2). And it paved the way for a series of judicial decisions that shifted power in state legislatures across the country. Rural interests declined in strength, their representatives replaced by legislators from cities and suburbs. In the early 1960s, most discussion of the decision focused on *Baker's* significance in enhancing urban representation, leading to the widespread belief that it would radically increase the power of political liberals. Later in the decade, however, it became clear that the rapidly growing suburbs might benefit comparably. Their voters are often quite as conservative as those in rural counties, making the ideological consequences of *Baker* less dramatic than Warren and many others may have anticipated at the time of the decision.

Baker itself only decided that matters of legislative apportionment can be decided by courts under the Fourteenth Amendment. Actual judicial standards for reapportionment had to await subsequent cases. A modest movement was under way seeking reapportionment before *Baker*, but the decision helped to spawn the creation of a more significant movement, as *Brown* v. *Board of Education* launched the civil rights movement.

The reapportionment movement, of course, shared few of the characteristics of the civil rights movement or of such progeny as the women's rights movement or the movement against the Vietnam war. The equal representation movement was largely composed of a relatively small number of state legislators, municipal officials, lawyers, and politically active and sophisticated citizens who devoted their energies to litigation and legislative lobbying and not to street demonstrations. The most important organizations providing leadership and support for their efforts were established bodies such as the National Municipal League and the Twentieth Century Fund, which sponsored scholarly studies on which the litigation and lobbying were based, convened conferences to bring together activists in the movement, and distributed literature on equal representation. A widely circulated Twentieth Century Fund pamphlet, *One Man— One Vote,* helped to popularize the phrase that became the movement's slogan. Although the style of this movement was staid and conservative, because it was believed at the time that reapportionment would profoundly alter the ideological character of the nation's legislatures, activists in the movement and close observers of it thought that the consequences of its success would be revolutionary. No doubt this view was shared by many of the judges deciding the early reapportionment cases, their willingness to take part in a revolution reflecting their sense of their own enhanced capacity in the early 1960s to exercise national leadership.

In 1964, two years after *Baker,* the Supreme Court decided *Reynolds* v. *Sims,*[25] a case requiring equality in representation in both houses of the Alabama legislature, along with five companion cases applying the same principle to other states. A measure of the significance sophisticated observers attached to the decision may be gleaned from a small incident that took place in the Supreme Court chamber as the decision was being read. The *New York Times* law correspondent, Anthony Lewis, passed a note to Archibald Cox, then solicitor general of the United States. "How does it feel," Lewis asked, "to be present at the second American Constitutional Convention?" Cox, who had filed a brief for the United States urging the Supreme Court to invalidate on narrow grounds the state legislative schemes that were being challenged, passed back a note saying, "It feels awful."[26]

Reynolds was brought to the Supreme Court by a group of young lawyers who were in some ways typical of those responsible for such litigation in almost every state in the period following *Baker* v. *Carr.* No national organization sponsored their litigation, though some of them attended conferences sponsored by the established groups that provided them with scholarly support. They were politically active political liberals from the state's biggest city, Birmingham, some of them involved in the civil rights movement, which reached its peak in intensity of activity in Alabama in the period from 1962, when *Baker* was decided, to 1964, when *Reynolds* was decided. This was the place and time of Martin Luther King, Jr.'s famous "Letter from Birmingham City Jail"; of the protest demonstrations which Birmingham police chief Eugene "Bull" Connor attempted to suppress with fire hoses and police dogs; and of the bombing at the 16th Street Baptist Church in Birmingham that killed four black girls. The atmosphere created by court decisions advancing the cause of the civil rights movement was reflected in a passage in the brief two of the young Birmingham lawyers filed in the Supreme Court. They described the federal district court that had originally considered *Reynolds* as "the only institution to which freedom in Alabama has been entrusted."[27] Another aspect of the litigation, its connection to the political activity of the lawyers involved in it, is reflected in the fact that one of them, David Vann, was elected mayor of Birmingham a decade or so later.

Reynolds put into practice the theory that the Court had found justiciable in *Baker* and made the standard for equal representation one-person, one-vote-because, as Chief Justice Warren wrote in the Court's opinion, "the Equal Protection Clause requires that a State make an honest and good faith effort to construct districts . . . as nearly of equal population as is practicable."[28] Representative government in the states would have to become numerically representative. *Reynolds* also inspired legislators who saw their ideological control—and, perhaps, their jobs—threatened to launch a major effort to amend the United States Constitution to permit states to apportion one house of each state legislature in accordance with factors other than population. Symmetry with the federal Constitution was a frequently cited argument for such an approach, though its actual purpose was plainly to permit rural interests to retain their power. The increasing identification of the cities as the home of racial minorities was a generally unspoken concern of some of the amendment's supporters.

The most visible and vigorous proponent of a constitutional amendment was Everett Dirksen of Illinois, leader of the Republican minority in the United States Senate. He quickly marshaled substantial political support for an amendment, but it never came close to adoption. In retrospect, the defeat of the Dirksen amendment seems inevitable. Constitutional amendments are difficult to pass, generally requiring both a substantial national consensus and strong support from a significant segment of the population that has interests directly at stake. The second of those conditions was met because many rural legislators and officeholders and others dependent on those legislators were directly affected. In addition, the proposed amendment attracted support from many political leaders, particularly in the South, who saw it as a means of expressing their outrage at the part the Supreme Court had played during the decade from *Brown* to *Reynolds* in reshaping American public policy. But a national consensus could not be obtained. Dirksen and company were unable to create a majoritarian backlash against a Supreme Court decision that enhanced the representativeness of representative government; the Supreme Court's prestige was too great to permit passage of a constitutional amendment that derived much of its support from anti-Court sentiment; and time was against the Dirksen amendment. As legislatures reapportioned in compliance with *Reynolds,* rural representation declined, leaving an ever smaller political base of support for the adoption of a constitutional amendment designed to perpetuate the power of rural interests.

As Robert B. McKay pointed out in a 1968 report by the Twentieth Century Fund, "Despite the delaying tactics of opponents of the one man, one vote decision, by the end of 1967 nearly all the states had brought their congressional districts and their state legislative districts in substantial compliance with the equal-population principle.... In nearly every instance of malapportionment, a judicial proceeding was initiated in federal or state court (sometimes in both) to invalidate the existing formula, and legislative action followed in partial or total correction."[29]

In the years since *Reynolds,* reapportionment cases have occupied much of the time of the federal courts. Village, town, city, and county councils, school boards, local boards of election, and many other public bodies have been required to conform to the one-person, one-vote principle.[30] Only public bodies exercising very limited powers, such as water district bodies, have been held exempt from the requirement to apportion representation according to population.[31] Some cases have acquired lives of their own, returning to court after each reapportionment in tests of their conformance to the principle of one-person, one-vote. Although it has proved difficult to secure compliance with this standard, as Victor Navasky points out, it "has avoided the morass of litigation a *less* mechanical standard might have precipitated."[32]

The year following *Reynolds,* the United States Congress adopted the Voting Rights Act of 1965.[33] One of the most significant achievements of the civil rights movement of the 1960s, the act is intended to implement the Fifteenth Amendment, which prohibits abridgement of the right to vote on account of race. It prohibits the use of "tests or devices" that have the effect of limiting voting, and it requires Justice Department approval of changes in some state and local voting laws to make certain that they do not abridge the rights of minorities. The act enhanced the significance of litigation in securing equal political representation, as Congress anticipated in adopting it, because much of its enforcement takes place in Court. The results have been dramatic, in many instances more important politically than the reapportionment required by *Reynolds.* In Mississippi, for example, voter registration among blacks rose from a little over 6 percent in 1964 to close to 60 percent three years later.[34] The law has also given litigators a ready means of challenging schemes adopted by many southern communities that were intended to limit the political power of newly enfranchised black voters.[35]

The most important continuing battles over equal representation involve at-large voting. Litigation challenging this practice proceeds under the Fourteenth and Fifteenth Amendments to the Constitution and under the Voting Rights Act. The Supreme Court considered this practice in 1971 in *Whitcomb v. Chavis*[36] and, in an opinion by Justice White, upheld at-large voting in Indiana because the plaintiffs proved neither that the practice had a racially discriminatory purpose nor a racially discriminatory effect and because "experience and insight have not yet demonstrated that multi-member districts are inherently invidious and violative of the Fourteenth Amendment. . . . [I]f the problems of multi-member districts are unbearable or even unconstitutional it is not at all clear that the remedy is a single-member district system with its lines carefully drawn to ensure representation to sizeable racial, ethnic, economic or religious groups."

Two years later, however, in *White v. Regester,*[37] in another opinion by Justice White, the Supreme Court found that a scheme for at-large election to the Texas House of Representatives was unconstitutional because its effect was to dilute minority voting strength. In contrasting the circumstances with those in *Whitcomb,* White stressed the history of voting discrimination in Texas, noting that the Democratic party organization that controlled elections in Dallas County "did not need the support of the Negro community to win elections" because of at-large voting and "did not therefore exhibit good-faith concern for the political and other needs and aspirations of the Negro community."[38] In Bexar County, at-large elections "excluded Mexican-Americans from effective participation in political life."[39]

In *White* v. *Regester* Justice White's stress was on the practical effect of at-large voting on equal representation for racial and linguistic minorities, but the grounds for the decision were somewhat ambiguous because the opinion referred to both "the design and impact" of such schemes.[40] The decision, predating *Milliken* v. *Bradley* and *Washington* v. *Davis,* which required proof of discriminatory purpose before the Court would invalidate segregation, encouraged litigators to bring cases challenging at-large voting when discriminatory effect could be proved, especially in communities with a history of disenfranchisement. As Laurence Tribe noted, despite the ambiguity of *White* "and despite a growing tendency to make discriminatory motive a sine qua non of equal protection challenges claiming other forms of racial injustice, it seems clear that a districting scheme which truly excluded a racial minority from a community's political life could not justifiably be upheld on the basis that the exclusion was accidental rather than intentional."[41]

In 1980, however, in *City of Mobile* v. *Boulden,*[42] the Supreme Court abandoned its focus on the effects of at-large voting requirements and required instead that litigators challenging such schemes prove that these effects resulted from discriminatory purposes. Since such a purpose could not be proved in the case before it, the Court upheld at-large municipal voting in Mobile, Alabama, even though the practice had resulted in no black ever having been elected to the City Commission.

Discriminatory purpose could not be shown in *Mobile* because at-large voting for members of the City Commission had been in effect since 1911. Black citizens of Alabama had been almost completely disenfranchised at the time, so Mobile had no need to rely on at-large voting to keep them from electing any members of the City Commission. Subsequent to the adoption of the Voting Rights Act of 1965, black voter registration in Mobile had come to reflect the black portion of the population, approximately 35 percent when *Mobile* v. *Boulden* was filed. Accordingly, despite the absence of discriminatory purpose when the at-large voting scheme was adopted—not allowing blacks to vote at all sufficed to serve Mobile's discriminatory purpose—its effect is to continue to deny equal representation when other barriers to equal representation have been swept away.

In Justice Stewart's opinion for the Court in *Mobile,* he reconciled the holding with *White* v. *Regester* by ignoring that case's primary emphasis on the discriminatory effect of at-large voting. Citing the language in the Court's opinion in *White* that could be interpreted to suggest a finding of discriminatory purpose, Stewart wrote that the earlier case was "consistent with 'the basic equal protection principle that the invidious quality of a law claimed to be racially discriminatory must ultimately be traced to a racially discriminatory purpose.'"[43] Only if such a purpose had been proved in *Mobile* would the at-large election of the City Commission have been invalidated.

In dissent, Justice White, the author of the earlier opinion, asserted that *Mobile* "is flatly inconsistent with *White v. Regester.*"[44] He accused the plurality of the Court that supported Stewart's opinion of ignoring the facts deemed relevant in *White,* among them, "a lack of minority access to the candidate selection process, unresponsiveness of elected officials to the minority interests, a history of discrimination."[45] Those conditions prevail in Mobile, Alabama.

In a separate dissent, Justice Marshall complained, with more than a touch of bitterness, that the Court had concluded that, "in the absence of proof of intentional discrimination by the State, the right to vote provides the politically powerless the right to cast meaningless ballots."[46] Marshall went on to point out the discrepancy between the

Court's approach to *Mobile* and the exacting scrutiny it had given to the reapportionment cases:

> *Reynolds* v. *Sims* and its progeny focussed solely on the discriminatory *effects* of malapportionment. They recognize that, when population figures for the representational districts of a legislature are not so similar, the votes of citizens do not carry as much weight in the legislature as do votes cast by citizens in smaller districts. The equal protection problem attacked by the "one person, one vote" principle is, then, one of vote dilution: under *Reynolds,* each citizen must have an "equally effective voice" in the election of representatives. . . . In the present cases, the alleged vote dilution, though caused by the combined effects of the electoral structure and social and historical factors rather than by unequal population distribution, is analytically the same concept: the unjustified abridgement of a fundamental right. It follows, then, that a showing of discriminatory intent is just as unnecessary under the vote-dilution approach . . . as it is under our reapportionment cases.[47]

At this writing, it is difficult to estimate all the consequences of *Mobile.* It will certainly hinder minorities in making further political gains in the South and the Southwest. Up until *Mobile,* those gains had been dramatic, with a proportionately larger number of blacks and Hispanics elected to public office than in other parts of the country. Yet, despite such gains, which give Mississippi and Louisiana the largest number of black elected officials of any states, by 1980 blacks held only 1 percent of elective offices nationwide.[48] At-large electoral schemes already in place are a major obstacle to significant changes, but they will probably be upheld by the courts unless their authors were foolish or careless enough to acknowledge openly that their purposes were discriminatory. Conceivably, the decision will also allow communities that presently have single-member districts to change to at-large elections, though that is not yet clear. Where minorities are equitably represented, they may be able to block such conversions. And the Court may find evidence of purposeful discrimination in conversions to at-large elections in the wake of its decision in *Mobile*.

Whatever the ultimate impact of *Mobile* on equal representation, the Court's decision is deferential to other branches of government in circumstances in which it should feel doubly obliged to scrutinize them exactingly. The scheme challenged in *Mobile* directly concerns the representativeness of representative government, both because it involves the rights of a discrete and insular minority and because it involves the electoral process. There could hardly be a more compelling case for judicial activism. A clear principle of corrective justice—making certain that citizens are "equal one amongst another" in access to political power—warrants judicial venture into political justice to invalidate an electoral scheme that concentrates all power in the hands of the white citizens of Mobile. Instead, the Supreme Court has required litigants to meet the difficult—and, in *Mobile,* impossible—task of proving discriminatory purpose where discriminatory effect is plain. Ironically, and without saying so, the Supreme Court seems to have reverted to the philosophy that inspired Justice Frankfurter's opinion in *Colegrove* v. *Green* and his dissenting opinion in *Baker* v. *Carr.*

Perhaps *Mobile* v. *Boulden* is an aberration. Perhaps not. But even if *Mobile* determines the way the Court considers equal representation cases in the future, the clock cannot be turned back all the way. The Court is a great teacher, and it has persuaded the nation that the one-person, one-vote principle is essential to democratic government. By entering the "political thicket" of legislative districting, the Court elicited approval that by now is near universal. Like *Brown* v. *Board of Education* and its progeny, the equal representation cases enhanced the prestige of the judiciary. The reason is similar: the role of the unrepresentative branch of government in shaping public policy is never so well accepted as when it cuts through impasses in the representative branches to make democratic government more democratic. It is a role the Court should have played in *Mobile*. Aside from that decision's unfortunate effects on the causes of racial equality and equal representation, *Mobile* tarnishes one of the Supreme Court's most lustrous achievements.

6

Sexual Equality and the Difficulties of Sisterhood

In 1869, Myra Colby Bradwell applied for admission to the Illinois bar. Although she passed the exam, the Illinois Supreme Court refused to admit her because she was a woman. She appealed to the United States Supreme Court, contending that the Fourteenth Amendment's prohibition on state abridgement of the privileges or immunities of "persons born or naturalized in the United States" entitled her to pursue the profession of her choice. If not, according to the brief her counsel filed in the Supreme Court, "then the Legislatures of the States may exclude colored men from all the honorable pursuits of life, and compel them to support their existence in a condition of servitude. And if this provision does protect the colored citizen, then it protects every citizen, black or white, male or female."[1]

The Supreme Court rejected the argument, ostensibly on the ground that admission to the bar is not a privilege or immunity of citizenship. Actually, the suspicion seems well-founded that the Court did not consider women to be "persons" within the meaning of the Fourteenth Amendment.

So much was implicit in a concurring opinion by Justice Joseph Bradley for three members of the Court:

> The civil law, as well as nature herself, has always recognized a wide difference in the respective spheres and destinies of men and women. Man is, or should be, woman's protector, and defender. The natural and proper timidity and delicacy which belongs to the female sex evidently unfits it for many of the occupations of civil life. . . .
>
> The paramount destiny and mission of woman are to fulfill the noble and benign offices of wife and mother. This is the law of the Creator. . . .
>
> It is the prerogative of the legislator to prescribe regulations founded on nature, reason, and experience for the due admission of qualified persons to professions and callings demanding special skill and confidence. This fairly belongs to the police power of the state; and in my opinion, in view of the peculiar characteristics, destiny, and mission of woman, it is within the province of the legislature to ordain what offices, positions, and callings shall be filled and discharged by men, and shall receive the benefit of these energies and responsibilities, and that decision and firmness which are presumed to predominate in the sterner sex.[2]

When *Bradwell* was decided, women could not persuade legislatures to ordain otherwise because they were denied the right to vote, a circumstance that prevailed until the Nineteenth Amendment was ratified in 1920.

If the great feminist movement that produced the Nineteenth Amendment had been sustained, with access to the ballot, women might have persuaded the representative branches of government to eliminate virtually all laws imposing disadvantages on them. But it was not sustained; it seemed to die on the morning after its triumph. It was reborn in the late 1960s as a child of the movement for civil rights for blacks. In that respect, as in many others, it resembled nineteenth-century feminism, which had its origins in the abolitionist movement. Women who played leading parts in efforts to obtain equality for blacks could hardly help noticing the parallels to their own situation. Their work for racial equality taught them organizational skills that served them well when they took up the feminist cause.

The racial equality movement of the 1960s relied heavily on litigation to advance its cause. Accordingly, it seemed natural for its offspring, the contemporary feminist movement, also to turn to the courts. Judicial response was quick. In 1971, the Supreme Court reviewed *Reed* v. *Reed,*[3] a case that confronted head-on the question that seemed to underlie *Bradwell:* are women "persons" who may invoke the protection of the Fourteenth Amendment to challenge discrimination against them by reason of their sex? At issue in *Reed* was an Idaho law regulating the designation of persons entitled to administer the estate of one who dies intestate. It provided that, "[of] several persons claiming and equally entitled to administer, males must be preferred to females." Implementing that law, an Idaho judge rejected Sally Reed as administrator of the estate of her deceased son in favor of the boy's father, Cecil Reed. The judge made no effort to determine which parent was more qualified.

Sally Reed was represented by an Idaho attorney but, when the Supreme Court granted review he was joined by an attorney for the American Civil Liberties Union, Ruth Bader Ginsburg, who wrote the brief submitted to the Court. At the time, professor of law at Rutgers University, subsequently at Columbia University, and, in 1980, appointed to a federal appellate judgeship, Ginsburg became the principal strategist and litigator on behalf of those attempting to secure equality for women through the courts. Her brief to the Supreme Court in *Reed* framed the arguments that have guided litigation on behalf of women's rights ever since.

According to Ginsburg's brief, "The sex line drawn by ... the Idaho Code, mandating subordination of women to men without regard to individual capacity, creates a 'suspect classification' for which no compelling justification can be shown." In the event that the Supreme Court did not agree that sex is a "suspect classification," Ginsburg proposed a fallback: "The line drawn by the Idaho legislature, arbitrarily ranking the woman as inferior to the man by directing the probate court to take no account of the respective qualifications of the individuals involved, lacks the constitutionally required fair and reasonable relation to any legitimate state interest in providing for the efficient administration of decedents' estates."[4]

In contending that sex should be treated as a "suspect classification" requiring exacting scrutiny, Ginsburg attempted to establish a precedent that would make it possible to wipe out virtually all legal obstacles to equality for women through litigation. There are few circumstances in which a state could demonstrate a compelling interest in discrimination. But, even though Ginsburg was able to demonstrate that women suffered from prejudice and were victimized because of their sex, she faced a difficult task in persuading the Supreme Court that classifications by sex should be considered suspect. Except in prohibiting abridgement of the right to vote, the Constitution does not mention discrimination on grounds of sex, and no suggestion could be made that any provision of the Constitution was intended by its authors to prevent such discrimination. A prohibition against discrimination could only be inferred from language intended to protect blacks. Previously, the Court had only held that race, ancestry, and alienage are suspect classifications. The situation of those other than blacks who had become beneficiaries of exacting scrutiny is more analogous than the situation of women to the situation of blacks. Racial minorities, minorities suffering discrimination because of ancestry, and aliens may readily be viewed as "discrete and insular minorities" unable to secure redress through the political process because of prejudice. Whatever prejudice women suffer, it may hardly be argued that the political process cannot fairly deal with their grievances. After all, they constitute a majority of the population. A half century after the adoption of the Nineteenth Amendment, they ought to be able to get the representative branches of government to deal with them fairly. If the rationale that inspired Justice Stone's footnote in *Carolene Products* is to define the limits on judicial ventures into distributive justice or political justice, discrimination against women would be invalidated by the courts only when necessary to render corrective justice.

In deciding *Reed,* the Supreme Court addressed only Ginsburg's fall-back argument. "The question presented by this case, then," Chief Justice Burger wrote for a unanimous Court, "is whether a difference in the sex of competing applicants for letters of administration bears a rational relationship to a state objective that is sought to be advanced by" the state laws regulating the administration of estates. Reviewing the grounds for discrimination cited by the Idaho courts, Burger found none rationally related to such a state interest. Accordingly, "by providing dissimilar treatment for men and women who are thus similarly situated, the challenged section violates the Equal Protection Clause."[5]

The year following *Reed,* 1972, the Congress of the United States approved the Equal Rights Amendment and submitted it to the states for ratification. The Amendment provides that "equality of rights under the law shall not be denied or abridged by the United States or by any state on account of sex." The vote in Congress suggested over-whelming support for this proposition: in the House of Representatives, the final vote was 354 to 23; in the Senate, the final vote was 84 to 8. Yet it seems likely that not many of those who voted on either side understood that, in the view of many legal scholars, the principal effect of the amendment would be to achieve what Ginsburg had been unable to achieve in *Reed*. As four of them wrote in an influential article published in the *Yale Law Journal:* "There are three methods of making changes within the legal system to assure equal rights for women. One is by extending to sex discrimination the doctrines of strict judicial review under the Equal Protection Clause of the Fourteenth Amendment. A second is by piecemeal revision of existing federal and state laws. The third is by a new constitutional amendment. These alternatives are not, of course, mutually exclusive."[6]

Congressional approval of the Equal Rights Amendment did not end the effort to secure the same result through litigation. As the authors of the *Yale Law Journal* article wrote, neither the two methods nor even a third—piecemeal legislative revision—is mutually exclusive. But a movement capable of obtaining lopsided congressional endorsement of a sweeping constitutional amendment seemed at last to fulfill its potential under the Nineteenth Amendment. To partisans of Justice Stone's approach to judicial activism, therefore, it might have been a good time for the judiciary to sit back and, except for providing corrective justice in cases of clear discrimination, let women vindicate their rights through the political process.

Whether or not there were theoretical contradictions in their manner of seeking rapid change simultaneously through the representative and judicial processes, women's rights activists pressed ahead on both fronts. Their movement seemed to be growing rapidly in strength. Litigators, again led by Ruth Bader Ginsburg, reached a high-water mark in 1973 in *Frontiero v. Richardson,*[7] a claim by a lieutenant of the United States Air Force that she had been denied equal protection of the laws because her husband did not get the same benefits that the armed services provided to the female dependents of male officers. The Supreme Court agreed. A plurality of the Court—four justices—held that sex is a suspect classification and, therefore, any discrimination must be subjected to exacting scrutiny. Justice Brennan, writing also for Justices William O. Douglas, White, and Marshall, explained that

> since sex, like race and national origin, is an immutable characteristic determined solely by the accident of birth, the imposition of special disabilities upon the members of a particular sex because of their sex would seem to violate "the basic concept of our system that legal burdens should bear some relationship to individual responsibility. . . ."
>
> And what differentiates sex from such nonsuspect statuses as intelligence or physical disability, and aligns it with the recognized suspect criteria, is that the sex characteristic frequently bears no relation to ability to perform or contribute to society. As a result, statutory distinctions between the sexes often have the effect of invidiously relegating the entire class of females to inferior legal status without regard to the actual capabilities of its individual members.[8]

Missing from this analysis was any suggestion that "those political processes ordinarily to be relied upon to protect minorities" were curtailed because of prejudice against women for the obvious reason that, though women might suffer from prejudice, they are not a minority.

One justice, William Rehnquist, dissented, but four other justices concurred in holding that Lieutenant Frontiero's husband was entitled to equal benefits. They did not agree, however, that sex should be considered a suspect classification. Justice Powell, writing for himself, Chief Justice Burger, and Justice Harry A. Blackmun, argued that there was a

> compelling reason for deferring a general categoriz-
> ing of sex classifications as invoking the strictest test
> of judicial scrutiny. The Equal Rights Amendment,
> which if adopted will resolve the substance of this
> precise question, has been approved by the Con-
> gress, and submitted for ratification by the States. . . .
> [D]emocratic institutions are weakened, and confi-
> dence in the restraint of the Court is impaired, when
> we appear unnecessarily to decide sensitive issues
> of broad social and political importance at the very
> time they are under consideration within the pre-
> scribed constitutional processes.[9]

Although Justice Douglas helped to make up the plurality of the Supreme Court in *Frontiero* that considered sex
a suspect classification, a year later he defected. Writing for
six justices in *Kahn* v. *Shevin,* Douglas upheld a property
tax exemption Florida granted to widows but not to widowers as "reasonably designed to further the state policy of
cushioning the financial impact of spousal loss upon the
sex for whom that loss imposes a disproportionately heavy
burden."[10] Only three justices held fast for scrutinizing the
Florida law more exactly. No subsequent Supreme Court
case has elicited more support for the suspect classification
standard requiring a state to justify sex discrimination by a
compelling state interest.

Douglas's refusal to adhere to the view that sex is a suspect classification had much to do with the circumstances
of *Kahn.* Widows in Florida, as elsewhere, generally were
employed less often and earned less than widowers. Accordingly, providing them with a special tax exemption appeared

to be a benign exercise in distributive justice by the Florida legislature tending to equalize their place in society. Except for the abstract proposition that all discrimination by sex is suspect, no principle of corrective justice required the Supreme Court to invalidate the law.

It also seems possible that the shifting political climate influenced the decision in *Kahn*. Just as judicial solicitude for women's rights reached its apex in 1973 in *Frontiero*, so support for women's rights by the representative branches of government crested at about the same time. Within six months of congressional approval of the Equal Rights Amendment in 1972 it was ratified by twenty-one states. Another ten states ratified the amendment before the end of 1973. With ratification by only seven more states needed, it appeared certain of quick adoption. Yet the amendment ultimately failed even though Congress extended the time for ratification in 1978. When it died, it was not clear how many state ratifications were still needed because several states that ratified before the end of 1973 subsequently rescinded their ratification, raising the unsettled question of whether they were constitutionally authorized to rescind. The issue became moot because the amendment died for failure to obtain the requisite thirty-eight states for adoption even if all the rescissions were invalid.

Whatever the reasons for the decline in the political strength of the women's rights movement following 1973, they do not seem to derive from defections from the feminist cause. Women committed to women's rights appear to be as committed as ever. More likely, the decline in the movement's capacity to influence the representative branches is attributable to the rise of a countervailing movement, symbolized by the emergence of Phyllis Schlafly's crusade against the Equal Rights Amendment, the rise of the Moral Majority, and the political strength of the National Right to Life

Committee. Some of these groups are female-dominated. The questions, for the purposes of this book, are, first, how should the courts respond when much of the strongest opposition to special judicial protection for a class of citizens comes from within that class and, second, to what degree was the emergence of this countermovement stimulated by the women's rights movement's reliance on litigation?

The first of these questions is very difficult. The fact that some women oppose equality for women would not, of itself, seem to diminish the entitlement of other women to equality. In that respect, it might seem that the proper response to the question is that the emergence of a female-dominated countermovement should be immaterial. Yet the question is not whether women are entitled to equality but to what extent courts should be the instrument for promoting equality. At the least, the size and vigor of the female antifeminist movement suggests that there is nothing "discrete" about women as a class of citizens. Not all women have interests in common or profess to share interests in common, the "sisterhood of all women" feminist ideology notwithstanding. Although a particular woman suffering from intentional discrimination that has already taken place should certainly be able to look to the courts for corrective justice, the emergence of a powerful antifeminist movement should probably restrain the courts when it comes to sweeping forward-looking decisions involving distributive justice. Since the members of the class profess not to have interests in common, courts should probably be slower and more flexible than otherwise in setting standards intended to regulate what happens in the future.

As to the second question, Supreme Court decisions almost certainly provided impetus to the development of the countermovement, although *Roe* v. *Wade*[11] and *Doe* v. *Bolton*,[12] invalidating criminal sanctions against abortion, probably played a larger part than any cases dealing directly with social equality. The abortion decisions provoked a backlash (see Chapter 7) that has helped to make "right to life" probably the most powerful popular movement in the country during the past decade. Just as feminists link equality for women and the right to obtain abortions, so opponents of abortions link the two causes. Some of the energy of the redoubtable antiabortion movement has been directed toward preventing ratification of the Equal Rights Amendment and toward preventing achievement of other feminist goals. Moreover, the prominence of the courts in advancing the feminist cause provides the countermovement with a ready basis for making common cause with other backlash movements against judicial decisions. Collectively, the movement opposed to Supreme Court decisions legalizing abortions, equalizing the status of women, requiring school desegregation, prohibiting prayer in the public schools, and invalidating censorship of pornography is "the new right" that played such a dominant role in the 1980 national elections.

The first signs that groups antagonistic to Supreme Court decisions were forming such a political alliance were evident as early as 1973 or 1974. This alliance that stopped cold the drive to ratify the Equal Rights Amendment had its counterpart in the treatment of women's rights cases by the Supreme Court, most notably in *Gedulig* v. *Aiello*,[13] decided in 1974. The decision upheld California's disability insurance scheme exclusion from coverage of disabilities resulting from pregnancy. In Justice Stewart's opinion for the Court, this is constitutionally permissible because "the State has a legitimate interest in maintaining the self-supporting nature of its insurance program."[14] The opinion went on to point out that "there is no risk from which men are protected and women are not,"[15] a statement that could be extrapolated to imply that any discrimination against women on grounds of pregnancy is justified so long as men are treated similarly if they become pregnant. Justice Douglas was among the three dissenters holding out for a stricter standard of scrutiny, his switch from *Kahn* probably based on the different circumstances. Whereas the tax exemption scheme attacked in *Kahn* favored women, the class that had suffered discrimination, the insurance scheme attacked in *Geduldig* disadvantaged women. Accordingly, Douglas would have had the Court dispense distributive justice in *Geduldig* even though he had written the opinion rejecting such a role for the Court in *Kahn*.

Two years later, in 1976, in another case involving disability benefits, *General Electric Company* v. *Gilbert*,[16] the Supreme Court extended its decision in *Geduldig* to cases arising from Title VII of the Civil Rights Act of 1964 forbidding employment discrimination.[17] In effect, the opinion for the Court written by Justice Rehnquist applied the "legitimate interest" reasoning of *Geduldig* to justify discrimination even though the case was decided under a law explicitly prohibiting sex discrimination. The decision aroused consternation among women's rights activists and, since they had lost so badly in the courts, they turned to Congress for a remedy. Their lobbying paid off in 1978 with the enactment of the Pregnancy Discrimination Act providing that such terms as "because of sex" or "on the basis of sex" in legislation prohibiting employment discrimination "include, because of or on the basis of pregnancy, childbirth, or related medical conditions; and women affected by pregnancy, childbirth, or related medical conditions shall be treated the same for all employment-related purposes, including receipt of benefits under fringe benefit programs, as other persons not so affected but similar in their ability and inability to work."[18]

Enactment of the Pregnancy Discrimination Act demonstrated that even though the feminist movement lacked
the strength to secure ratification of the Equal Rights
Amendment, it retained substantial capacity to influence
the representative branches of government. Hardly any other
group that seriously contended that the courts should subject legislation specially affecting it to exacting scrutiny
would simultaneously be capable of persuading Congress
to enact legislation directly providing it with a benefit it
was denied by an adverse Supreme Court decision. Yet the
Pregnancy Discrimination Act could not have passed except
that feminists persuaded the antiabortion movement not to
oppose it. That was done by arguing that the availability of
disability benefits for pregnancy would make it necessary
for fewer women to obtain abortions and by inserting in
the law an exception that troubles many feminists providing
that the law did "not require an employer to pay for health
insurance benefits for abortion, except where the life of the
mother would be endangered if the fetus were carried to
term, or except where medical complications have arisen
from an abortion."[19]

Two years after *Geduldig*, and on the heels of *Gilbert*, the
Supreme Court decided *Craig* v. *Boren*,[20] establishing a novel
standard for reviewing sex discrimination. *Craig* involved a
challenge to an Oklahoma law prohibiting the sale of non-
intoxicating 3.2 percent beer to males under the age of
twenty-one and to females under the age of eighteen. Justice Brennan wrote the opinion for the Court, holding that
"to withstand constitutional challenge . . . classification by
gender must serve important governmental objectives and
must be substantially related to achievement of those objectives."[21] This was neither so difficult a standard as necessary
to achieve a compelling state interest nor so easy as rationally
related to a legitimate state interest. Four justices—Marshall,

White, Blackmun, and John Paul Stevens—concurred in approving the intermediate standard; Justice Powell would have invalidated the Oklahoma law because it "does not bear a fair and substantial relation to the object of the legislation,"[22] a lower standard than employed by Brennan but higher than a mere rational relationship to a state interest; Justice Stewart would have invalidated the law as not rationally related to a state interest; and Justices Burger and Rehnquist dissented because they found the law rational and thought a rational relationship to a legitimate state interest should be the test.

Rehnquist's dissent highlighted an obvious shortcoming of the Court's new intermediate standard. "I would think we have had enough difficulty," he wrote, "with the two standards of review which our cases have recognized—the norm of 'rational basis,' and the 'compelling state interest' required where a 'suspect classification' is involved. . . . How is this Court to define what objectives are important? How is it to determine whether a particular law is 'substantially' related to the achievement of such objective; rather than related in some other way to its achievement? Both of the phrases used are so diaphanous and elastic as to invite subjective judicial preferences or prejudices."[23]

Despite this weakness, the intermediate standard seems the best yet devised for evaluating sex discrimination, even—though most feminist litigators would disagree—from the feminist standpoint. It recognizes that women suffer prejudice solely because of their sex and, accordingly, deserve judicial intervention to ensure that they count equally. The political strength of women, despite their number, is limited because of prejudice. Yet women enjoy enough political clout to make the representative branches of government respond, as they did in passing the Pregnancy Discrimination Act, when an evident injustice is done to women, when the energies of the feminist movement are effectively mobilized and focused, and, perhaps most important, when organized movements of antifeminist women can be persuaded not to oppose that which is sought by feminists. The intermediate standard permits gender discrimination in circumstances where a too rigid standard might actually injure the cause of equality for women. This is especially true in circumstances when the interests of different groups of women diverge, as is evident when considering the question of athletic opportunities for women.

Sport occupies a central place in American life. Male dominance of sport and male assumption of exclusive comprehension of its rituals and mysteries is an important part of male dominance of society and unwillingness to recognize women as equals. But is the cause of equality served by sexual desegregation of school athletic programs—at least, noncontact sports—or by requiring schools to provide separate but equal facilities? Or is some hybrid the best path to equality?

In a substantial number of instances, female athletes have gone to court to obtain the right to compete against males. One such case, *Brenden* v. *Independent School District*,[24] involved an attempt by two female high school students to compete against males in tennis, cross country running, and skiing. A United States Court of Appeals said that they had a right to an "individual determination"[25] of their ability to compete. This decision benefits such exceptional female athletes as Nancy Lopez (now Nancy Lopez Melton), who was at first denied the right to compete against her New Mexico high school's male golfers. It seems likely that Lopez's phenomenal professional career has been enhanced by the opportunity she had to compete against the best golfers in her high school.

But what of women eager to take part in sports who lack the exceptional abilities of a Nancy Lopez? Physical differences would exclude most if the only opportunities to take part in competitive athletics required them to compete against men. In a high school of a thousand students in which two hundred students comprised various teams, perhaps only five or ten females would qualify if all teams were sexually desegregated. The cause of equality for women would hardly be served by permitting only so small a number to take part in competitive athletics. Separate male and female teams with equal facilities are needed to provide as many females as males with athletic opportunities.

If the courts considered sex a suspect classification, they would probably prohibit schools from maintaining separate athletic teams for males and females in noncontact sports. The plaintiff in an engagingly named case, *White v. Corpus Christi Little Misses Kickball Association*,[26] would have prevailed in his claim that he was entitled to try out for an all-female team. No compelling state interest would justify denying him an individualized determination of his qualifications.

On the other hand, if a mere rational relationship to a state interest is sufficient to validate sex discrimination, a court would have no ground for requiring a school to allow a female athlete with the qualifications of a Nancy Lopez to compete against males. Only a few females can compete successfully against males in athletic contests. Accordingly, a court would be forced to find that there is a rational relationship between sex discrimination in athletics and a legitimate state interest in providing both males and females an opportunity to compete against their peers.

The *Craig* intermediate standard is flexible enough to permit courts to require that exceptional female athletes should be allowed to compete against males and, simultaneously, to require equivalent facilities for separate male and female teams. Providing separate but equal facilities may not serve a compelling state interest but it serves the important governmental objective of providing athletic opportunities to large numbers of athletes of both sexes. Requiring equivalent facilities is substantially related to achieving that objective. On the other hand, unlike the rational relationship test, the *Craig* standard does not require a court to keep hands off when an exceptional female athlete seeks an individualized determination of her capacity to compete against male athletes.*

Subsequent to *Craig*, the Supreme Court adhered to the intermediate standard in invalidating provisions of the Social Security Law that discriminated on the basis of sex.[27] Even though the discrimination reflected differences between the wage-earning and family-supporting roles of women and men, the Court found it unconstitutional because it is not substantially related to achieving important governmental objectives. The Social Security cases make it plain that the *Craig* standard can effectively serve the cause of equality for women. On the other hand, the Court applied the *Craig* standard in more troubling fashion in determining that absolute lifetime preference given to veterans in state hiring does not involve unlawful discrimination even though

---

*Of course, if the Equal Rights Amendment had been ratified, the *Craig* standard would probably have lapsed and sex would be considered a suspect classification. Separate but equal facilities in noncontact sports probably could not be maintained unless considered a form of temporary affirmative action to be abolished when females generally achieved athletic parity with males. Since athletic differences appear to be physiological as well as sociological, however, a new concept of affirmative action would be required to perpetuate separate but equal athletic facilities. Separate but equal facilities in such contact sports as wrestling present a different question entirely because maintaining privacy for males and females would probably be viewed by the courts as a compelling state interest.

the effect is to disadvantage women.[28] The *Craig* standard seems particularly inadequate to some women's rights litigators, however, because the Court has not applied it to prohibit all discrimination based on pregnancy, as it made clear by deciding *Gilbert* adversely to their cause contemporaneously with *Craig*. But the fault here is not with the standard but with the Court's failure to comprehend the significance of discrimination on grounds of pregnancy as an attribute of sex discrimination. As Justice Stevens pointed out in his dissent in *Gilbert*, "It is the capacity to become pregnant which primarily differentiates the female from the male."[29] Accordingly, Stevens did not see any need to inquire into the motive for discrimination; he believed it was plainly forbidden by the federal law prohibiting sex discrimination in employment. By way of analogy (not suggested by Stevens), the capacity to become pregnant differentiates females from males as skin color and hair texture differentiate blacks from whites and as linguistic heritage differentiates Hispanics from Anglos. The Court would certainly invalidate discrimination based on the attributes that distinguish racial minorities; so in circumstances when sex discrimination is forbidden by law it should invalidate discrimination based on the attribute that distinguishes the sexes. Requiring that pregnant women receive the same disability benefits as men and women suffering disabilities for other reasons involves distributive justice. Yet it seems a necessary concomitant of providing corrective justice to women.

On the other hand, the logic of this approach is that women should rely on the representative branches of government for distributive justice in many other circumstances. For example, women are aggrieved because jobs traditionally held by them, such as nursing, are paid less than jobs requiring comparable skills traditionally performed by males. Other issues they consider important include day care for children and recognition of household work as a form of employment that should be covered by Social Security. Although some litigation has been initiated on these questions, the access women enjoy to the political process suggests that these matters of distributive justice are best dealt with by the representative branches of government.

The contention that the courts should leave to the representative branches much of the job of bringing about equality assumes, of course, that women generally share an interest in equality. That seems valid insofar as such matters are concerned as the right of women to be paid equally for equally demanding work. Even Phyllis Schlafly probably does not quarrel with that proposition. The assumption breaks down, however, when applied to questions such as day care and compensation for household work. To prevail through the political process on such matters, feminists must enlist on their side women not presently aligned either with their movement or with the countermovement or even, as in the case of the Pregnancy Discrimination Act of 1978, women aligned with the countermovement. The prospect that they could persuade such women to side with them makes clear why feminist women, themselves a minority suffering from prejudice, should not be regarded by the courts in the same manner as a "discrete or insular minority." It lies within the capacity of feminist women to reach out to other women and make them political allies. If they succeed in such efforts, they enjoy the strength to provide themselves with distributive justice through "those political processes ordinarily to be relied upon."

7

Abortion: Retreating under Fire

If surveys could identify the most controversial court decision of the past decade, it is likely that general public opinion
and scholarly legal opinion would be found to coincide. The
choice would be *Roe* v. *Wade*,[1] the United States Supreme
Court decision in 1973 holding that the state may not prohibit abortions performed during the first two trimesters
of pregnancy. Popular sentiment is reflected in the emergence of the powerful "right to life" citizen movement; in
the rise of "single issue politics" in which abortion figures
even more conspicuously than taxes, busing, gun control,
or the Equal Rights Amendment; and in repeated crises in
Congress and in state legislatures caused by impasses over
budgets because of provisions involving the funding or failure to fund abortions for poor women. The divisive question
politically is the morality of abortion. Scholarly dispute, on
the other hand, concerns the propriety of judicial policy
making. More than any other Supreme Court decision, *Roe*
symbolizes judicial entry into territory ordinarily reserved
to the representative branches of government. This aspect

of *Roe* is debated at length in textbooks, treatises, and law review articles. One argument, however, has been almost entirely missing: that although women generally and feminist women in particular should not be able to invoke the most exacting scrutiny by the courts, poor women seeking abortions are a discrete and insular minority suffering from prejudice, and judges should examine legislation and practices affecting them accordingly.

Two unrelated events of the early 1960s foreshadowed the twin, interlocking debates inspired by *Roe*. The public debate got its start in 1962 when an Arizona television performer, Sherri Finkbine, the mother of four children, announced publicly that she was seeking an abortion. She had taken the tranquilizer drug Thalidomide during the early stages of her pregnancy and discovered later that other pregnant women who took the drug had given birth to deformed children. When Finkbine failed in efforts to get an abortion in Arizona, California, or New Jersey, she went to Sweden for the operation (the fetus was deformed).[2] The episode generated wide discussion of what had been a taboo subject since the adoption of state antiabortion laws in the second half of the nineteenth century.

The debate among legal scholars started with a dissenting opinion by Justice John Marshall Harlan in a case decided by the United States Supreme Court in 1961, *Poe* v. *Ullman*.[3] Two married couples in Connecticut and the physician for the two wives challenged the constitutionality of the Connecticut law forbidding the possession or distribution of contraceptives. Both women had been informed by the physician that their health would be endangered if they became pregnant, but the doctor would not provide them with contraceptives for fear of prosecution. The Supreme Court refused to rule on the constitutionality of the law because no prosecution had been initiated. Justice Harlan dissented, however, holding that the due process clause of the Fourteenth Amendment prohibited such "an intolerable and unjustifiable invasion of privacy in the most intimate concerns of an individual's personal life."[4]

Harlan's opinion was based on a more expansive reading of the due process clause than had become customary. He wrote:

> Were due process merely a procedural safeguard it would fail to reach those situations where the deprivation of life, liberty or property was accomplished by legislation which by operating in the future could, given even the fairest possible procedure in application to individuals nevertheless destroy the enjoyment of all three. . . . [I]t is not the particular enumeration of rights in the first eight Amendments which spells out the reach of Fourteenth Amendment due process, but rather, as was suggested in another context long before the adoption of that Amendment, those concepts which are considered to embrace those rights "which are . . . *fundamental*; which belong . . . to the citizens of all free governments."[5]

Harlan's dissent breathed new life into "substantive due process," a concept associated with the era in which the Supreme Court invalidated legislation that conflicted with its laissez-faire economic philosophy and discredited since the Court repudiated it to forestall Roosevelt's court-packing plan. The rights protected by "due process" are not only procedural in both the Harlan view and the view of the *Lochner*[6] Supreme Court. Instead of protecting substantive economic rights, in Harlan's formulation due process protects "fundamental" rights—rights the Court holds to be implicit in the concept of ordered liberty. The privacy of the marriage relationship, in Harlan's view, is such a fundamental right. He held that it encompasses the right to make decisions about contraception free of state interference.

Four years later, in 1965, the Supreme Court decided another case involving the Connecticut law against contraception, *Griswold v. Connecticut*.[7] This time, arrests of officials of the Planned Parenthood League of Connecticut had been made and the Court as a whole considered on its merits the constitutionality of the law. This time, the majority held the law unconstitutional, though Justice Harlan's reasoning—that the due process clause of the Fourteenth Amendment prohibits such a law because it violates fundamental rights—did not carry a majority of the court. Delivering the opinion of the Court, Justice Douglas wrote that the Constitution protects the privacy of the marriage relationship because

> specific guarantees in the Bill of Rights have penumbras, formed by emanations from those guarantees that help give them life and substance.... Various guarantees create zones of privacy. The right of association contained in the penumbra of the First Amendment is one, as we have seen. The Third Amendment in its prohibition against the quartering of soldiers "in any house" in time of peace without the consent of the owner is another facet of that privacy. The Fourth Amendment explicitly affirms the "right of the people to be secure in their persons, houses, papers and effects against unreasonable searches and seizures." The Fifth Amendment in its Self-Incrimination Clause enables the citizen to create a zone of privacy which government may not force him to surrender to his detriment. The Ninth Amendment provides: "The enumeration in the Constitution of certain rights, shall not be construed to deny or disparage others retained by the people."...

The present case, then concerns a relationship lying within the zone of privacy created by several constitutional guarantees.[8]

Justice Arthur J. Goldberg, joined by Justices Warren and Brennan, concurred, but added that the Connecticut law also violated the Ninth Amendment, which provides that "the enumeration in the Constitution, of certain rights, shall not be construed to deny or disparage others retained by the people." He wrote:

> I do agree that the concept of liberty protects those personal rights that are fundamental, and is not confined to the specific terms of the Bill of Rights. My conclusion that the concept of liberty is not so restricted and that it embraces the right of marital privacy though that right is not mentioned explicitly in the Constitution is supported both by numerous decisions of this court . . . and by the language and history of the Ninth Amendment. . . .[9]
>
> To hold that a right so basic and fundamental and so deep-rooted in our society as the right of privacy in marriage may be infringed because that right is not guaranteed in so many words by the first eight amendments to the Constitution is to ignore the Ninth Amendment and to give it no effect whatsoever.[10]

Dissenting, Justice Black, joined by Justice Stewart, wrote that "the law is every bit as offensive to me as it is to my Brethren." But Black protested against what he saw as an attempt to incorporate the justices' personal values into the Constitution, whether through "the Due Process Clause or the Ninth Amendment or any mysterious and uncertain natural law concepts." Comparing the decision to *Lochner*, he wrote:

> Apparently my Brethren have less quarrel with state economic regulations than former Justices of their

persuasion had. But any limitation upon their using the natural law due process philosophy to strike down any state law, dealing with any activity whatever, will obviously be only self-imposed. . . .[11]

The late Judge Learned Hand, after emphasizing his view that judges should not use the due process formula suggested in the concurring opinion today or any other formula like it to invalidate legislation offensive to their "personal preferences," made the statement, with which I fully agree, that: "For myself it would be most irksome to be ruled by a bevy of Platonic Guardians, even if I knew how to choose them, which I assuredly do not."

So far as I am concerned, Connecticut's law as applied here is not forbidden by any provision of the Federal Constitution as that Constitution was written.[12]

When *Griswold* was decided in 1965, litigators did not seriously contemplate challenging in the courts the constitutionality of laws imposing criminal sanctions on abortion. By the mid-1960s, the Connecticut law was an anachronism. No other state made possession of contraceptives a crime, and in most states they could be readily purchased at drugstores. The Supreme Court's reasoning in *Griswold* might be shaky—"emanations,""penumbras," and the catch-all Ninth Amendment made a fragile foundation—but the result nevertheless seemed inevitable. Judicial invalidation of a law punishing the possession or dissemination of contraceptives was one thing. Getting the courts to invalidate laws against abortion was quite another thing. It was not considered hyperbolic in 1966 for a book to begin with the sentence: "Abortion is the dread secret of our society."[13] Hundreds of thousands of women obtained abortions each year; indeed, according to Dr. Christopher Tietze, a demographer noted for his studies of abortion, the number was about 1,200,000 a year.[14] Yet the stigma was so great that women frequently concealed their abortions from their immediate families and their closest friends. Fearful to identify themselves, they could not speak out in their own interests or mobilize to seek political change to advance their rights. Much public discussion seemed necessary before the abortion laws could be changed, but those whose interests were directly at stake were not likely to take part in such discussion.

Legislative consideration of proposals to change abortion laws did get under way in 1965 and 1966 in California, Colorado, New York, and North Carolina. The novelty, however, was still evident in March 1966 at what was probably the first legislative hearing on abortion law reform in the twentieth century. Under the auspices of the New York Assembly Committee on Health, about a dozen witnesses testified on a bill that would have made what now seem only modest changes in the law.[15] The prospect of the bill's passage seemed so remote, however, that the Roman Catholic church, ordinarily an active body in the New York legislature, refused to send a representative to testify. To do so, church lobbyists made clear, would only dignify proceedings that did not deserve to be taken seriously. And the speaker of the assembly refused to allow the customary use of state funds to pay for a transcript of the hearing.[16]

Legislative hearings mitigated the strangeness of the issue. They also galvanized legal, medical, church, and civic organizations—but not organizations representing women seeking abortions because there were none—to adopt positions on abortion so that they could present testimony. By 1967, a substantial movement to change the abortion laws had taken shape. Litigation came under serious discussion, the turn to the courts inevitable at that moment of high tide for judicial policy making.

At first, it seemed necessary to those contemplating litigation to wait until prosecution was initiated, as in *Griswold*. Several doctors disclosed that they were performing abortions, thereby inviting arrest. In addition, a Clergy Consultation Service was organized in New York in 1967, and later nationally, that publicized its defiance of state criminal laws in referring women to doctors who would abort their pregnancies.[17] Few prosecutions were brought, but the cases that resulted helped to pave the way for *Roe* v. *Wade*.

The most significant prosecution started on May 1, 1968, when Washington, D.C., police arrested Dr. Milan Vuitch for violating the District's abortion law. He had been openly performing abortions for two years, many of them for women referred by clergy affiliated with consultation services. In 1969, a federal district court ruled that the law under which Vuitch had been arrested was unconstitutional. In 1971, the United States Supreme Court reversed the decision invalidating the law but held, nevertheless, that Vuitch should go free.[18] The Court read the provision of the District of Columbia law permitting abortions to save a woman's health to encompass "psychological as well as physical well-being." Since the prosecution had not proved that Vuitch had not acted out of a concern for the woman's health—so defined—his conviction was overturned. *Vuitch* made it plain that prosecutions of doctors for performing abortions would be difficult to sustain.

As *Vuitch* demonstrated, the courts had quickly become more receptive to abortion litigation than organizers of the movement for change had anticipated in 1965 and 1966. By 1968, sensing the opportunities, litigators in several states brought cases challenging abortion laws. Because their clients had not been prosecuted, they ran the risk that the courts would decline to rule on the merits of their cases as the Supreme Court majority had declined to consider the constitutionality of the Connecticut contraceptive law in *Poe* v. *Ullman*. But by the end of the 1960s, the courts were less inclined than at the beginning of the decade to dismiss litigation on such procedural grounds. Starting with a couple of suits that sought to invalidate the New York abortion law, lawsuits challenging the constitutionality of the laws were soon under way in most states.

The emergence of the contemporary feminist movement provided impetus for change. In 1965 and 1966, there had been no discernible feminist movement and abortion was rarely discussed as a women's rights issue. In those years, advocates of change focused primarily on intrusions on privacy in criticizing the abortion laws. They also criticized churches for imposing on others their doctrine that human life commences at conception. Issues raised included the freedom of doctors to practice medicine; the suffering and humiliation of women who were compelled to obtain illegal abortions; and the economic discrimination in the availability of abortions, despite the laws, to those who could afford premium costs. The laws of some states that permitted abortions to save a woman's life or health were criticized as too vague. Starting in 1968, feminist thinking began to shift the argument to a woman's right to control her own body.

Missing from the arguments advanced by advocates of change was the contention that women who are seeking abortions are a discrete and insular minority suffering from prejudice and deserving of special judicial solicitude for their rights. There seem to be several reasons for this omission. In the prefeminist period, advocates of change derived their main arguments from those that had been used successfully against legal restrictions on the possession or distribution of contraceptives. Establishing that abortion belongs within the zone of privacy that the Supreme Court said protects decisions about contraception seemed most promising. In the feminist period, some of the emphasis shifted to the rights of women as women. Feminist litigators contended that the courts should recognize sex itself as a suspect classification and that all laws discriminating on grounds of gender could be justified only by a compelling state interest. Implicitly, this approach reflected the contemporary feminist movement's insistence on the sisterhood of all women. The idea that women seeking abortions are a special class deserving of still greater judicial protection contradicts both the attempt to establish sex itself as a suspect classification and a central tenet of feminist ideology.

Yet if it is conceded (as I contend in the previous chapter) that gender is not a suspect classification because women generally do not share interests in common, it still may be that *some* women who share interests should be viewed as a discrete and insular minority. If anything, such a perception seems to derive greater validity from a frank acknowledgment that discrimination by gender, by itself, is not always suspect. Several aspects of discrimination against pregnant women who do not want to bear children make it analogous to discrimination against other discrete and insular minorities. The prejudice against this minority is frequently intense. The group suffering from prejudice is genuinely a minority. The minority is politically powerless because of its numbers; because of the youth, poverty, and lack of political experience of most of its members; and because the intensity of prejudice makes members fearful to identify with each other and fearful to reveal to others that they are members of this minority.

It is true, of course, that the discrete characteristic of women seeking abortions—pregnancy—is temporary. On reflection, however, that does not seem sufficient reason to deny such women exacting judicial scrutiny of discrimination against them. Alienage, which the Supreme Court has considered a suspect classification, is also usually temporary, though its duration is longer than pregnancy. And, for women denied the opportunity to obtain abortions, the consequences are long-lasting: they have children they did not want. What is genuinely brief is the period when anything can be done to abort a pregnancy, too brief, even if the minority had greater political clout, to permit women seeking abortions to exert influence over the representative branches of government while their own interests are at stake.

On the surface, the feminist argument that restrictions on abortion discriminate improperly against women generally played only a small part in judicial decisions on abortion and figured only a little more in the pleadings by lawyers seeking change. Intrusions on privacy and due process violations because of the vagueness of the laws were their main focus. But feminism created a sense of urgency to which officials of all branches of government responded. Its impact was evident, for example, in the New York State legislature, where the leadership seeking change in 1965 and 1966 had been provided by men: Assemblymen Percy Sutton and Albert Blumenthal and Senator Basil Paterson. In 1968, it shifted to a woman, Assemblywoman Constance Cook. By 1969, it was not surprising to read a headline in the *New York Times* reporting, "WOMEN BREAK UP ABORTION HEARING." The story that followed said that the disruption began when a former judge (male) finished testifying and a woman shouted, "All right, now let's hear from some real experts—the women!"[19] In 1970, New York repealed its law against abortion, the second state to take this step (Hawaii preceded New York by a month). A change that seemed unthinkable a few years earlier was brought about because the emerging feminist movement had radically changed the political climate. In those salad days of feminism, no significant countervailing movement opposed it.

The Roman Catholic church, which did not take the possibility of change in the abortion law seriously enough to present legislative testimony in New York in 1966, had not mobilized sufficiently by 1970 to be able to prevent its outright appeal.

In 1971, the year in which the Supreme Court decided *Vuitch* and the year in which the Court first held that the Fourteenth Amendment's guarantee of equal protection of the laws applied to women, the Court also agreed to review cases challenging the constitutionality of the abortion laws in Georgia and Texas. After hearing arguments twice, the Supreme Court decided the two cases in 1973.[20] The "fundamental" right to privacy, Justice Harry Blackmun wrote in the opinion of the Court, "whether it be founded in the Fourteenth Amendment's concept of personal liberty and restrictions upon state action, as we feel it is, or, as the District Court determined, in the Ninth Amendment's reservation of rights to the people, is broad enough to encompass a woman's decision whether or not to terminate her pregnancy."[21] The fetus is not a person with rights to protect, and the state, according to Blackmun, first acquires a "compelling" interest in protecting potential life at "viability" and, accordingly, may prohibit abortions only in the final trimester of pregnancy.[22] A "compelling" interest in the health of the mother does not begin until the end of the first trimester of pregnancy, when abortion becomes a dangerous operation. Accordingly, the state may regulate—but not prohibit—abortion during the second trimester "to the extent that the regulation reasonably relates to the preservation and protection of maternal health."[23] Blackmun's opinion invalidating the abortion laws was in no respect based on the nature of the class claiming abrogation of its rights; rather, it was exclusively based on the nature of the right that was abrogated.

The vote in the abortion cases was 7–2, though not all the justices in the majority subscribed to Blackmun's reasoning. In dissent, Justice Rehnquist contended, "As in *Lochner* and similar cases applying substantive due process standards to economics and social welfare legislation, the adoption of the compelling state interest standard will inevitably require this court to examine the legislative policies and pass on the wisdom of these policies in the very process of deciding whether a particular state interest put forward may or may not be 'compelling.' The decision here to break the terms of pregnancy into three distinct terms and to outline the permissible restrictions the State may impose in each one, partakes more of judicial legislation than it does of a determination of the intent of the drafters of the Fourteenth Amendment."[24]

Stronger attacks were to come. In a petition for rehearing, Texas compared the Blackmun view that the fetus is not a person with Justice Taney's holding in *Dred Scott* that a Negro is not a person with rights that whites are bound to respect.[25] That comparison quickly became a favorite with groups opposed to the decision. An important scholarly attack on *Roe* appeared a few months after the decision in an article by John Hart Ely of Harvard Law School in the *Yale Law Journal*. Ely found *Roe* "frightening" because

> this super-protected right is not inferrable from the language of the Constitution, the framers' thinking respecting the specific problem in issue, any general value derivable from the provisions they included, or the nation's governmental structure. Nor is it explainable in terms of the unusual political impotence of the group judicially protected vis-a-vis the interest that legislatively prevailed over it. And that, I believe is a charge that can responsibly be leveled at no other decision of the past twenty years. At times the inferences the Court has drawn from the values

the Constitution marks for special protection have been controversial, even shaky, but never before has its sense of an obligation to draw one been so obviously lacking.[26]

Focusing particularly on whether those whose rights were enhanced by the decision deserved special judicial protection, Ely added: "I'm not sure I'd know a discrete and insular minority if I saw one, but confronted with a multiple choice question requiring me to designate (a) women or (b) fetuses as one, I'd expect no credit for the former answer."[27] It does not seem to have occurred to Ely that women seeking abortions could be differentiated from women generally in determining whether they are a class warranting special judicial solicitude for their rights.

John Ely's suggestion that fetuses might be at least as deserving of protection as a discrete and insular minority as women seeking abortions indicates, of course, that he regards the fetus as a human being. In *Roe*, on the other hand, the Supreme Court regarded the fetus only as a potential human being. The question is central and simultaneously not susceptible to resolution. But Ely's quarrel with the Court on this underlying issue indicates that he might not have criticized *Roe* so severely had he been persuaded, like the Court, that the countervailing interest is potential life, not actual life.

A colleague of Ely's at the Harvard Law School, Laurence Tribe, writing at about the same time in the *Harvard Law Review*, had a different view of the decision:

> The Court was not, after all, choosing simply between the alternatives of abortion and continued pregnancy. It was instead choosing among alternative allocations of decision-making authority, for the issue it faced was whether the woman and her doctor, rather than an agency of government, should have the authority to make the abortion decision

> at various stages of pregnancy. . . . [T]he result [the
> Court] reached was not the simple substitution of
> one nonrational judgment for another concerning
> the relative importance of a mother's opportunity
> to live the life she has planned and a fetus's oppor-
> tunity to live at all, but was instead a decision about
> who should make judgments of that sort.[28]

Tribe found attempts to derive guidance on such allocations of decision-making roles from the Constitution "inescapably value-laden,"[29] but legitimate all the same.

Restating Ely's argument in the terms used in this book, he contends that the Court engaged in policy making to bring about what it determined to be political justice without grounding its decision on principles of corrective justice. By contrast, Tribe argues, in effect, that the decision was no more than an exercise in corrective justice, albeit "value-laden" corrective justice. Absent from the responses to Ely has been any serious dispute of his assertion that the decision "is not explainable in terms of the unusual political impotence of the group judicially protected."

One obvious indication of the prejudice against women seeking abortions is that the lawsuits challenging abortion laws were almost invariably brought by plaintiffs using pseudonyms such as Roe and Doe. Courts have discretion whether to allow the parties to litigation to conceal their identities. In permitting women not to reveal their names, judges all across the country implicitly recognized the stigma attached.

Hundreds of thousands of women, otherwise law-abiding, annually obtained abortions even when state laws made such abortions criminal. Yet they could not advance their own interests effectively through the political process because, given the prejudice against them, they feared to reveal their identities to each other. Without identifying themselves, they could not possibly organize to bring about change. It is true, of course, that change had begun to take place in the legislatures by the time the Supreme Court decided *Roe*. Yet because those whose interests were at stake played no part in bringing about change, legislative relief was possible in only a handful of states. A discrete and insular minority suffering from prejudice should not be denied exacting scrutiny of legislation restricting its rights just because in a few places prejudice has abated sufficiently to provide it with its rights through the political process. Indeed, the natural conservatism of the judiciary makes it unlikely that courts will provide a serious hearing to an argument until it loses some of its novelty. Often, it is only when the other branches of government begin to respond to an argument that it acquires sufficient respectability to become persuasive to courts.

Roe did not eliminate the stigma. Indeed, apparently understanding its significance, opponents of abortion devoted much of their effort in the period following the decision to exploiting the stigma. They had a good deal of success in perpetuating its effects.

"Right to life," the antiabortion movement, first appeared in the mid-1960s but, lacking organizational structure for several years, remained relatively ineffectual politically. A lay Catholic backlash against the church's laxity in opposing the repeal of the New York law against abortion provided impetus to its growth and to its development of political sophistication. The church responded, as in Cardinal Terence Cooke's proclamation of "Right to Life Sunday," April 16, 1972. It was celebrated by sermons against abortion in churches throughout several archdioceses and by a parade down New York City's Fifth Avenue.

Following *Roe*, "right to life" grew stronger nationwide and persuaded legislatures and executive agencies to impede abortions by measures exploiting stigma and ensuring its inescapability. These measures were issuance of fetal death certificates; requirements of spousal and parental consent; public disclosure of the identities of doctors collecting Medicaid reimbursements for performing abortions; and requirements that doctors inform women seeking abortions of the human characteristics of the fetus. In addition, some abortion opponents resorted to extralegal methods, such as advertising "abortion counseling," luring women seeking abortions to reveal their identities to opponents, and ostentatiously photographing women entering abortion clinics. Such tactics have intimidated women from identifying themselves as exercising their right to obtain abortions. Prevented from organizing, these women found their influence on the representative branches of government curtailed. Such prejudice, like prejudice against other discrete and insular minorities, requires women who wish to get abortions to continue to rely on the judiciary to protect their rights.

Under pressure from "right-to-life" and other opponents of abortion in the period following *Roe*, several states and municipalities cut off public funding for abortions for poor women and refused to allow abortions to be performed in public hospitals. In *Beal* v. *Doe*,[30] the Supreme Court upheld Pennsylvania's refusal to provide Medicaid reimbursement for nontherapeutic abortions. In *Maher* v. *Roe*,[31] the Court upheld Connecticut's policy of providing reimbursement only for medically necessary abortions in the first trimester. And, in *Poelker* v. *Doe*,[32] the Court upheld refusal by two St. Louis municipal hospitals to perform abortions except when there is a threat of grave physiological injury or death to the pregnant women. The common theme of the three decisions was that a state decision to fund normal childbirth but not nontherapeutic abortions may influence a woman's choice between the two alternatives but does not unduly burden the woman's fundamental right to choose. The state need not be neutral. It can decide to favor normal childbirth, and policies rationally related to this goal, such as those in Pennsylvania, Connecticut, and in St. Louis, will be upheld. Although such a decision would have been inconsistent with a holding that practices affecting the rights of women who seek abortions must be exactingly scrutinized because of the nature of the class affected, it is also inconsistent with the Court's holding in *Roe* that the decision to choose an abortion is a "fundamental" right. That holding should also, according to the Supreme Court's prior decisions, trigger exacting scrutiny. Yet the Court did not hold that the state had demonstrated a compelling interest in encouraging childbirth as should have been necessary to uphold practices restricting exercise of a fundamental right.

The reasoning of *Beal, Maher*, and *Poelker* undercuts *Roe*. It implies, without saying so, that the Court no longer considers a decision to choose abortion to be a fundamental right. From the standpoint of women seeking abortions, this makes it all the more urgent that they differentiate themselves from women generally and persuade the courts that they are a discrete and insular minority. As such they would be able to argue that restrictions of their rights weigh most heavily on women who require public funding to pay for abortions.

The inconsistency of the three 1977 cases with *Roe* is, of course, susceptible to more than one explanation. It may indicate that the present Supreme Court is especially reluctant to dispense distributive justice, as is involved in allocating public funds to pay for abortions for poor women. Or it may reflect the Court's sensitivity to public opinion. The women's rights movement was riding high when the Court considered *Roe*. By 1977, it no longer appeared politically potent, as its inability to secure ratification of the Equal Rights Amendment demonstrated. By contrast, "right to life" was growing in strength and appeared able to sway the outcome of elections for many state and national offices. Its nationwide power was evident when, several months before the Court's decisions upholding restrictions on state funding, Congress adopted the Hyde Amendment imposing drastic limits on federal funding of abortions.[33] A federal court had quickly enjoined implementation of this restriction on federal expenditures,[34] but the Supreme Court vacated the injunction when it decided *Beal* and *Maher*.[35]

The three organizations that sponsored the litigation against the Hyde Amendment, the American Civil Liberties Union, the Center for Constitutional Rights, and Planned Parenthood Federation of America, did not abandon the battle in the courts following the 1977 decisions. They were forced to concentrate, however, on the issue left open by the Supreme Court: whether government refusal to fund therapeutic abortions—probably about one-third of all abortions involving the poor—is constitutional if the government funds all other medically necessary operations. Their lawyers proceeded as if required to prove all over again that compelling principles of corrective justice required judicial intervention to invalidate the acts of the representative branches of government. Anything less seemed unlikely to persuade the Supreme Court to dispense distributive justice by requiring Medicaid reimbursement of the costs of medically necessary abortions for poor women.

The principal case in which this effort was made was *Harris* v. *McRae*.[36] Evidentiary hearings commenced immediately following the 1977 Supreme Court decisions and involved testimony by more than sixty witnesses and submission of some five hundred exhibits to the Court. Two and a half years later, Judge John J. Dooling handed down a

350-page opinion holding the Hyde Amendment unconstitutional and ordering the federal government to fund
medically necessary abortions for poor women.[37] Among
the reasons for special judicial solicitude for those affected
by the legislation, he noted:

> Pregnant teenagers, particularly the younger teen-
> agers, are a disadvantaged class, recognized as such
> by Congress; they are disadvantaged by the conver-
> gence of their unwanted pregnancies of physical and
> psychological immaturity, poverty and dependence,
> and a high risk of serious pregnancy-connected
> physical and psychological complications that
> threaten permanently to undermine the health. . . .
> No legislative interest outweighing the interest in
> the teenagers' health can be advanced to justify the
> discriminating denial of necessary medical care.[38]

Continuing along lines indicating that he saw parallels
between the class affected by restrictions on funding medically necessary abortions for the poor and those minorities
requiring special judicial protection, Dooling noted: "The
medical relevancy of poverty itself is a factor increasing the
risks of pregnancy complications for the health of poor
women; they are the class least able to sustain withdrawal
of the procedure from the physician's battery of procedures.
The indigent younger teenager who becomes pregnant represents the extreme of need."[39]

Although several other grounds for invalidating the
law were cited in the decision, it was in documenting the
hardship to a disadvantaged class that Dooling's opinion in
McRae differed most dramatically from the Supreme Court's
1977 decisions. The fact that medically necessary abortions
rather than nontherapeutic abortions were at issue, of course,
enhanced the disadvantagement that would result if the courts
deferred to the judgment of the representative branches.

The Supreme Court was not persuaded by Judge Dooling's reasoning. In Justice Stewart's opinion for the Court, there was no recognition that poor women who seek abortions are distinguishable from the poor generally. Accordingly, Stewart wrote, though "the principal impact of the Hyde Amendment falls on the indigent ... that fact does not itself render the funding restriction constitutionally invalid, for this Court has held repeatedly that poverty, standing alone, is not a suspect classification."[40] In dissent, Justice Marshall complained, unavailingly,

> I am unable to understand how the Court can afford the same level of scrutiny to the legislation involved here—whose cruel impact falls exclusively on indigent pregnant women—that it has given to legislation distinguishing opticians from opthalmologists, or to other legislation that makes distinctions between economic interests more than able to protect themselves in the political process.... And while it is now clear that traditional "strict scrutiny" is unavailable to protect the poor against classifications that disfavor them ...I do not believe that legislation that imposes a crushing burden on indigent women can be treated with the same deference given to legislation distinguishing among business interests.[41]

In the wake of *Harris* v. *McRae*, women who wish abortions are concentrating their efforts to provide funding for those who cannot afford the cost of abortions on litigation in state courts under state constitutional provisions. At the same time, the "right to life" movement is concentrating its efforts on an attempt to pass a constitutional amendment prohibiting abortion entirely or, if that proves impossible, an amendment leaving it to the states to determine whether abortion should be punished criminally. Under pressure from this movement, and under continuing scholarly fire, it seems conceivable that the Supreme Court—with new members who may be appointed by President Reagan—will reverse its decision in *Roe*.

Some critics of *Roe* contend that the Court dissipated its own prestige and authority by dealing with a politically charged question without establishing a stronger constitutional foundation for its decision. Whatever the merits of this view, the loss of prestige and authority will be incommensurably greater if a Court with Reagan appointees reverses *Roe* under pressure from "right to life" and its allies on the new right. Although the Court has not persuaded most Americans that it was right in *Roe*, neither are most Americans persuaded that it was wrong. Reversal would not bring the Court more into line with public opinion; it would merely align the Court with a different segment of public opinion. Reversal would destroy the image of resoluteness that the Court created by its own decisions on school segregation in the decade and a half after *Brown*, thereby inflicting lasting damage to the Court as an institution.

8

Ending Poverty: Too Great a Task

From the Progressive era until the late 1950s, enlightened public opinion ascribed poverty in America to two preeminent causes: economic cycles and migration. The New Deal suggested that the way to deal with the poverty caused by an economic depression was to create jobs and to devise measures to tide Americans over during periods of temporary unemployment. As for the migrants—among them, black migrants from the rural South—it was widely believed that in a matter of time they would be absorbed into the American economic mainstream. Antidiscrimination measures would speed the process by removing artificial barriers. Poverty did not seem to be an insuperable problem in the 1950s. It was a period of relatively full employment; we thought we knew how to avoid another great depression; and the nation had a champion, the Supreme Court, to help rid it of discrimination.

In 1958, John Kenneth Galbraith challenged accepted thinking about poverty with the publication of *The Affluent Society*.[1] "Poverty does survive,"[2] he announced, and he divided it into two new categories: "case poverty" and "insular poverty." Case poverty is caused by "some quality peculiar to the individual—mental deficiency, bad health, inability to adapt to the disciplines of modern economic life, excessive procreation, alcohol, insufficient education, or perhaps a combination of several of these handicaps."[3] Insular poverty is attributable to residence in an island, like the exhausted coal-mining region of West Virginia, where "everyone or nearly everyone is poor. . . . [A] homing instinct causes them to bar the solution, always an individual remedy in a country without barriers to emigration, to escape the island of poverty."[4]

Although Galbraith advanced American thinking about poverty, his analysis did not require him to propose a very radical solution. "The first and most strategic attack on poverty," he wrote, "is to see that it is no longer self-perpetuating. This means insuring that the investment in children from families presently afflicted be as little below normal as possible."[5] In addition, he called for "slum clearance and expansion of low and middle income housing"[6] to attack insular poverty. Case poverty, said Galbraith, should be dealt with by "treat[ing] those characteristics which cause people to reject or be rejected by the modern industrial state. Educational deficiencies can be overcome. Mental deficiencies can be treated. Physical handicaps can be remedied."[7]

Four years later, Michael Harrington published *The Other America*.[8] Acknowledging a debt to Galbraith for opening up discussion of poverty in America, Harrington pointed out that the title of Galbraith's book had been misinterpreted and contributed to the view in some quarters that everybody in America was affluent. This mistaken view could be held, according to Harrington—who estimated that there were fifty million poor in America—because the poor were invisible. They lived in rural slums that outsiders never visited and in urban slums quickly bypassed by commuters to the suburbs. Harrington helped to make them visible, pointing out that the problem went beyond insular and case poverty because "poverty in America forms a culture, a way of life and feeling, that makes it a whole. . . . There are people in the affluent society who are poor because they are poor; and who stay poor because they are poor."[9] Without proposing a blueprint, Harrington called for a "campaign" against poverty to be mounted by the "one institution in the society capable of acting to abolish poverty. That is the Federal Government."[10]

Harrington's proposal for a campaign against poverty became Lyndon Johnson's "war on poverty." The model the Johnson administration looked to for conducting the war was Mobilization for Youth (MFY), an aggressive anti-poverty program established on the lower East Side of New York City in 1962 with the help of funds appropriated under the federal Juvenile Delinquency Act of 1961 and with additional support from the National Institute for Mental Health, the Ford Foundation, and New York City.

The intellectual parents of MFY were sociologists Frances Fox Piven and Richard Cloward. They believed in helping the poor fight for their rights under existing welfare laws, at the time an innovative way of combating poverty. MFY opened storefront service centers—also an innovation—to encourage the neighborhood poor to visit and to seek help. Piven and Cloward describe what took place: "The center staff became skilled in fighting the welfare department. They totaled up scores of welfare budgets to detect underbudget-ing; they placed telephone calls to a bewildering number of functionaries and sometimes accompanied families to see officials in person. They argued and cajoled; they bluffed and threatened. . . . 'When I go to welfare,' one Stanton Street staff member declared,'I don't wait around for the stall. If I don't get treated with respect, I start hollering for the supervisor, and then I threaten legal action.'"[11]

In 1963, MFY made its threats of legal action credible by hiring two lawyers. Two more were employed the following year. They were the first poverty lawyers, and their success in vindicating the rights of the poor, combined with the growing faith in the courts as an agent for social change brought about by *Brown* v. *Board of Education* and its progeny, inspired the designers of the war on poverty in 1965 to incorporate a federally funded legal services program in the Office of Economic Opportunity. Many veterans of the "freedom summer" air lift of attorneys to the deep South the previous year left private practices to go to work in the neighborhood legal services offices established all across the country. It was another way of joining the civil rights movement. In publications like the *Yale Law Journal*, the new poverty lawyers were told that they would be the leading edge of change: "As in the case of the Negro the avenue of [social welfare] reform must be through law. In a society that is highly organized, institutional and bureaucratic, law is the essential means by which individuals are protected; law alone can ensure the fairness and lack of oppression that is essential to individual independence. The field of social welfare has grown up with no participation by lawyers at the level where individual rights are at stake. Lawyers are desperately needed now."[12] Nothing seemed beyond the reach of litigation in the mid-1960s, even solving the newly discovered problem of mass poverty.

MFY's first legal director was Edward Sparer, subsequently director of the Center on Social Welfare Policy and Law, chief counsel for the National Welfare Rights Organization (NWRO), and now professor of law at the University of Pennsylvania. In 1966, Sparer, the father of the poverty law movement, circulated a memo to the newly hired lawyers in the neighborhood legal services offices out-lining a strategy.[13]

Sparer's goal was to transform government assistance for the poor from a privilege (i.e., something that the government may withhold or reduce at will) to a right (i.e., an enforceable contractual obligation) under the Fourteenth Amendment's guarantee of equal protection of the laws. This right, in Sparer's words, would be a "right to live." Other liberties, such as those protected by the First Amendment, are dependent on this right, he contended, because, "Let the unemployed man lie starving, let the sick woman die because an affluent society won't provide her with minimal medical treatment, and you have killed off the speaker, the writer and the worshipper. You have preserved those rights only for the comfortable and the affluent. The reason we need a constitution is to protect the rights of the weak, the powerless and the dispossessed."[14]

To establish a right to live through litigation would require the judiciary to dispense distributive justice not only when necessary to provide corrective justice but for its own sake. The courts would have to do what Alexander Hamilton said they could not do: exercise "influence over the purse" and "direction of the wealth of the society."[15] At any other time, such a task could not have been seriously contemplated. In the mid-1960s, however, it appeared to many that the country was being transformed by the civil rights movement; that the courts were the movement's ally; and that old rules about the limitations of the courts might be overcome. The nation had accepted the leadership of the courts in ending legal segregation of the races. It would accept the leadership of the courts in another great moral cause: ending poverty.

The transformation of government assistance to the poor was to come about as the cumulative consequence of a series of court decisions. Sparer outlined ten areas in which litigation was to be brought: challenges to (1) such procedures as "man in the house rules," which deprived families of Aid to Families with Dependent Children (AFDC) if an unemployed father had not deserted or if a "substitute father" had a relationship with the mother and was presumed to have taken on responsibility for child support; (2) welfare department "midnight raids" to discover whether a man was in the house; (3) residence laws, which required that welfare residents live in the state or county for a set period (often several years) before obtaining assistance; (4) "maximum family grants," which provided that AFDC payments not be increased when the number of children in a family rose beyond a particular number; (5) relatives' liability statutes, providing for state recovery of welfare payments from grandparents, grandchildren, and other relatives; (6) work relief statutes that did not adequately define the standards under which welfare recipients could decline particular kinds of work; (7) criminal penalties imposed on welfare recipients for violations of moral standards, such as illegitimate births; (8) the absence of standards for discretionary decision making (e.g., what is an "employable mother" or a "suitable home"); (9) the denial of fair procedures for determining eligibility for welfare; and (10) the failure of the states to enforce uniform practices in the administration of welfare.

Sparer distributed sample legal pleadings and offered back-up services through the Center on Social Welfare Policy and Law. He encouraged the newly opened legal services offices to undertake a great many cases that fundamentally challenged the assumptions of the prevailing welfare system. An important contributing factor was the birth of the welfare rights movement, which coalesced around the storefront centers established by the Office of Economic Opportunity. In 1966, that movement acquired a leader, Dr. George Wiley, a black former chemistry professor at Syracuse University, who had left that post earlier in the decade to become associate director of the Congress of Racial Equality (CORE). He left CORE when it was taken over by black nationalists and became director of an antipoverty organization in Washington, D.C. Attracted to Piven and Cloward's theories about mobilizing the poor to fight poverty, Wiley used his Washington post as a base to create the National Welfare Rights Organization.

Daniel P. Moynihan, who clashed with Wiley over Richard Nixon's Family Assistance Plan (FAP) (which Moynihan devised), acknowledged Wiley's achievement in creating NWRO:

> Wiley's genius was to see that this segment of the black population had interests which could never be served by a strategy of avoidance designed more to maintain the self-esteem of those who did not need help than to help those who did. At a moment of much separatist activity he saw that dependency was an experience that united rather than divided: *half* of all AFDC mothers were white. He and his associates, and of course the women who followed him, made an imaginative leap that seemed to have regenerative qualities. Instead of denying dependency, they asserted it. In asserting dependency they ceased in ways to be dependent. . . . Two years after [NWRO was founded] it was the unchallenged spokesman for blacks with respect to an issue which four years earlier the civil-rights movement had denied existed, but which was now the center of national politics.[16]

As a result of his experience in CORE in the early 1960s, Wiley was a skilled organizer of demonstrations; he knew their value to the civil rights movement in stimulating social change. His faith in demonstrations as a way of advancing the interests of the poor was enhanced by a historical analysis produced by Piven and Cloward showing that government aid to the poor rose in periods of turmoil by the poor.[17] They "thought it likely that a huge increase in the relief rolls would set off fiscal and political crises in the cities, the reverberations of which might lead national political leaders to federalize the relief system and establish a national minimum income standard."[18] This became known as the welfare rights movement's "crisis theory."

The civil rights movement where Wiley had gotten his training had, however, its greatest gains through litigation in the federal courts, gains not limited to what was actually provided in court orders. Litigation had served an organizing role, as well, encouraging southern blacks to challenge their oppressors. Many blacks had been to court to listen as sheriffs, police chiefs, and mayors who had lorded it over them all their lives were cross-examined by civil rights lawyers. They had seen those officials humbled by federal judges. After such visits to courts, many more blacks were ready to insist on their rights. Litigation, Wiley understood, could serve the same purpose in making the poor insist on their rights when dealing with public officials who had previously seemed all-powerful.

NWRO's operating style embodied Wiley's experience. It did most of its work in two arenas: in the streets and in the courts. As in the case of the civil rights movement, the court battles were divided between defenses of the actions in the streets, lawsuits to redress the individual grievances of constituents, and lawsuits seeking social change, that is, the changes spelled out in Sparer's memo. If the social change litigation were to succeed, of course, the relief rolls would be greatly expanded and government budgetary allocations would be insufficient. This fitted Piven and Cloward's "crisis theory." As a consequence of such a crisis, Piven, Cloward, Sparer, and Wiley hoped to force abandonment of the welfare system as it then existed and its replacement by a federally guaranteed income.

The litigation made substantial headway in a very short period. In its 1968 term, the Supreme Court invalidated state "substitute father" regulations because they violated federal law;[19] in its 1969 term, the Court invalidated durational residency requirements because they violated the Fourteenth Amendment's guarantee of equal protection of the laws and, following the reasoning of the equal protection of the laws and, following the reasoning of the Court's 1954 decision in *Bolling* v. *Sharpe* striking down school segregation in Washington, D.C., invalidated the D.C. residency requirement because it violated the Fifth Amendment's guarantee of due process of law;[20] and in its 1970 term, the Court invalidated state regulations that permitted welfare officials to discontinue or suspend welfare payments prior to a hearing because such procedures violated the Fourteenth Amendment's guarantee of due process of law.[21] Lower court cases put a stop to midnight raids.[22]

The residency requirements decision, *Shapiro* v. *Thompson*, raised most directly the question of whether the courts could provide distributive justice. By requiring the inclusion in welfare programs of recent arrivals in a state, the Court forced the states either to increase their total expenditures on welfare or to reduce the benefits accorded to long-term residents. Writing for the Supreme Court's majority, Justice Brennan faced this question: "We recognize that a State has a valid interest in preserving the fiscal integrity of its programs. It may legitimately attempt to limit its expenditures, whether for public assistance, public education, or any other program. But a State may not accomplish such a purpose by invidious distinctions between classes of its citizens."[23]

What made a distinction based on residence invidious? Its purpose and effect, the Court found, was to deter the poor from migrating to a particular state to take advantage of the benefits offered. This was impermissible because, as Brennan explained "This Court long ago recognized that the nature of our Federal Union and our constitutional concepts of personal liberty unite to require that all citizens be free to travel throughout the length and breadth of our land uninhibited by statutes, rules or regulations which unreasonably burden or restrict this movement."[24] In other words, to provide corrective justice by removing an impediment to the right to travel, it was necessary for the court to dispense distributive justice by requiring welfare payments to new residents. Brennan cited previous Court decisions going back to 1849 to demonstrate that interference with travel from one state to another was impermissible. The earlier cases, however, all involved more direct limits on the right to travel.

The following year, the Supreme Court considered *Dandridge* v. *Williams*, a challenge to state regulations that set ceilings on the size of the grant any family could receive under the federally funded Aid to Families with Dependent Children. A poor family with eight children could receive no more assistance than a poor family with five children, penalizing those children with the misfortune to be born into large families. The redistribution of income required by success of the challenge would resemble that required by *Shapiro* v. *Thompson*. If benefits were paid to each additional child in a large family, it would have to be at the expense of other children who received AFDC or the total expenditure on welfare would have to be increased at the expense of other public programs or at the expense of the taxpayer. An amicus curiae brief, filed by Sparer's Center on Social Welfare Policy and Law on behalf of the National Welfare Rights Organization and several other groups, argued that the regulations challenged made invidious distinctions because they were

> subversive of, the dual purposes of Title IV of the Social Security Act fulfilling the financial needy dependent children and their caretakers and promoting the care of such children in the family home. As to the former, the grant maximum ignores a significant portion of the needs of those families affected by it; as to the latter, the grant maximum encourages the placement of children outside the family home and in the custody of a relative eligible to receive benefits on their behalf unaffected by the maximum. The grant maximum and the classification it creates warrants the strict scrutiny of this Court for a number of reasons: the classification affects appellees' ability to obtain the fundamental necessities of existence; it reaches a class characterized by political powerlessness; it undermines the integrity of the basic family unit, and it creates a class of children based on a status over which they have no control.[25]

The Supreme Court was not persuaded. Justice Stewart, writing for the majority, conceded that the federal Social Security Act was concerned with keeping children in a family environment, but,

> Given Maryland's finite resources, its choice is either to support some families adequately and other less adequately, or not to give sufficient support to any family. We see nothing in the federal statute that forbids a State to balance the stresses that uniform insufficiency of payments would impose on all families against the greater ability of large families—because of the inherent economies of scale—to accommodate their needs to diminished per capita payments. The strong policy of the statute in favor of preserving family units does not

prevent a State from sustaining as many families as it can, and providing the largest families somewhat less than their ascertained per capita standard of need. Nor does the maximum grant system necessitate the dissolution of family bonds. For even if a parent should be inclined to increase his per capita income by sending a child away, the federal law requires that the child, to be eligible for AFDC payments, must live with one of several enumerated relatives. The kinship tie may be attenuated but it cannot be destroyed.[26]

Perhaps most important, Stewart's opinion for the Court rejected the claim by welfare recipients that they are entitled to exacting scrutiny of legislation affecting them. In effect, thereby, the Court seemed to reject Michael Harrington's perception that the poor "are poor because they are poor" and "stay poor because they are poor." That formulation by Harrington suggests an analogy to discrete and insular minorities warranting special judicial solicitude. By asserting that poverty or receipt of welfare does not warrant exacting scrutiny, the Court implicitly aligned itself with the traditional American view that the poor are not a discrete class. Another possible interpretation of the Court's position, of course, is that whatever its view of the nature of poverty, it shied away from a finding that, according to the Court's own lights, would require it to scrutinize exactingly legislation and administrative practices dealing with the poor. The burden of dispensing distributive justice that the Court would have assumed had it decided otherwise, given the vast size of this minority, may simply have seemed too heavy—heavier by far than any the Court had previously tried to carry.

Despite the Court's finding that poverty is not a suspect classification warranting special judicial concern, the different results in *Shapiro* and *Dandridge* seem inexplicable on the merits of the cases. Preserving the integrity of the family is at least as compelling a principle of corrective justice as protecting the right to travel. Perhaps still more compelling is the principle that each person—child in this instance—is entitled to be protected by the law without regard to his affiliation with a large or small family. The right to travel from state to state was certainly no more impaired by an attempt to remove the attraction of moving to take advantage of welfare benefits than the right to preserve family units or than the right to be protected equally by the law without regard to family affiliation were impaired by a regulation that required either sending a child to live with relatives to obtain payments to cover the necessities of life or diminished payments per child. The different result cannot be explained by a change in the personnel of the Court. Warren Burger replaced Earl Warren as chief justice in the period between the two cases, but no other changes occurred in the Court's makeup. And, since Warren dissented in *Shapiro* and Burger concurred in *Dandridge*, the vote from that seat remained constant.

The most likely explanation for the shift from *Shapiro* in 1970 to *Dandridge* in 1971 is the one identified by Justice Marshall, dissenting in a 1972 case challenging discrimination against a class of applicants for government assistance to the poor. AFDC, he noted, "is not a politically popular program" and there was evidence "of a stigma that seemingly attaches to AFDC recipients."[27] AFDC had become extremely unpopular politically by the time *Dandridge* was decided, apparently dissuading the Court from pursuing the course of providing distributive justice to the poor that it had embarked on a little while earlier in *Shapiro*. A backlash was under way, in part inspired by the urban riots of the late 1960s. It was marked by special antagonism to those who seemed to mock what Richard Nixon was calling the "work ethic." The nonworking poor—that is, welfare recipients—became a special target of this backlash.

The political unpopularity of welfare recipients was evident in a decision by the Supreme Court the year following *Dandridge*. In *Wyman v. James*, the Court considered an appeal of a lower court decision holding that a welfare recipient had a right to prohibit a warrantless search of her home by a welfare worker without forfeiting welfare benefits. A few years earlier, the Supreme Court had held that a building manager could bar a building inspector without a warrant from entering an apartment building to make a routine annual inspection for possible housing code violations.[28] No issue of distributive justice was involved in that case, and at least on the surface no issue of distributive justice was involved in *Wyman*. A welfare recipient's right to the privacy of her own home would seem to be at least as great as a building manager's right to privacy in his place of work, but the Supreme Court did not see it that way. No warrant was required, according to Justice Blackmun's opinion for the Court, because, "One who dispenses purely private charity naturally has an interest in and expects to know how his charitable funds are utilized and put to work. The public, when it is the provider, rightly expects the same. It might well expect more, because of the trust aspect of public funds, and the recipient, as well as the caseworker has not only an interest but an obligation."[29] In other words, because welfare recipients are beneficiaries of distributive justice provided by the representative branches of government, they do not enjoy the same rights as others to corrective justice. Within a scant two years, the Supreme Court had stood on its head the approach it followed in *Shapiro*.

Wyman made it plain that the Court saw governmental assistance to the poor as a privilege—or "charity" as Justice Blackmun put it—rather than as a right. Despite the victories of Sparer and the welfare rights movement early in their campaign, they had lost their effort to establish judicially a right to live. Welfare rights advocates have since won a few victories in the Supreme Court (subsequent to their losses in *Dandridge* and *Wyman*)[30] but the main goal of their campaign could not be achieved through the courts.

Writing after *Dandridge*, Sparer contended that

> a contrary result in *Dandridge* would have permitted wholesale challenges to the barriers created by state legislators and Congress to deny welfare assistance to groups of needy people. Distinctions between grant levels of individuals in equal need, whether because of differences in categories or their state of residence, might have been brought down. Traditional divisions between state and federal authority, and between the three branches of government, would doubtless have been altered. The equal protection clause would have become the vehicle for establishing a constitutional guarantee of human life. In these and other ways affirmative judicial scrutiny to guarantee equal protection could have led to a different America.[31]

This view assumes, of course, that the other branches of government and the American people would have tolerated a judicial excursion so deep into the territory of distributive justice as to create such "a different America"—which seems improbable. *Wyman*, which denied welfare recipients the same right to privacy in their own homes as everyone else, reflects better what most Americans wanted the courts to do to welfare recipients in the 1970s.

The political unpopularity of welfare recipients is reflected in the way the other branches of government dealt with them in the 1970s. In 1969, President Nixon proposed the elimination of the AFDC and its replacement with a guaranteed annual income paid by the federal government.

Nixon's plan was attacked by the NWRO because the payments were too low—$1,600 a year for a family of four (with provisions allowing wage-earning families to receive supplementary benefits up to a maximum total income of $3,920 a year for a family of four). The program's architect, Daniel Moynihan, contends that the NWRO opposed the FAP for its own organizational reasons. "NWRO represented the aristocracy of welfare recipients,"[32] he says, those living in New York and other industrial states where welfare support levels were already much higher than would be provided by the FAP. The plan would have benefited welfare recipients in the South and some of the working poor, who would get supplementary benefits.

In Moynihan's view, the NWRO, Wiley, Piven, and Cloward were instrumental in defeating the FAP by persuading liberals and civil rights groups to withhold the support the plan needed to resist attacks from conservatives in Congress who opposed the idea of a guaranteed annual income for the poor. Piven and Cloward, never enthusiastic about the FAP because of its low payments, attribute its defeat to lack of support from the White House. Whichever view is correct, the FAP was dead by 1971. Nixon formally abandoned the plan in 1972 and exploited the political unpopularity of welfare recipients in the presidential campaign of that year. No significant possibility of overhauling the nation's way of dealing with the poor arose during the rest of the decade. Welfare payments did not keep pace with inflation, and the standard of living of the poor declined.

By the time *Dandridge* and *Wyman* were decided and the FAP abandoned, the National Welfare Rights Organization itself was collapsing. George Wiley resigned in 1972 (and died a few months later in an accident), and the organization formally expired in 1975. At its high point in 1969, it had only twenty-two thousand dues-paying members,[33] though its activism in the streets and the courts sometimes conveyed an impression of greater numbers. Newspaper accounts regularly credited it with a membership of one hundred thousand or more. When the NWRO collapsed, the welfare rights movement ceased to exist. Litigation on behalf of welfare recipients continues, but with no likelihood that it will be an important agent of change.

What did the movement and the litigation in its behalf accomplish? One view is that the genuine advances won by welfare recipients, such as the elimination of residence requirements, could not have come about any other way. Lacking political power, they could make headway only in the courts. Another view is that the court cases that established fairer procedures and expanded the welfare rolls, asserting public assistance as a right and not a privilege, aroused a backlash that made greater reform impossible. That backlash may have helped to bring about the Reagan era cutbacks on welfare benefits.

It seems possible that both views are valid. There would have been no welfare rights movement were it not for the assertion of dependency that Daniel Moynihan identified as a crucial step toward ceasing to be dependent. Yet, paradoxically, although that assertion was necessary to establish government assistance to the poor as a right it was also crucial in bringing about the rejection expressed in David Stockman's frequent statements that the Reagan administration recognizes no entitlements. The resort to litigation to transform the situation of the poor seems warranted because, short of massive social upheaval, no other strategy could have succeeded. Moreover, the poor made headway through litigation. Yet, in retrospect, the idea that poverty in America might be ended through litigation seems hopelessly naive. That it did not appear so naive in the late 1960s suggests the heady atmosphere of the time. Litigation did not seem then, as it seems now, too puny an instrument with which to undertake a task of such magnitude. The Supreme Court could take on the enormous task of ending legal segregation of the races because of the apparent morality of the cause. In the process, the Court greatly enhanced its own prestige and authority. But the Court would not and could not take on the even larger task of establishing for the poor a right to live. The task was perceived as impossible because of its magnitude and, even more important, because most Americans were never persuaded by Harrington's argument that the poor are poor because they are poor. Accordingly, the claim by the poor that they had a right to assistance appeared to most Americans to lack morality.

9

Challenging War: A Futile Effort

The idea of putting a war on trial in court would have occurred to few Americans before the mid-1960s. It did not seem so strange at that time. Every other public policy dispute was going to court. The Supreme Court enjoyed unprecedented authority because of the prestige it had earned in the school segregation cases. Many active opponents of the war in Vietnam were veterans of the civil rights movement accustomed to judicial resolution of their grievances; and lawyers who had played leading roles in the civil rights struggle had developed the habit of thinking boldly about what could be done through litigation.

Yet the legal precedents were not encouraging. The courts had long made it plain that they were unwilling to challenge the representative branches of government on matters involving the war power or national security. Indeed, on several important occasions, the judiciary had evaded its responsibility to dispense corrective justice in war-related matters.

The most notorious instance of judicial evasion of responsibility took place during World War II when the Supreme Court considered several cases involving discriminatory treatment of Americans of Japanese ancestry. The leading case, *Korematsu v. United States*,[1] involved a Japanese-American's appeal of his criminal conviction for violating a military order issued under the authority of an Executive Order by President Roosevelt that excluded anyone of Japanese descent from the West Coast. The constitutionality of the order was upheld by the Supreme Court in 1944.

The opinion in *Korematsu* was written for the Court by Justice Hugo Black, who acknowledged at the outset that "all legal restrictions which curtail the civil rights of a single racial group are immediately suspect."[2] Having determined that the Court was required to employ the most exacting scrutiny, Black went on to write that restriction of the rights of Japanese-Americans was warranted by a compelling state interest. Even though the exclusion order was directed at all Japanese-Americans, "most of whom we have no doubt were loyal to this country,"[3] all could be excluded from the West Coast because the military had not found it possible "to bring about an immediate segregation of the disloyal from the loyal."[4] Justice Black concluded, "Our task would be simple, our duty clear, were this a case involving the imprisonment of a loyal citizen in a concentration camp because of racial prejudice," but to "cast this case into outlines of racial prejudice, without reference to the real military dangers which were presented merely confuses the issue."[5]

With the advantage of hindsight, it seems plain that the decision fits Justice Frank Murphy's characterization of it in dissent as a "legalization of racism."[6] No one demonstrated that Americans of Japanese descent were more dangerous to the national security than Americans of German decent or Italian descent. Yet though the United States was at war simultaneously with the countries from which those citizens originated, it was never seriously proposed that they be excluded from the East Coast. The distinguishing characteristics of the Japanese-Americans were their separate race, their relatively small number, and the intensity of racial antagonism against them, that is, the characteristics of a discrete and insular minority suffering from prejudice.

The willingness of the courts to uphold war or national security measures that violate clearly defined rights has sometimes ended when the emergency, or the national sense of emergency, has passed. That happened after the Civil War when the Supreme Court invalidated the suspension of habeas corpus during the war.[7] Similarly, as the post–World War II cold war thawed in the late 1950s, the Supreme Court began to invalidate measures restricting civil liberties similar to those it had upheld a few years earlier.[8] At other times, however, as in cases involving prosecutions for speech during World War I, the wartime mood persisted even after the war ended. For example, in *Schenck* v. *United States*, a case involving the prosecution of a man for circulating a leaflet attacking military conscription, Justice Holmes wrote for the Supreme Court a year after the war ended that, "when a nation is at war many things that might be said in time of peace are such a hindrance to its effort that their utterance will not be endured so long as men fight, and that no Court could regard them as protected by any constitutional right."[9]

The poor record of the courts in providing corrective justice in cases involving free speech, habeas corpus, and racial discrimination during times of war made it seem a foregone conclusion that litigation challenging the legality of a war could not succeed. But because the 1960s were different, many challenges were mounted. The first, or one of the first, was brought by David Mitchell, a young draft resister who refused induction into the armed services in

1965. He sought dismissal of the prosecution against him for violating the draft law on the ground that the law implemented a war that was illegal both under international agreements prohibiting aggressive war and under the constitutional requirement that only Congress may declare war. Federal Judge William Timbers, who presided at Mitchell's trial, greeted these arguments scornfully. In language reflecting both the novelty of the questions and his own character, Timbers supplemented his legal reasoning with a comment about "the sickening spectacle of a 22 year old citizen of the United States seizing the sanctuary of a nation dedicated to free speech to assert such tommyrot."[10] Timbers's decision was reversed on a question involving Mitchell's procedural rights. The appellate court took note of Timbers's comments to the extent of suggesting that he might assign the case to another judge for retrial.[11]

In 1967, the United States Supreme Court declined to review *Mitchell*.[12] Only one justice (four are required to grant review), William O. Douglas, expressed interest in hearing it.[13] Later that year, with public opposition to the war mounting rapidly, Douglas was joined by Justice Potter Stewart in stating a willingness to consider another challenge to the war, in *Mora v. McNamara*, involving three soldiers at Fort Hood, Texas, who had been court-martialed for refusing to obey orders transferring them to Vietnam. Stewart set forth some questions that he thought the Supreme Court should try to resolve:

I. Is the present United States military activity in Vietnam a "war" within the meaning of Article I, Section 8, Clause 11, of the Constitution?

II. If so, may the Executive constitutionally order the petitioners to participate in the military activity, when no war has been declared by the Congress?

III. Of what relevance to Question II are the present treaty obligations of the United States?

IV. Of what relevance to Question II is the Joint Congressional ("Tonkin Gulf") Resolution of August 10, 1964?

    (a) Do present United States, military operations fall within the terms of the Joint Resolution?

    (b) If the Joint Resolution purports to the Chief Executive authority to commit United States forces to armed conflict limited in scope only by his own absolute discretion, is the Resolution a constitutionally impermissible delegation of all or part of Congress' power to declare war?[14]

These were all critical questions. Indeed by 1967, the entire country was debating them. But should they be resolved by the courts?

In Justice Brennan's famous enumeration of the characteristics of a "political question,"[15] first place was accorded to "a textually demonstrable constitutional commitment of the issue to a coordinate political department." The issue of war is clearly committed by the text of the Constitution to Congress. In that sense, it is certainly a political question. But as the issues were framed by the young men resisting shipment to Vietnam, that textual commitment could not be considered dispositive. They did not ask the Court to determine whether the United States should carry on the war. Rather, they said that it should decide whether the executive branch of the government had disregarded the textual commitment of the issue to Congress. The Constitution does not textually commit to another branch of government the power to decide whether one of the representative branches has usurped the powers of the other. In that sense it was not a political question, at least so far as the first of Brennan's criteria was concerned.

There was, of course, a powerful precedent for judicial determination whether the executive had usurped the powers of the legislative branch in a war-related case: *Youngstown Sheet and Tube Co. v. Sawyer*,[16] the 1952 steel seizure. The Supreme Court had invalidated an Executive Order of President Harry Truman directing the secretary of commerce to take control of the steel industry and to keep it running despite the strike. The Korean War was under way, and Truman said it was essential to keep the steel mills going because steel is an indispensable component of weapons and other war materials. "The order cannot properly be sustained as an exercise of the President's military power as Commander in Chief of the Armed Forces," the Supreme Court had said. "This is a job for the Nation's lawmakers, not for its military authorities.... And the Constitution is neither silent nor equivocal about who shall make laws which the President is to execute."[17]

In the steel seizure case, the Supreme Court succeeded in making the president comply with its decision. Were the circumstances different in 1967? Both cases involved the authority of the president to conduct a war. The president in 1952, Harry Truman, like the president in 1967, Lyndon Johnson, was not hesitant about using the powers of his office. Both cases involved major questions of political justice. The Supreme Court's prestige was relatively high in 1952, fifteen years after the court-packing plan, but it was far higher in 1967 after more than a decade of presiding over school desegregation. By 1967 (and certainly later on), the war was unpopular with a substantial section of the population, just as the steel seizure had been in 1952. And on both occasions compliance with a decision adverse to the president did not necessarily mean cessation of the activity at issue; it would have meant only that the president could not continue to act unilaterally but, in either instance, Congress could have decided to pursue the same course. Of course, Congress did not continue the steel seizure in 1952 and it might not have continued the war in 1967 if it had been required to face the question directly. Yet far from intimidating the judiciary, the possible unwillingness of the Congress to sustain the course charted by the president might have encouraged the Court to act.

Yet there were crucial differences. The seizure of the steel industry was characterized by Truman as a war measure, but it did not involve the actual conduct of the war. And the prestige of the president was at stake during the Vietnam war as it never was in the steel seizure. The war had been building for several years, and successive presidents became ever more deeply enmeshed in it. The steel seizure was a quick—some might say impulsive—response to what President Truman considered an emergency. American involvement in the Korean War was not repudiated by *Youngstown* nor was Truman's entire presidency. The Vietnam war would have been repudiated and Johnson's presidency and, subsequently, Nixon's presidency would have been repudiated by a Supreme Court decision holding that the president was not authorized to conduct the war. Truman complied with *Youngstown*, but it seems likely that Johnson or Nixon would have defied a Supreme Court decision that held the war unconstitutional. In defiance, inevitably the president would attack the Court for usurping authority it lacked. However great its prestige, the Supreme Court probably could not prevail in such a fight. In the process, the Court probably would have lost much or all of the authority it had accumulated since the mid-1950s.

The campaign by antiwar activists to get the Supreme Court to rule on the constitutionality of the war got a powerful boost in April 1970, when the Massachusetts legislature adopted a statute directing the state's attorney general to challenge the president's power to wage the war on behalf of soldiers from Massachusetts ordered to Vietnam. Under the provision of the Constitution conferring original jurisdiction on the Supreme Court in cases "in which a State shall be a party,"[18] the Massachusetts attorney general attempted to bypass the lower federal courts. In November 1970, the Supreme Court declined to accept the case, sending Massachusetts back to a federal district court.[19] This time, Justice Harlan joined Douglas and Stewart in expressing a willingness to consider the case, making it necessary for those litigating against the war to pick up just one more vote to obtain Supreme Court review.

These developments, it is important to recall, took place against a backdrop of escalating antiwar sentiment. Antagonism to the war peaked following the American invasion of Cambodia and the Kent State shootings in May 1970. On college campuses, feelings ran so high that many schools stopped functioning. Final exams and graduation ceremonies were simply canceled. If ever there was a time when the courts might have prevailed in a struggle with the president over the constitutionality of a war not declared by Congress, this was it.

An increasing number of soldiers joined the movement against the war. Thousands went to Canada; others disappeared; others did not flee but openly defied orders to go to Vietnam. Malcolm Berk of New York went to court, enlisting Theodore Sorensen as his counsel in challenging an order to report for shipment to Vietnam in June 1970. Formerly a principal aide of President John F. Kennedy, Sorensen was then a partner in a leading New York law firm and a candidate for the United States Senate. The willingness of lawyers such as Sorensen to get involved was a fair measure of the respectability that such litigation was acquiring.

In court, the arguments proceeded along lines that were becoming familiar:

> Sorensen: To say that this is a political issue—that it is not a justiciable case—is to say that there is no such thing as an unconstitutional war; that there is no restraint on the exercise of the powers of the President who wishes to send American forces into combat anywhere in the world.
>
> The Court: The District of Columbia Court of Appeals, with Judge Burger concurring [since that opinion, Burger had been appointed chief justice of the United States], says it is difficult to think of an area less suitable for judicial decision.
>
> Mr. Sorensen: But in the *Youngstown* case the Court was willing to exercise restraint upon the executive branch for the very reason that the founding fathers put a checks-and-balances system together.
>
> The Court: But that did not involve a war problem.
>
> Mr. Sorensen: In part.
>
> The Court: Indirectly, yes. All right. Go ahead.[20]

The Federal District court judge with whom this colloquy took place was Orrin Judd, who declined to enjoin Berk's shipment to Vietnam. The American Civil Liberties Union, which had just resolved, after a long internal debate, to oppose the war as unconstitutional, joined Berk's lawyers in an appeal. On June 7, just two days after Sorensen's colloquy with Judge Judd, Supreme Court Justice Byron White—not one of those who had previously expressed a willingness to consider a challenge to the war—issued an order staying Berk's shipment to Vietnam until all the issues could be fully considered. White's action was unexpected and attracted nationwide press attention. Suddenly, Berk's case was the focus of an intensified litigation campaign to declare the war unconstitutional.

Within a week following the stay issued by Justice White, another hearing on a soldier's attempt to resist shipment to Vietnam was held in the Eastern District of New York where *Berk* was proceeding. Salvatore Orlando's case was heard by Judge John J. Dooling, who acknowledged that "I was, as I think all of us were, surprised by Justice White's action after there had been so many denials of stays by so many of the Justices, other than Mr. Justice Douglas." That it was White who issued the stay was especially significant because, Dooling noted, he was regarded as "one of the swing justices," indicating "that there is something that he is concerned about that has not been apparent before."[21]

White never said publicly why he shifted, but it seems fair to speculate that heightened popular antagonism against the war was a factor. If he was concerned about the capacity of the judiciary to withstand a contest with the president, the national mood in the wake of Cambodia suggested that the Court was no longer so certain a loser. Perhaps with such considerations in mind, Judge Dooling stayed Orlando's shipment to Vietnam. From then on, *Orlando* proceeded through the courts alongside *Berk*.

The United States Court of Appeals for the Second Circuit permitted the *Berk* and *Orlando* cases to go forward by ruling that the legality of the war was justiciable, "but must still be shown to escape the political question doctrine."[22] After a full-scale trial in *Orlando*, however, Dooling ruled that the participation of Congress in making it possible for the United States to engage in combat was sufficient to refute any contention that the president had usurped the war power. Responding to critics of this view, Dooling wrote:

It is passionately argued that none of the acts of the Congress which have furnished forth the sinew of war in levying taxes, appropriating the nation's treasure and conscripting its manpower in order to continue the Vietnam conflict can amount to authorizing the combat activities because the Constitution contemplates express authorization taken without the coercions exerted by illicit seizures of initiative by the presidency. But it is idle to suggest that the Congress is so little ingenious or so inappreciative of its powers, including the power of impeachment, that it cannot seize policy and action initiatives at will, and halt courses of action from which it wishes the national power to be withdrawn.... [T]he reality of the collaborative action of the executive and the legislative required by the Constitution has been present from the earliest stages.[23]

Dooling's decision was followed in short order by Judge Judd's decision in *Berk*, which also concluded that "Congress repeatedly and unmistakably authorized the use of armed forces of the United States to fight in Vietnam."[24] These rulings placed opponents of the war in the worst possible situation. The central question of the presidential usurpation of powers had been confronted on the merits by two federal court judges, both highly respected and noted for greater receptivity than most of their colleagues to litigation to advance causes. Both ruled that no usurpation had taken place. The two decisions not only set back litigation against the war; they also threatened to undermine an important political argument against it.

Briefs submitted to the Second Circuit Court of Appeals debated at great length whether congressional appropriations for military expenditures, congressional approval of the draft, and other such acts fulfilled the constitutional mandate that only the Congress may declare war. The appellate court, which had previously ruled that the constitutionality of the war was justiciable, disposed of the dispute by blending affirmation of the reasoning of Dooling and Judd with a finding that a political question was at issue:

> Beyond determining that there has been some mutual participation between the Congress and the President, which unquestionably exists here, with action by the Congress sufficient to authorize or ratify the military activity at issue, it is clear that the constitutional propriety of the means by which Congress has chosen to ratify and approve the protracted military operations in Southeast Asia is a political question. The form which congressional authorization should take is one of policy, committed to the discretion of the Congress and outside the power and competency of the judiciary, because there are no intelligible and objectively manageable standards by which to judge such actions.[25]

The Court of Appeals decision in *Berk* and *Orlando* came down on April 20, 1971. It caused a stir in Congress, where Senator William Fulbright protested on June 4, that "I do not like to think that by voting for the draft, which we have had on many occasions prior to the Vietnamese war, the court would infer from that decision that I am thereby endorsing the policy which we are now following in Vietnam. . . . I had never dreamed of not voting money for the Defense Department."[26] Even Senator John Stennis, a supporter of the war, concurred, pointing out, "When you vote for a bill, there are a lot of ingredients in it, and for the Court to single out that this is an endorsement of war, it seems to me, misses the mark and is too broad by any standard."[27] Senator Jacob Javits picked up the discussion a few weeks later, when a conscription bill was being discussed on the Senate floor, and asked Stennis, as its manager, "Is there anything in this act which would be deemed to constitute an authorization by the Congress for the conduct of military hostilities in Southeast Asia pursuant to the war powers of Congress as specified in article I, section 8 of the Constitution?" Stennis replied, "I do not think there is anything in the bill that would authorize the conduct of the war in Southeast Asia." Pressing further, Senator Thomas Eagleton said, "I assume the Senator from Mississippi [Stennis] does not regard this bill, which provides for the conscription of young men to serve in the Armed Forces to provide for the national defense, as authority for the President to use them in any other way than the Constitution states. For instance, if young men are sent into Indochina war, does not Congress have to authorize such hostilities in accordance with the Constitution?" Stennis responded, "My answer to that question is yes. Yes, that is correct."[28]

Despite such congressional disavowal of the reasoning of the Second Circuit Court of Appeals, the Supreme Court declined to review *Berk* and *Orlando*. Only Justices Douglas and Brennan dissented. Passions had cooled since Justice White's stay fifteen months earlier had set off a flurry of litigation. Cambodia and Kent State had receded somewhat in memory, and the Nixon administration's claim that it was winding down the war had begun to gain public acceptance. Justice Harlan had retired from the Court. Justice Stewart, who earlier expressed an interest in hearing a challenge to the constitutionality of the war, and Justice White, who had stayed Malcolm Berk's shipment to Vietnam, voted with the majority. Perhaps they reasoned that, if the war was ending anyway, there was no cause to plunge the Court into a momentous and, perhaps, ineffectual struggle with the president. The Court had just taken on the president in another war-related case, overruling his attempt to prohibit publication of the Pentagon Papers.[29] That case involved traditional judicial responsibility for rendering corrective justice by dealing with censorship of the press. In the wake of that case, Stewart and White may have decided that another great struggle with the president was inadvisable, especially on a matter less clearly within the Court's territory. Conceivably, it occurred to them that if they squandered the prestige and authority of the Court in a vain effort to stop the war on the ground that the president had usurped authority, the charge of usurpation of authority would be turned back on them. Wounded in such a struggle, the Court might fare less well if another clear case of corrective justice like the Pentagon Papers case were to come along.

Passionate opposition to the war was rekindled briefly by the Christmas 1972 bombing of North Vietnam and the 1973 bombing of Cambodia. Those bringing new litigation against the Cambodian bombing included a member of Congress, Representative Elizabeth Holtzman, who secured a ruling from Judge Judd on July 25, 1973, that the escalation of the war had not been authorized by Congress and was illegal.[30] When the order was stayed by the Second Circuit Court of Appeals before it took effect, Holtzman's ACLU lawyers went to Justice Marshall, the member of the Supreme Court responsible for reviewing emergency appeals from the Circuit during the Court's summer recess. On August 1, Marshall refused to vacate the stay.[31] The Court's procedures permit applications to any other justice in such circumstances. On August 4, the attorneys persuaded Justice Douglas, whom they found at his cabin, where there was no telephone, on a mountain at Goose Prairie, Washington, to vacate the stay.[32] That same day, however, Justice Marshall arranged a conference call among all the justices (except Douglas, who was still at his cabin without a phone), and Douglas was overruled.[33] The few hours that elapsed between the time Douglas vacated the stay and the full Court overruled him were the only period during the war when a court order enjoining it actually took effect. So far as anyone knows, there was no interruption of military activity during that period.

As director of the ACLU at the time *Orlando*, *Berk*, and *Holtzman* were underway, I enthusiastically supported the litigation. In retrospect, it deserved to fail. That judgment reflects no second thoughts about American involvement in the war—now, as then, I think it was catastrophic. Nor does it reflect any change of opinion about presidential usurpation of the war power—now, as then, I think it was flagrantly unconstitutional. It does reflect, however, a revision of my thinking about the power that should be exercised by the judiciary. Opponents of the war suffered from no handicaps in pursuing their goals through the political process. Though serious issues of corrective justice were involved because young men were forced to fight in a war that had not been constitutionally declared, the effort to obtain political justice should have been directed to the representative branches of government. Had opponents of the war "won" a court decision, almost certainly it would have had no effect on the war, but it could have seriously impaired the judiciary.

The ACLU attorneys who conducted the main part of the litigation, Burt Neuborne (now a professor of law at NYU) and Leon Friedman (now a professor of law at Hofstra), have argued that the litigation achieved several valuable results, among them, that "the principle of judicial review of Executive warmaking was explicitly recognized for the first time by the courts"; that "the myth of inherent presidential authority to wage war was utterly destroyed"; that "Congress was put on notice that it could no longer avoid its constitutional responsibilities by abdicating them. . . . No longer could critics of a war be dissuaded from debating its merits during the appropriations process by assurances that paying the bills for a war did not constitute approval"; and that the litigation was "a catalyst in spurring Congress to take effective action to insure that the tragedy of Vietnam can never be repeated."[34] Although much of this argument is necessarily speculative, there is evidence to support some of the attorneys' conclusions. In its report on what became the 1973 War Powers Law, the Senate Foreign Relations Committee took note of the judicial holding that appropriations for the armed forces could be construed as congressional authorization for war.[35] Accordingly, the legislation provided that authority for the use of military force shall not be inferred from "any provision contained in any Appropriations Act, unless such provision specifically authorizes the introduction of . . . forces into hostilities . . . and states that it is intended to constitute specific statutory authorization." Whether any president will pay any attention to this provision in the law, however, is not clear. El Salvador may be viewed as a test, though President Reagan's caution about using American soldiers in combat there may have more to do with the persisting strength of popular feeling about the Vietnam war than with the War Powers Law. It is still far from certain that it is possible to adopt general legislation that will inhibit presidential warmaking. The very existence of such legislation suggests that its enforcement would have to be sought through litigation at a moment when Congress is not prepared to use its powers to cut off support for that particular war.

In retrospect, the litigation against the Vietnam war seems to confirm the conventional wisdom of an earlier age that the direct exercise of the war power is not susceptible to judicial limitation. The most that the courts can do is to limit the representative branches of government when they invoke the war power to deny corrective justice or justify acts that do not clearly derive from the war power. It was a role the courts failed to perform—to their discredit—when

Japanese-Americans were interned. It was a role they did perform—to their credit—when President Truman seized the steel industry and when President Nixon tried to stop publication of the Pentagon Papers. Judicial attempts to challenge the direct exercise of the war power not only seem futile but may also compromise the capacity of the courts to limit excesses in the name of the war power.

10

Challenging the National Security State: A Not-So-Futile Effort

Opponents of "the national security state"—as they label it—pursue twin goals through litigation: they want the government to stop political surveillance of dissenters, and they want the government to reveal information that it tries to keep secret. The underlying theory is that government power over citizens diminishes as government is denied information about citizens and that citizen control of government is enhanced as citizens discover information about their government. Both political surveillance and government secrecy have long been issues in litigation. The connection between these practices and such larger questions as whether American military policy and foreign policy are subject to democratic control began to emerge in the late 1960s when discontent with the Vietnam war reached its peak. The concept of a national security state was first discussed at that time, but it was not instantly apparent that anything might be done about it in the courts. A role for a litigation campaign became clear, however, in January 1970, when a former United States Army intelligence officer, Christopher Pyle, revealed publicly that the military had conducted systematic surveillance of the political activities, beliefs, and associations of American civilians.[1]

Pyle's revelation caused a sensation and prompted the United States Senate Subcommittee on Constitutional Rights, headed by Senator Sam Ervin, to conduct hearings that brought into the open a great deal of additional information on political surveillance by the federal government. It also inspired the American Civil Liberties Union to launch a litigation campaign against political surveillance. The first major lawsuit in that campaign sought an injunction against political surveillance by the army and the destruction of all the political dossiers it had compiled on civilians.

The plaintiffs in the suit against the army were Arlo Tatum, a prominent pacifist, and other individuals and organizations Pyle had identified as targets of political surveillance. They claimed that their exercise of their First Amendment rights was "chilled" by the government's collection of data because the data could be used to smear their reputations, deny them jobs, and harass them in other ways. Filed in 1970, *Tatum v. Laird* was decided by the United States Supreme Court in 1972.[2] Chief Justice Burger, writing for the Court's five-member majority, delivered what seemed to be a deathblow to the infant litigation campaign against political surveillance by holding that "allegations of a subjective 'chill' are not an adequate substitute for a claim of specific present objective harm or a threat of specific future harm."[3] Accordingly, the plaintiffs lacked standing to bring the matter before the judiciary, and there was no occasion for the Court to consider whether the army's political surveillance program was constitutionally permissible. As Justice Douglas pointed out in dissent, "To withhold standing to sue until that time arrives [when the "harm" referred to by Burger had taken place] would in practical effect immunize from judicial scrutiny all surveillance activities, regardless of their misuse and their deterrent effect."[4]

Civil libertarians were appalled by *Tatum*. It ran directly counter to their view that the judiciary has a special duty to scrutinize exactingly activities by the other branches of government that restrict the political process. Certainly, the political process is restricted when the government compiles dossiers on the peaceful political activities of its citizens. Yet the Court had asserted that a large-scale government program unmistakably intended to empower the government to limit political activity was not susceptible to challenge in the courts by those against whom it was directed unless they could also demonstrate some additional injury. *Tatum* was judicial restraint with a vengeance.

That the Supreme Court's decision in *Tatum* did not provide political surveillance complete immunity from judicial scrutiny is in some part attributable to the ingenuity of lower court judges who devised ways to limit its impact. An example is a dissenting opinion the following year by Judge James L. Oakes of the Second Circuit Court of Appeals in *Fifth Avenue Peace Parade Committee* v. *Gray*.[5] The majority followed Chief Justice Burger's reasoning in *Tatum* in dismissing a political surveillance suit against the FBI by participants in an antiwar demonstration. Oakes distinguished the case from *Tatum*, however, on the ground that the FBI had turned over a summary of the information it obtained through surveillance to other government agencies, among them the Internal Revenue Service. Since this action exposed the demonstrators to selective harassment by the IRS, Oakes said that it met Burger's specific harm test. Attorneys such as John Shattuck, who directed the ACLU's political surveillance litigation, and one of the counsel in both *Tatum* and *Fifth Avenue Peace Parade Committee*, were quick to realize that opinions like Oakes's suggested "a way of formulating challenges to political surveillance which does not rely on proof of an elusive 'chilling effect.'"[6] If they could show that the agency conducting surveillance had disseminated what it gathered to another agency or had labeled the data in some stigmatizing way, judges would have a basis for distinguishing *Tatum*.

A case decided on the basis of reasoning similar to Oakes's dissent was *Yaffe v. Powers*,[7] handed down by the First Circuit Court of Appeals just a few months after the Supreme Court decided *Tatum*. Erna Yaffe was photographed by the police of Fall River, Massachusetts, as she took part in an antiwar demonstration. The police arranged for the photo to appear on the front page of a local newspaper shortly before election day when her husband was running for Congress. He lost; she sued. The Court of Appeals decision sustaining her effort to enjoin police surveillance avoided the "subjective chill" reasoning of *Tatum* because the police had disseminated the photo to damage her husband.

In *Paton v. La Prade*,[8] decided in 1975, the Third Circuit Court of Appeals upheld a challenge to surveillance even though no dissemination of information outside the FBI had taken place. The case involved a schoolgirl, Lori Paton, in New Jersey, who wrote to the Socialist Workers party for information she needed for a social studies paper. Since the party had been an ongoing target of FBI surveillance for some thirty years, her letter prompted the bureau to investigate her. Lori Paton learned about the investigation from a teacher who was asked for information about her. She sued. The Court distinguished her case from *Tatum* on the ground that the bureau had placed her dossier in a file on "subversives," thereby stigmatizing her.

The willingness of lower federal courts to distinguish *Tatum* may have reflected their dismay at what was widely regarded as one of the Burger Court's worst decisions. It also reflected the sophistication acquired by litigation organizations by the 1970s. In the two decades that had elapsed since *Brown*, the American Civil Liberties Union alone had undertaken more cause litigation than had been brought by litigators for causes of every sort throughout American history prior to *Brown*. The ACLU's approach to a setback like *Tatum* was to bring cases designed to circumscribe its effects. Another factor in making it possible to win cases like *Paton* surely was the Watergate scandal that erupted a year after *Tatum*. It aroused widespread public alarm about political surveillance, prompting Congress to adopt the Federal Privacy Act of 1974[9] that restricted the right of federal agencies to collect political data and the 1974 amendments to the Freedom of Information Act (FOIA)[10] that enhanced the ability of citizens to discover the contents of government dossiers on themselves. Support for such measures was so strong in the aftermath of Watergate that the amendments to the FOIA were adopted by Congress over President Gerald Ford's veto.

From the standpoint of opponents of political surveillance, the cases that upheld their right to sue had a consequence that frequently proved even more valuable than the actual court decisions won. They were permitted "discovery" in connection with their lawsuits, which proved to be a powerful research tool in finding out how previously secret political surveillance programs operated and in identifying those engaged in surveillance and the targets of surveillance. By publicizing information they obtained through discovery they were able to discredit the surveillance programs and the officials responsible for them. As litigators began to realize what they could achieve in this way, they stopped calling for the destruction of the files as in *Tatum*; instead, their lawsuits sought preservation of the files so that the subjects of surveillance would be furnished with their own dossiers and could determine whether to publicize their contents.

The law enforcement agencies that were the defendants in the litigation also shifted tactics as they realized the embarrassment they would suffer if their files were discovered. They began to destroy their surveillance files. In New York City, for example, dossiers on the political activities and associations of about a million persons were destroyed by the police while litigation was underway.[11] In Memphis, the struggle over whether the dossiers were to be destroyed took on comic-opera qualities. While attorneys for the ACLU were in federal court seeking an order against destruction of the files, police in the city hall basement shoveled them into a furnace. When a federal judge enjoined their destruction, one of the attorneys raced across the street and burst past the city hall guards (who followed him with drawn guns) to serve the order on the mayor. Some of the files had not yet been burned and were preserved.[12]

Twin cases challenging political surveillance in Chicago by the Police Department's Red Squad[13] illustrate the significance of the discovery process. They required the city to turn over to the plaintiffs some four hundred thousand dossiers, including many chronicling the activities and associations of citizens prominent in public life. This made the police look ludicrous and paranoid. Though the Chicago litigation may eventually produce an injunction against future surveillance and money damages for those on whom the police spied, from the standpoint of the police most of the damage to their operations has already been done by the exposé brought about by the litigation. Similarly, from the standpoint of the plaintiffs, if they fail to obtain injunctive relief or damages, they have already accomplished much by discrediting political surveillance by the Chicago police. Similar results have been achieved in litigation against police red squads in several other communities and in litigation against federal agencies such as the FBI and the CIA.

Litigation under the Freedom of Information Act has complemented discovery as a method of exposing political surveillance by agencies of the federal government. Information discovered through litigation has aided the work of several congressional committees that have investigated the CIA and the FBI and, in turn, investigations by those committees has unearthed additional information. In effect, therefore, the proceedings of the judicial and legislative branches of government have been mutually reinforcing in exposing abuses by the executive branch. In combination, these exposés provided the impetus for efforts to adopt charters for the FBI and the CIA that would prohibit them from conducting domestic political surveillance.

At this writing, Congress has not acted on the charter proposals and, in the case of a charter for the CIA, there seems little likelihood that it will be adopted any time soon. A proposed charter was considered by Congress in 1980 but the seizure of the American hostages in Iran and the Soviet invasion of Afghanistan doomed it. The public mood resulting from those events was more concerned with "unleashing" and "revitalizing" the CIA than with placing new restraints on it. Indeed, in some quarters, there was a tendency to blame restraints on the agency for events in Iran and Afghanistan. Any extended consideration of those questions is beyond the scope of this book, but it seems worth nothing that no actual legal restraints had been placed on the CIA beyond a requirement that it report covert operations to certain members of Congress. Nevertheless, a sense of restraint prevailed from about 1975 to 1980 because the agency had been discredited. Litigation played a central part in discrediting the CIA, almost entirely through discovery rather than through court orders. There were few of the latter, and their effect was minimal.

Enactment of a charter for the FBI seems more likely, though the momentum to do so has been lacking in the Reagan era. Exposés of past surveillance embarrass the bureau's present-day leadership, which seems eager to change the image of the FBI by concentrating on such matters as "Abscam." That sense of embarrassment is a direct consequence of litigation. In 1979 and 1980, bureau officials supported enactment of a charter that would place some limits on the FBI's power to engage in political surveillance, although less stringent limits than civil libertarians favor. Most of the resistance to restrictions came from outside the bureau—from the White House and from members of Congress who want the bureau to perform much in the way it did in the days of J. Edgar Hoover.

Probably the most important consequence of the litigation is that the targets of political surveillance do not feel helpless. Knowing that they embarrass police spies by exposing them, political dissenters are encouraged to maintain their activities. The litigation has not been an external remedy for an interference with the political process; it has functioned as an integral part of the political process in mitigating the effects of interference. By forcing the spies to try to hide from discovery, litigation turns the tables on them. Police spies are chilled by litigation and, in the process, political dissenters escape some of the chilling effects of surveillance. If the litigation campaign had come to a halt with *Tatum*, the chill which the Court failed to find a sufficient injury for federal court litigation might well have become a deep freeze. As it is, Americans seem less hesitant to take part in political activity for fear that Big Brother may be watching them at any time in the last forty years. Bedeviled by the interrogatories to which they must respond in the discovery process, police spies no longer seem so fearsome as when they managed to keep most of their work secret.

The litigation campaign against government secrecy paralleled the campaign against political surveillance; it often involved the same government agencies and, occasionally, proceeded in the same court cases. Among government agencies, the foremost target has been the Central Intelligence Agency.

Although the CIA was established in 1947 as an outgrowth of the wartime Office of Strategic Services it largely escaped public scrutiny and almost entirely escaped litigation during its first twenty years. In 1967, *Ramparts* magazine caused a stir by disclosing that the agency had secretly financed a large number of organizations and publications, many with "liberal" reputations. The following year, a Pennsylvanian named William B. Richardson initiated the first significant lawsuit against the agency that sought public disclosure of its receipts and expenditures. He claimed a taxpayer's right to know this information under the constitutional provision that "no money shall be drawn from the Treasury, but in Consequence of Appropriations made by Law; and a regular Statement and Account of the Receipts and Expenditures of all public Money shall be published from time to time."[14]

Richardson's suit was dismissed on jurisdictional grounds,[15] but he reinstituted it in 1970 and, two years later, won a ruling from the Third Circuit Court of Appeals that he had established a satisfactory jurisdictional basis.[16] The government appealed the ruling to the United States Supreme Court. Richardson, who had represented himself up to this time, enlisted the American Civil Liberties Union to provide him with counsel, shifting from a lonely crusade to become part of a larger litigation campaign. The representation provided did not avail Richardson, however, because the Supreme Court voted 5–4 in 1974 to reverse the Appeals Court decision. Writing for the majority, Chief Justice Burger dismissed Richardson's suit on grounds similar to *Tatum's*. Allegation of "a subjective chill" was insufficient to confer standing to sue. In *Richardson*, Burger held that a claim that a tax-payer who was denied information on CIA expenditures could not exercise his duties of citizenship was a too "generalized grievance" to confer standing to sue.[17] As in *Tatum*, Burger's approach ran directly counter to the idea that courts have a special duty to scrutinize exactingly those acts of the representative branches that cannot be cured through ordinary political processes because they restrict the political process itself. Uninformed about the size of the CIA budget, citizens could hardly use the political process to curb waste.

The decision in *Richardson* did not affect a broad class of litigation as did the decision in *Tatum*. But even more than *Tatum* it placed a violation of constitutional rights beyond the reach of litigation. No one has yet devised a way to circumvent the holding in *Richardson*, although there have been several attempts.[18] The Supreme Court's decision in *Richardson* is characteristic of judicial response to attempts to litigate challenges to CIA secrecy. The major cases have been lost by the opponents of secrecy; even so, many consider their litigation campaign worthwhile, especially in light of the lack of alternative remedies. By its nature, secrecy is difficult to challenge through the representative branches of government because the secrecy itself prevents the revelations of abuses that would supply political momentum for change. Secrecy maintained perpetuates itself.

In 1972, while *Richardson* was still in the courts, another matter posed a more potent challenge to CIA secrecy. A former CIA agent, Victor Marchetti, contracted with Alfred Knopf, Inc., to publish a book about the agency. Like all other employees of the CIA, Marchetti had signed an agreement with the agency not to publish about it without submitting a manuscript for clearance. The CIA sued Marchetti to make him submit his manuscript for censorship and persuaded the Fourth Circuit Court of Appeals to uphold a prior restraint on publication. Chief Judge Clement Haynesworth wrote for a unanimous Court that "the Government's need for secrecy in this area lends justification to a system of prior restraint against disclosure by employees and former employees of classified information obtained during the course of employment. One may speculate that ordinary criminal sanctions might suffice to prevent unauthorized disclosure of such information, but the risk of harm from disclosure is so great and maintenance of the confidentiality of the information so necessary that greater and more positive assurance is warranted. Some prior restraints in some circumstances are approvable of course."[19] The Supreme Court declined to review this decision.

When Marchetti and co-author John Marks submitted their manuscript for review, the CIA demanded 339 deletions. In the course of litigation, the agency backed down on 171 of those deletions. In the published version of the book, the 171 restored items appear in bold type, and blank spaces appear where the remaining 168 items would have appeared.[20] Knopf's manner of publishing proved embarrassing to the CIA because the passages it had attempted to delete and then agreed to restore were clearly identified and it was possible to guess what was said in some of the passages entirely deleted. Many of the deletions appeared ridiculous. Although the litigation was a dismal failure from the standpoint of challenging the principle of prior restraint, it was a success because it provided the opportunity for Knopf to embarrass the CIA and its secrecy system.

Despite the CIA's litigation victory, several other former agents followed Marchetti's lead in publishing books about the agency without submitting them for censorship. Philip Agee evaded censorship by staying out of the country and publishing his book overseas before it was issued in the United States.[21] John Stockwell[22] and Frank Snepp[23] published books which the CIA did not discover until it was too late for prior restraint. The CIA had won its suit against Marchetti, but it seemed to be losing its battle to hold onto its secrets. Fighting back, the CIA escalated the struggle by suing Frank Snepp for all his earnings from *Decent Interval* (that is, all his income for a period of several years), for damages, and for an injunction to compel him to submit for censorship everything else that he wrote.[24]

It is likely that the CIA would have won its suit against Snepp in any circumstances; still, the timing of the Supreme Court's consideration seems to have been a factor in determining the manner in which the Court decided the case and in determining the content of its decision. The case was considered in early 1980, hard upon the heels of the Soviet Union's invasion of Afghanistan and the seizure of the American hostages in Iran, events creating a national mood of hostility to betrayers of CIA secrets and a widespread public demand to "revitalize" and "unleash" the CIA. President Carter, who had called for restraints on the CIA and a reduction in government secrecy when he campaigned for the presidency in 1976, now led the nation in demanding fewer restraints and more secrecy.[25] Inevitably, the public clamor affected the Supreme Court.

The Court also had its own special reason for concern about secrecy. Bob Woodward and Scott Armstrong's *The Brethren* had just been published,[26] infuriating several of the justices by revealing many of the Court's own secrets. Moreover, the manner of disclosure resembled the revelations of CIA secrets: employees who had been entrusted with confidences disclosed them. Unlike Marchetti, Agee, Stockwell, and Snepp, the Supreme Court clerks had not committed themselves to secrecy in writing. But the Court diverged from the facts before it in *Snepp* to encompass other government employees like the clerks who violated confidences by revealing them to Woodward and Armstrong. "Even in the absence of a written contract," the Court's six-member majority wrote in a *per curiam* opinion, "an employee has a fiduciary obligation obtained during the course of his employment."[27] This fiduciary obligation, the Court said, is sufficient to warrant prior restraint.

There were many extraordinary features to *Snepp*. The Court decided the case without the benefit of either briefs or oral argument; it did this by granting Snepp's petition for a writ of certiorari and the government's conditional cross-petition for certiorari and by simultaneously issuing its *per curiam* opinion. As Justice Stevens complained in a dissenting opinion for himself and Justices Brennan and Marshall, "The Court's decision to dispose of this case on the Government's cross-petition for *certiorari* is just as unprecedented as its disposition of the merits."[28] Writing in the *New York Times*, Anthony Lewis, a close student of the Court not known for using intemperate language when discussing it, said that in *Snepp* the Court "showed contempt for the rule of law."[29]

The procedural irregularity of the decision, as Stevens noted, was matched by its substance. The government never contended that Snepp disclosed classified information, the only kind he was forbidden to divulge by the agreement the CIA made him sign when he quit the agency in 1976, although an agreement that he signed when he started work for the CIA in 1968 was broader in scope, prohibiting him from publishing "any information or material relating to the Agency, its activities or intelligence activities generally . . . without specific prior approval by the Agency." Snepp contended that the 1968 agreement was superseded by the narrower termination agreement of 1976 under the ordinary rule of contract law that a later contract supersedes an earlier contract. The Supreme Court made short shrift of this argument. Snepp never got a chance to elaborate it either in a brief or orally. "Whether Snepp violated his trust," the Supreme Court's majority held, "does not depend upon whether his book actually contained classified information."[30] Prior restraint was warranted, the Court found, because "the Government has a compelling interest in protecting both the secrecy of information important to our national security *and the appearance of confidentiality essential to the effective operation of our foreign intelligence service.*"[31] Taken together with the holding that the written agreement was not essential to upholding prior restraints, the Court seemed to say that all government employees in positions of trust may be required to submit their writing for censorship regardless of whether they disclose confidential information in all circumstances where the government has a compelling interest in the appearance of confidentiality—whatever that means.

By employing a "compelling interest" test, the Court ostensibly conformed to its own prior decisions holding that nothing less justifies government interference with a fundamental right that directly affects the operation of democratic political processes. Even so, *Snepp* is astonishing. The Supreme Court's insistence that it will exactingly scrutinize any interference with a fundamental right to determine whether a compelling interest requires its abridgement is mocked by the procedural irregularity in this case. How can there be exacting scrutiny without either briefs or oral arguments? Perhaps even more important, the decision flatly contradicts the approach the Court had taken previously in determining the existence of a compelling interest. Previously, such a determination was made by the legislature in adopting a restriction on rights. The role of the Court was to scrutinize exactingly the decision of the legislature and to uphold the restriction or not depending on its evaluation of the legislative determination. By contrast, in *Snepp* there had been no finding by the legislature that the government had a compelling interest in prior restraint. That finding was made independently by the Court which, by the language of its decision, extended it to other government employees in different circumstances who never had an opportunity to take part in the deliberations that produced *Snepp*. Probably more than any other decision in the post-*Brown* era, *Snepp* betrayed the responsibility the Court had assumed of using its authority to enhance the representativeness of representative government.

No one seriously believes that the Court meant everything that it said. If it did, the flow of memoirs and articles by former employees of government would stop entirely. Almost certainly, future decisions will narrow the application of *Snepp*. But the decision stands as a monument to the Court's susceptibility to the passions of the moment as does the Supreme Court's decision a year and a half later to abandon a quarter century of its own reasoning in right to travel cases in order to strip the most reprobate of former CIA agents, Philip Agee, of his passport.[32] Since the remedy the Court imposed allowed the government to take away all Snepp's earnings from *Decent Interval*, the decision may prove more potent than the Fourth Circuit's ruling in *Marchetti* in stopping the disclosure of CIA secrets.

The *Marchetti* and *Snepp* cases, of course, did not directly involve questions that go beyond the traditional judicial role of dispensing corrective justice. They are a crucial part of a discussion of a litigation campaign to challenge the national security state, however, because of the way the litigators on both sides represented their clients. The ACLU, which represented Marchetti and Snepp as well as the other CIA agents who litigated questions involving their right to publish, used the cases to embarrass the CIA for practicing censorship. Throughout the 1970s, much of the public criticism of the CIA and of its role in American public life was generated through the *Marchetti* and *Snepp* litigation. On the other side, the Justice Department, representing the CIA, proceeded with special vindictiveness against Snepp. The Justice Department insisted on collecting from Snepp all that the Supreme Court said the government was entitled to collect. The amount, about $140,000, constituted Snepp's entire earnings for a period of several years. As a consequence, he was left flat broke and in debt. Since his offense was relatively minor, even from the CIA standpoint, insofar as his actual disclosures were concerned, it seems evident that the Justice Department's purpose was to make an example of Snepp. The intent was to deter other CIA agents and employees of other government agencies from disclosing what the government does not want disclosed.

The agency has not fared as well in protecting its secrets against court-ordered discovery. The leading case in the area is *Halkins* v. *Helms*,[33] an ACLU suit against Operation CHAOS, the CIA's major program for collecting domestic political information. The documents obtained during discovery reveal, among other things, that the CIA did not inform a committee of the United States Senate—the "Church Committee"[34]—of the magnitude of CHAOS. They demonstrated that the CIA continued to use the information collected in the program after it said it had stopped. The documents reflected a great internal controversy about the program within the agency. They reveal the extent to which the CIA exchanged information with local police departments and the concealment of CHAOS from Office of Management and Budget (OMB) auditors.[35] The capacity of litigation to pry loose even more information than a congressional committee that conducted a major investigation could do indicates the potency of discovery as a weapon against secrecy.

Freedom of Information Act litigation has also helped to force disclosure of CIA secrets. The American Civil Liberties Union and the Center for National Security Studies have filed several FOIA lawsuits against the agency. Although this litigation has not directly forced many major revelations,[36] it has compelled the CIA to comply more fully than it might like with requests for information it receives under the act. For example, the agency was forced to disclose sixteen thousand pages on its MKULTRA program describing its experiments with exotic drugs.[37] As a consequence, when the national mood shifted in the 1980s in favor of protecting CIA secrecy, the agency and its friends in Congress and the White House made exempting the agency from the Freedom of Information Act a top priority.[38] They were unable to rally the requisite support, however, and this proposal was still pending in early 1982.

Several important lessons emerged from the decade-old litigation campaign against political surveillance and government secrecy. Although these practices go to the heart of the democratic process, much of the judiciary has resisted the effort to get it to scrutinize them exactingly. The issues are so politically charged that some judges put aside the concerns that they display in other circumstances for the representativeness of representative government. Despite the difficulty in persuading some judges to exercise their powers to limit politically sensitive antidemocratic practices, litigation is an effective weapon against such practices. Litigation discredits political surveillance and government secrecy merely by exposing them to the light of the day. Court-ordered discovery is especially significant. What happens in court in this area is closely intertwined with concurrent events in the legislature. Litigation gains for opponents of surveillance and secrecy may be consolidated in the legislature, as through the enactment of a charter limiting such practices; or, they may be overturned, as through exemption of the CIA from the Freedom of Information Act. Accordingly, a litigation campaign's chances for success depend on mounting a legislative campaign simultaneously. By the same token, a legislative campaign is enhanced by pursuing the same goals through litigation because the information obtained through discovery helps to generate legislative momentum. Decisions by the United States Supreme Court are not all-important in determining the effects of a litigation campaign. Decisions like *Tatum* certainly have significant consequences, but in an area where the process of litigation matters as much as or more than actual court decisions, lower courts play an even more important part than they do generally.

Litigation against surveillance and secrecy differs crucially from litigation against the exercise of the war power. Although national security is invoked by the executive branch of government as the justification in each instance, it is widely accepted that courts may limit surveillance and secrecy yet they may not interfere with the war power. The war power is textually committed to the other branches in the Constitution. Judicially manageable standards for regulating the exercise of the war power are extremely difficult to discover, especially when a war is under way, the only time litigation against it is brought. Furthermore, the exercise of the war power is usually overt (the secret bombing of Cambodia is an obvious exception) and implicates much of the government and the society at large, and the war power directly and centrally involves the president. Those who challenge the exercise of the war power are not hampered in their use of ordinary political processes. By contrast, the Constitution does not authorize either secrecy or surveillance, and credible arguments can be made that the First Amendment's guarantees of freedom of speech and assembly and the Fourth Amendment's restrictions on searches and seizures forbid these practices. It is fairly easy to formulate judicially manageable standards for regulating these practices. By their nature, these practices are covert and directly implicate only a select group of trusted officials. Although the president may be involved, when these practices are exposed to the light of the day he is more likely to shirk responsibility than to engage in a test of strength with the judiciary. Most important, surveillance and secrecy restrict the operation of ordinary political processes.

Judicial avoidance of questions involving surveillance and secrecy, accordingly, is not wise conservation of judicial prestige and strength. Rather, decisions like *Tatum, Richardson*, and *Snepp* reflect the Supreme Court's acceptance of the national security rationale for surveillance and secrecy. Though lower courts must operate within bounds established by Supreme Court decisions, many judges have encouraged the maintenance of litigation against surveillance and secrecy. The important role that their rulings play in curbing antidemocratic practices in the name of national security demonstrates that it lies within the power of the judiciary to challenge the national security state.

11

Reforming Asylums: No Other Way

"A judge . . . should not be compelled to listen to such non-sense," was a 1951 opinion of a judge of the United States Court of Appeals for the Ninth Circuit concurring in the dismissal of a suit by the Birdman of Alcatraz.[1] The "non-sense" was the prisoner's claim than the First Amendment protected his right to correspond with a publisher.

Judges had been reacting the same way to complaints from prisoners and inmates of other asylums since time immemorial. As George Bernard Shaw wrote in 1922, "Judges spend their lives in consigning their fellow creatures to prison; and when some whisper reaches them that prisons are horribly cruel and destructive places, and that no creature fit to live should be sent there, they only remark calmly that prisons are not meant to be comfortable; which is no doubt the consideration that reconciled Pontius Pilate to the practice of crucifixion."[2]

The judicial view that what takes place inside prisons, mental hospitals, schools for the retarded, and juvenile institutions is of no concern to the courts prevailed until the

1960s. Those confined in such institutions, especially those confined in institutions other than prisons, are so weak and suffer from so much prejudice that for generations they were unable to get the attention either of the representative branches of government or of the courts. Then, like many other judicial traditions, the practice of ignoring inmates of asylums was swept away by the forces set in motion by the Supreme Court's school desegregation decisions, the change hastened by the confinement of new classes of prisoners. The civil rights demonstrators, Black Muslims, draft resisters, and antiwar demonstrators confined in the 1960s were more insistent about their rights than their predecessors and better able to enlist lawyers to take up their causes. Muslims, many of them converts to their faith in prison, made the first breakthroughs, winning judicial recognition that they are entitled to the same opportunities to worship in their own way as adherents of other religions. After courts held that prisoners enjoyed First Amendment rights to practice their religion, it seemed obvious to prisoners and their lawyers that they could also obtain judicial protection for other constitutional rights. Inmates of other institutions followed in the footsteps of prisoners, the modest lapse of time before they too presented their grievances to courts probably attributable to their inexperience in dealing with lawyers. Courts now devote much of their time to reviewing and regulating institutional practices. Indeed, some federal court judges are preoccupied for years on end with such cases and with attempts to secure compliance with their orders.

The volume of litigation involving the rights of inmates of asylums raises the question of whether other methods should not be pursued to reform conditions. One of those raising this question is Chief Justice Burger, who posed it this way in a 1981 address to the American Bar Association: "How much chance do you think there is of changing or rehabilitating a person who is encouraged to keep up years of constant warfare [i.e., litigation] with society?" Yet in the same address, Burger deplored that "after society has spent years and often a modest fortune to put a single person behind bars, we become bored. . . . Our humanitarian concern evaporates. In all but a minority of the states we confine the person in an overcrowded, understaffed institution with little or no library facilities, little if any educational program or vocational training."[3] The implication is that there might be some way of overcoming public boredom about what takes place in asylums other than by challenging abuses in court. Short of a riot, however, it is difficult to imagine anything other than litigation that might be capable of drawing attention to abuses. The essential characteristic of asylums, after all, is that they isolate their inmates from society, making it extraordinarily difficult to pursue strategies other than litigation to bring about reform. Indeed, it is only by litigating and thereby establishing attorney-client relationships with inmates of asylums that it is ordinarily possible to get inside asylums and find out what is taking place.

No aspect of litigation about asylums engages the courts more extensively than the effort to make them regulate treatment. Some cases are based on the theory that there is a legally cognizable right to receive treatment; others on the theory that there is a right not to be treated in certain ways. Important questions arise as to whether these rights are compatible with each other and with principles of liberty. Even though some litigators may not resolve these questions for themselves, the cases they bring to regulate treatment produce great changes in the operations of institutions and in the lives of inmates and their keepers. Litigation challenging the practices of asylums has produced many of the deepest judicial ventures into the territory of distributive justice. The political consequences of this litigation are far-reaching, occasionally forcing major revisions in state budgets.

The suggestion that treatment is a matter of right is generally believed to have originated in 1960 in an article by Morton Birnbaum, a physician and a lawyer.[4] This was about the time that Piven and Cloward began to articulate the view that receipt of welfare is a right, not merely a privilege. Birnbaum offered what seemed to many versed in constitutional thinking a more plausible basis for proposing a right to treatment than something grounded on an all-encompassing right to live. He argued that patients confined in mental hospitals because they are deemed by law to require treatment have a legal right to secure treatment because, if it is not provided, the mental hospitals simply incarcerate them as in a prison. Patients confined for purposes of treatment who do not receive treatment, according to Birnbaum, are entitled to go free. Treatment is the *quid pro quo* the State must offer in exchange for confining those not convicted of crime.

As an abstract proposition, Birnbaum's theory was initially popular with the psychiatric profession. It provided a rationale to seek additional funding for mental hospitals. With the population of such institutions at a peak of about 650,000 in the early 1960s, most mental hospitals were snake pits. Even assuming that psychiatric treatment in a mental hospital is beneficial and with the best of intentions, the typical institution of the 1960s could only harm its inmates. The physical conditions were appalling; the staff was inadequate to protect patients from each other; and the ratio of psychiatrists to patients was far too small to furnish treatment. It was in the interest of psychiatrists to favor new theories that might make it possible for them to provide better care to the confined.

Judicial recognition of this right began in 1966. Chief Judge David Bazelon of the United States Court of Appeals for the District of Columbia, long noted for his interest in the relationship between law and psychiatry, wrote an opinion holding that Washington, D.C.'s giant St. Elizabeth's Hospital was required "to show that initial and periodic inquiries were made into the needs and condition of the patient with a view to providing suitable treatment for him" and that the treatment must be "adequate in light of present knowledge." If it is not provided, according to Bazelon, "Unconditional or conditional release [of the patient] may be in order."[5]

Bazelon's holding was based on a law adopted by Congress requiring that patients in the District of Columbia be provided "medical care and treatment in accordance with the highest standards accepted in medical practice."[6] The opinion's reasoning, however, also suggested the existence of a constitutional right that could be claimed by patients confined in state mental hospitals under laws that made no mention of treatment. The opinion had profound distributive justice implications because of the expense that would be required to furnish "adequate" treatment, but Bazelon provided the District of Columbia with a way out. If it was not prepared to meet the expense, the court would rely on a traditional corrective justice remedy: release of the patient complaining of inadequate treatment. The choice rested with the representative branches of government.

Whether a right to treatment is protected by the Constitution and not merely by a statute such as the one in the District of Columbia was debated in the law reviews in the 1960s, but no court recognized such a right until the next decade. The organized psychiatric profession's attitude helped to make the courts reluctant to act. Despite enthusiasm for the extra expenditures on mental hospitals that might flow from recognition of a right to treatment, psychiatrists were unhappy with the prospect that courts might review their professional judgments. Bazelon's 1966 opinion in *Rouse* had indicated that if there is a right to treatment, courts would judge the adequacy of treatment to determine whether inmates had been accorded their rights. In a 1967 policy statement, the American Psychiatric Association (APA) acknowledged that "final authority with respect to interpreting the law on the subject rests with the courts," but insisted that "the definition of treatment and the appraisal of its adequacy are matters for medical determination." The association welcomed "constructive criticisms of the relative adequacy of a psychiatric facility," but objected to any attempt by an "outside" agency, "to interpose its judgments on the professional managerial affairs of that facility."[7]

The interposition of such judgments under the Constitution began almost by accident. In October 1970, an Alabama lawyer, George Dean, filed a lawsuit in federal court on behalf of employees of Bryce State Mental Hospital who had been dismissed from their posts in a state budget-cutting move. Even before it reduced expenditures, Alabama ranked last in the nation in per capita expenditures on mental patients. In seeking restoration of his clients' jobs, Dean claimed that the budget denied the inmates of Bryce their right to receive treatment.

It was Dean's fortune that the case he filed, *Wyatt* v. *Stickney*,[8] arose in the Middle District of Alabama in the jurisdiction of Judge Frank Johnson. An Eisenhower appointee, Johnson had clashed frequently over civil rights and civil liberties matters with state officials including Governor George Wallace. Johnson had ordered federal marshals and federal troops to protect Martin Luther King, Jr., and those who marched with him from Selma to Montgomery in 1965 after an earlier attempt to march was aborted when state troopers under orders from Wallace attacked and beat the marchers. If the United States Supreme Court symbolized the determination of the nation to rid itself of legal segregation of the races, Johnson was the high Court's embattled outpost deep in the heart of the most hostile territory. Time and again, Johnson demonstrated his readiness to use the authority of the federal courts innovatively to correct injustices that he determined violated federal constitutional rights. Far from leaving him gun-shy, his frequent conflicts with state officials made him readier to face the wrath of the organized psychiatric profession than judges who had previously considered requests that they interfere in the administration of mental hospitals.

In March 1971, Johnson ruled that "to deprive any citizen of his or her liberty upon the altruistic theory that the confinement is for humane therapeutic reasons and then fail to provide adequate treatment violates the very fundamentals of due process."[9] The inmates of Bryce were not receiving adequate treatment, according to Johnson, and he gave Alabama officials six months to make it adequate. He said he would order release of the patients or appoint experts to run the institution if such treatment was not provided.

Johnson did not then set standards for evaluating the treatment provided by Alabama; standards would have to be established in a separate court proceeding. George Dean, one of the ablest and most experienced trial lawyers in the state, required assistance in coping with this proceeding. His inquiries led to two young lawyers knowledgeable about treatment in mental hospitals: Charles Halpern in Washington, D.C., a founder of a pioneer public interest law firm who had been involved in statutory right-to-treatment litigation before Judge Bazelon; and Bruce Ennis, a lawyer employed since 1968 by the New York Civil Liberties Union and the first anywhere to devote full time to constitutional litigation on behalf of the rights of mental patients. They came into *Wyatt* as lawyers for three organizations that entered as amici curiae: the American Orthopsychiatric Association, the American Psychological Association, and the American Civil Liberties Union. Judge Johnson granted them full right to participate as if they were direct parties to the litigation.

Halpern and Ennis helped to arrange a hearing, at which, as Johnson noted in an opinion he handed down in April 1972, "the foremost authorities on mental health in the United States appeared and testified to the minimum medical and constitutional requisites for public institutions."[10] Their testimony made it plain that inmates of Bryce were not being treated adequately by any possible stretch of the imagination. Indeed, the treatment was barbarous. Johnson's opinion spelled out in detail minimum constitutional standards for adequate treatment of the mentally ill. The extent of his venture into distributive justice can be gathered by reproducing a section of the opinion. Point 24, for example, provided:

> The hospital shall have the following minimum numbers of treatment personnel per 250 patients. Qualified Mental Health Professionals trained in particular disciplines may in appropriate situations perform services or functions traditionally performed by members of other disciplines. Changes in staff deployment may be made with prior approval of this Court upon a clear and convincing demonstration that the proposed deviation from this staffing structure will enhance the treatment of the patients.

Classification	Number of Employees
Unit Director	1
Psychiatrist (3 years residency training in psychiatry)	2
MD (Registered physicians)	4

Nurses (RN)	12
Licensed Practical Nurses	6
Aide III	6
Aide II	16
Aide I	70
Hospital Orderly	10
Clerk Stenographer II	3
Clerk Typist II	3
Unit Administrator	1
Administrative Clerk	1
Psychologist (Ph.D.) (doctoral degree from accredited program)	1
Psychologist (M.A.)	1
Psychologist (B.S.)	1
Social worker (MSW) (from accredited program)	2
Social Worker (B.A.)	5
Patient Activity Therapist (M.S.)	1
Patient Activity Aide	10
Mental Health Technician	10
Dental Hygienist	1
Chaplain	5
Vocational Rehabilitation Counselor	1
Volunteer Services Worker	1
Mental Health Field Representative	1
Dietitian	1
Food Service Supervisor	1
Cook II	2

Cook I	3
Food Service Worker	15
Vehicle Driver	1
Housekeeper	10
Messenger	1
Maintenance Repairman	2[11]

Johnson allowed the Alabama Mental Health Board six months to "prepare and file with this Court a report reflecting in detail the progress on the implementation of this order."[12]

Along the way, the litigation was broadened to deal with the rights of inmates in all institutions administered by the Alabama Mental Health Board, including those in the Partlow State School and Hospital for the retarded. Ennis, who had never been inside an institution for the retarded, found that Partlow was worse than any mental hospital. Of his first visit, he wrote:

> There were eighty to ninety [inmates] to a ward, often staffed by only one attendant. Partlow was so crowded that many residents had to sleep on floor mats. The conditions were barbaric. We saw a man who had been locked in solitary confinement for seven years. A little girl in the nonambulatory ward was tied to her bed—otherwise she would try to stand—because there was no one there to catch her if she fell. Agitated residents stuffed dirt and rocks down their throats or lapped garbage water like dogs; we saw one woman in a straitjacket trying to spit the flies out of her mouth. Helpless children lay for hours in pools of urine. Everywhere was hopelessness, neglect and despair.[13]

Johnson ruled that the evidence presented to him "vividly and undisputedly portrayed Partlow State School and

Hospital as a warehousing institution, which, because of its atmosphere of psychological and physical deprivation, is wholly incapable of furnishing [habilitation] to the mentally retarded and is conducive only to the deterioration of the residents."[14] In April 1972, Johnson ordered an end to peonage in the institution; he set minimum staffing ratios, detailed physical and nutritional standards, and directed the preparation and implementation of individualized training programs to meet the needs of each inmate. As in the part of the case dealing with the mentally ill, he gave Alabama six months to report to him on compliance.

Despite outraged reactions by some public officials, a special session of the Alabama legislature was convened to increase the appropriation for the Alabama Mental Health Board from $14 million the year before the decree to $58 million in the year after. George Dean, a canny politician as well as a skilled lawyer, helped bring about this appropriation by filing a legal memorandum with Judge Johnson pointing out that Alabama's budget contained substantial appropriations for a White House of the Confederacy, an Alabama Junior Miss Pageant, a livestock coliseum, and a sports Hall of Fame. He suggested that the legislature would find funds for the retarded if they could be transmuted into "athletic or photogenic cows of Confederate ancestry."[15] The memorandum was widely publicized. Despite the increased allocation procured in this manner and many more since, the state had not yet by 1982 complied substantially with Johnson's 1972 order. On October 25, 1979, after the case had been before him almost continuously for nine years—seven and a half years having elapsed since he set minimum standards—Johnson ruled that the Alabama Mental Health Board was "in substantial and serious noncompliance with orders entered in this case [in 1972] in several critical areas."[16] He ordered the appointment of a receiver to take over the functions of the board, a move initially urged by the inmates' lawyers eight years earlier; he had resisted such a move while attempting to secure compliance by other means. If the executive branch would not comply with the court's order to provide the inmates with distributive justice, the court would try to give meaning to the order by taking over the executive function.

Although Johnson had good grounds for finding noncompliance, developments in legal doctrine and shifts in the thinking of the *Wyatt* lawyers and of Johnson himself gave the case a different focus in 1979 than in 1972. By 1979, the lawyers and the judge were explicitly concerned with moving inmates outside institutions like Bryce and Partlow and in helping them stay out by providing them with services in community residences. Deinstitutionalization had been a goal of some of the litigators from the start, but they had tried to achieve it by indirection. In forcing Alabama to comply with the standards set by Johnson, they had hoped to increase the costs of confinement, thereby forcing the state to release those best able to function in the community. The state would not provide the *quid* of treatment, they assumed, and therefore could not maintain the *quo* of confinement. Writing in 1973, historian David Rothman labeled this the "noble lie" tactic. He described the reasoning of its practitioners: "Courts, they claim, will never decide in favor of a litigant if the case is presented as a step toward shutting down the institution. Judges are comfortable with the rehabilitation ideal, and the more enlightened among them will force administrators to meet their responsibilities. But tell judges that rehabilitation is a sham, that nothing works, that we had better begin to dismantle this cruel and expensive system, and they will avoid the issue, dismiss the contentions as too radical, and deny the inmates all relief."[17]

Rothman's article raised important questions about the goals of lawyers for the confined. Was deinstitutionalization, by itself, a traditional corrective justice goal? Were they trying to achieve this goal by confronting the state with insupportable distributive justice remedies as an alternative? Or were they also concerned with ameliorating conditions for those remaining in institutions? Could they advance both goals simultaneously? Most of the litigators would have answered yes to all questions. The right-to-treatment theory served all these purposes, as they then saw it, not only because the cost of improving conditions of confinement would make it economically unfeasible for the states to confine such large numbers. The goal of deinstitutionalization would be served also by designing institutional treatment to help inmates live outside afterward. Yet if treatment can serve that purpose, Rothman pointed out, confinement for purposes of treatment may be justified. Ultimately, the goal of deinstitutionalization could be subverted by providing judicial sanction to a theory to which some litigators bringing right-to-treatment cases did not subscribe: that institutional treatment, designed and managed well, rehabilitates deviants and dependents and helps them to live self-sufficiently outside.

The Mental Health Law Project (MHLP), a public interest organization that grew out of the association between Ennis and Halpern in *Wyatt* and that has been engaged in litigation on behalf of the mentally ill and the retarded ever since, has never resolved its stand on the issues raised by Rothman. (Along with Halpern, Ennis, and this writer, Rothman served as one of its trustees.) Divergent views coexist peacefully within the MHLP because those most skeptical of the right to treatment believe that the project's cases establishing such a right have not actually impeded deinstitutionalization. It remains to be seen whether peace could be maintained if and when the right to treatment is turned around, as Rothman suggested it could be, and becomes a rationale for confinement.

Bruce Ennis, one of those who became most skeptical about the right to treatment, served as lead counsel in two cases that proceeded through the courts at the same time as *Wyatt*, which began partly as right-to-treatment cases but in which the "noble lie" was abandoned in favor of direct challenges to confinement. In *O'Connor v. Donaldson*,[18] Ennis brought a suit for damages on behalf of Kenneth Donaldson to compensate him for fifteen years during which he was confined custodially in a Florida mental hospital even though the institution was aware he was dangerous neither to himself nor to others. In *New York Association for Retarded Children, Inc. v. Rockefeller*,[19] Ennis challenged the conditions in which the inmates of Willowbrook, a giant institution for the retarded in New York City, were confined. He began work on the Willowbrook suit within the week following his return to New York from the hearing in Alabama before Judge Johnson about conditions at Partlow.

When Ennis commenced litigation on behalf of Kenneth Donaldson in 1971, the suit coupled a claim that Donaldson had been improperly deprived of liberty with Morton Birnbaum's concept of a right to treatment. Birnbaum himself served as Ennis's co-counsel. The trial judge accepted the right-to-treatment theory, telling the jury:

> 37. You are instructed that a person who is involuntarily civilly committed to a mental hospital does have a right to receive such individual treatment as will give him a realistic opportunity to be cured or to improve his mental condition.

> 38. The purpose of involuntary hospitalization is treatment and not mere custodial care or punishment if a patient is not dangerous to himself or

> others. Without such treatment there is no justifica-
> tion, from a constitutional standpoint, for continued
> confinement.[20]

The jury decided that the psychiatrists who confined Donaldson without treatment should pay him damages of $38,500. In 1974, the propriety of the trial judge's instructions and the award of damages were upheld by the United States Court of Appeals for the Fifth Circuit which asserted that "where a nondangerous patient is involuntarily civilly committed to a state mental hospital, the only constitutionally permissible purpose of confinement is to provide treatment, and that such a patient has a constitutional right to such treatment as will help him to be cured to improve his mental condition."[21]

From there, the case went to the United States Supreme Court, where Ennis's arguments shifted the focus. Instead of persisting with the contention that Florida had denied Donaldson his right to treatment, Ennis told the high Court that it should decide the case solely on the other argument he had raised in the lower courts: Florida should compensate Donaldson for improperly depriving him of liberty, that is, entirely on corrective justice grounds.

Several factors combined to bring about the shift. Ennis's own fear that the right to treatment would become a new justification for confinement was reinforced by Rothman's argument and by the hostility of a newly emerged former patients' movement. The development of such a movement, like other rights movements, had been stimulated by the litigation. Its primary concern was the right to refuse such treatment as shock therapy or medication with tranquilizers. Following the Court of Appeals decision in *Donaldson, Madness Network News*, a publication associated with the leading organization of former patients, the Network against

Psychiatric Assault, said that "the primary impact of the right [to treatment] for inmates whose release it cannot secure, would be to provide an impetus for state departments of mental hygiene and mental institutions to *impose* treatment on individuals who generally have no established right to *refuse* it."[22]

The shift was also tactical, dictated by an assessment of the attitudes of the members of the Supreme Court. Cases seeking distributive justice, like *Dandridge* v. *Williams* on behalf of welfare recipients (see Chapter 8), had fared badly. Moreover, Chief Justice Burger, an antagonist of his erstwhile colleague on the District of Columbia Court of Appeals, Judge Bazelon, could be counted on to be especially hostile to a claim of a right first judicially recognized by Bazelon. (In *The Brethren*, Woodward and Armstrong tell us. "The Chief's intention was clearly to beat the right to treatment concept to a bloody pulp."[23])

Recognizing that he could probably count on the votes of the Court's "liberal" members, Justices Brennan, Douglas, and Marshall, and that he might get the votes of Justices Blackmun or Powell, Ennis pitched his argument to Justice Stewart. The argument best calculated to appeal to Stewart was the denial of liberty to Donaldson. It worked. Stewart wrote the opinion for a unanimous Court holding that "a state cannot constitutionally confine without more a nondangerous individual who is capable of surviving safely in freedom by himself or with the help of willing and responsible family members or friends. Since the jury found, upon ample evidence, that O'Connor [superintendent of the hospital where Donaldson had been confined], as an agent of the State, knowingly did so confine Donaldson, it properly concluded that O'Connor violated Donaldson's constitutional right to freedom."[24] Stewart sidestepped any consideration of the right to treatment. That "difficult issue" did not have to be faced, he wrote, because, "as we view it, this case raises a single, relatively simple, but nonetheless important question concerning every man's right to constitutional liberty."[25] No venture into territory ordinarily off limits for the courts was necessary.

Stewart's opinion vacated the award of damages to Donaldson and remanded that issue to the lower courts. A friend of the court brief submitted by the American Psychiatric Association probably influenced that part of the decision.

The APA had divided over whether to file a brief because of the conflict between its support for a right to treatment and its reluctance to see the courts adjudicate treatment. A tie vote (8–8) within the APA Executive Committee was broken by the president, Dr. Alfred Freedman, who supported filing. The brief called on the Supreme Court to uphold the right to treatment but not to require psychiatrists to pay damages, reflecting the APA's view that "it would be unjust and unreasonable for courts to hold psychiatrists personally and individually responsible for resource deficiencies which are actually the responsibility of society."[26] Stewart reworked this opinion so that it meshed with the Court's holding that Donaldson had been improperly denied liberty, not treatment—though had the APA realized that liberty would become the basis for the Supreme Court decision it probably would not have entered the case. (Eventually, a settlement was reached in which the psychiatrists paid Donaldson $20,000 for fifteen years of improper confinement.)

Chief Justice Burger joined in Stewart's opinion for the Court but also wrote a separate concurring opinion attacking the right to treatment:

> I cannot accept the reasoning of the Court of Appeals and can discern no basis for equating an involuntarily committed mental patient's unquestioned constitutional right not to be confined

without due process of law with a constitutional right to treatment. Given the present state of medical knowledge regarding abnormal behavior and its treatment, few things would be more fraught with peril than to irrevocably condition a State's power to protect the mentally ill upon the providing of "such treatment as will give [them] a realistic opportunity to be cured." Nor can I accept the theory that a State may lawfully confine an individual thought to need treatment and justify that deprivation of liberty solely by providing some treatment. Our concepts of due process would not tolerate such a "trade off." Because the Court of Appeals' analysis could be read as authorizing those results, it should not be followed.[27]

Whether or not concepts of due process would tolerate a "trade off"—the *quid* of treatment in exchange for the *quo* of deprivation of liberty—the theory proved to have another deficiency that emerged only after the passage of time. Even when the practical effect of asserting a right to treatment is to free inmates from confinement, the freedom won is generally temporary. Few of the freed are provided with the services they require to survive outside. Because deprivation of liberty is a prerequisite for getting courts to require the provision of services in the right-to-treatment theory, the theory has no value in obtaining services for those not confined. The theory leads logically to the provision of distributive justice within institutions, not outside. Yet without services outside, the fate of many former inmates is a return to confinement.

Ennis's other major case, Willowbrook, also abandoned the right-to-treatment theory, but it did not abandon the effort to provide distributive justice. Far from it. The Willowbrook case pioneered in finding a way to secure distributive justice for inmates of asylums, or at least for the retarded, following their release.

The trial judge in Willowbrook, the late Orrin Judd, rejected the right-to-treatment approach at the outset. The *quid pro quo* rationale was inappropriate, according to Judd, because most inmates of Willowbrook were not involuntarily confined. They "entered because they had no alternative, and none have been denied a right to release."[28] But Judd accepted another argument advanced by Ennis: that those in state custody had a "right to protection from harm." Such a right involved established principles of corrective justice. Certainly, those claiming the right, the retarded, are the least able of any citizens to employ the political processes ordinarily to be relied upon to redress their grievances.

There are some difficulties in suggesting that prisoners should be treated by the courts as a discrete and insular minority since their crimes are responsible for their incarceration. There may even be objections to proposals that the mentally ill should be so regarded since mental illness is an elusive concept and, whatever it is, it may be brief. In this respect, the situation of the mentally ill resembles the situation of pregnant women who do not want to bear children. In both instances, the consequences of brief disability are likely to be long-lasting. Mental retardation, on the other hand, is a clearer case because it is generally a lifelong condition and it is not caused by any act of the retarded. The retarded suffer from enormous prejudice and, almost by definition, cannot fend for themselves in the ordinary political process. They are even weaker than prisoners or the mentally ill. Although Judge Judd's approach to the complaint of the retarded was not grounded in such thinking, to vindicate their rights he had to invade the territory of distributive justice. He ordered Willowbrook to hire at least eighty-five more nurses, at least thirty more physical therapists, fifteen additional physicians, and so on.[29] Differentiating these remedies from those ordered by Judge Johnson, however, Judd said, "The court will not include medical screening in the order, since this relates to the right to treatment rather than to the right to protection from harm."[30]

The following year, in October 1974, another stage in Willowbrook got under way before Judge Judd, a trial to decide what additional steps New York State would be required to take to protect the retarded from harm. After more than fifty witnesses testified over a three-month period describing in horrifying detail the primitive and barbaric conditions of confinement, Ennis and the other attorneys signed a consent decree with the state of New York.

New York State signed the consent decree in part because it seemed that Judge Judd would otherwise have ordered the state to take measures comparable to those to which it consented and in part because Willowbrook became a political issue in the state. Robert F. Kennedy, whose sister was retarded and whose family had long been identified with care for the retarded, had conducted a well-publicized tour of Willowbrook some years earlier. In addition, a television newscaster, Geraldo Rivera, had made his name with a filmed exposé. The litigation added to the public interest in Willowbrook aroused by Kennedy and Rivera exposed still greater horrors and pinned responsibility on state officials. Rivera questioned the 1974 gubernatorial candidates about the case and elicited a televised pledge from the winner, Hugh Carey, that a visit to Willowbrook would be his first order of business as governor. Ennis took Carey up on the pledge and conducted a tour for him. Carey was shocked. As Ennis recalls it, the incident that seemed to disturb Carey most was discovery of a man tied spread-eagled to a bed at a spot in the institution where Ennis predicted he would be because the man had been kept in that position for several years. Flies crawled over the man's face, making Carey turn to officials of Willowbrook in exasperation to demand whether the state could afford a fly swatter.

Following the tour, Carey directed an aide, Peter Goldmark, to negotiate a settlement with Ennis. After prolonged discussion, they jointly submitted to Judge Judd a twenty-nine-page consent decree providing that "protection from harm requires relief more extensive than this court originally contemplated, because harm can result not only from neglect but from conditions which cause regression or which prevent development of an individual's capabilities."[31] Custodial confinement itself was identified as a cause of regression in the retarded. To protect "developing organisms" from harm, therefore, the state must "take all steps necessary to develop and operate a broad range of non-institutional community facilities and programs to meet the needs of Willowbrook's residents."[32] These steps included a responsibility each year to request the New York legislature to "appropriate sufficient additional funds for the development and operation of community facilities and programs to serve the needs of the class."[33] In effect, therefore, the protection-from-harm theory accepted by Judge Judd, unlike the right-to-treatment theory, provided a rationale for the court to require the expenditure of state funds for services to provide distributive justice to inmates freed from Willowbrook living in the community.

In the Willowbrook case, the court had not only a rationale grounded in principles of corrective justice but, because of the consent decree, the unquestioned power to require community services. As a consequence, Willowbrook's population had declined from more than 5,000 when the litigation commenced to fewer than 1,500 at this writing. The consent decree had required that the number must go down to 250 by April 30, 1981. Although that goal was not achieved, Willowbrook has no new inmates and thousands of former inmates are living relatively normal lives in supervised apartments, group homes, and foster homes in the New York area. The case remains under the supervision of the court before which frequent hearings have been held. In one ruling, the court required the state to pay stipends to natural parents to allow them to care for former Willowbrook inmates at home.[34] Judge Judd's protection-from-harm theory, therefore, has served the deinstitutionalization purpose that had attracted some litigators to the right-to-treatment theory. Since institutional confinement was identified as a cause of harm, Judge Judd's theory did not provide a rationale for confinement. And, because freed Willowbrook inmates receive extensive services in the community, they manage well and hardly any have been reconfined. For them, up to now, deinstitutionalization has worked.

At this writing, it is not clear whether deinstitutionalization will continue to work. The future of compliance with the Willowbrook consent decree was thrown into doubt by the refusal of the New York legislature at its 1980 session to continue to provide funds to implement one of the least expensive provisions of the decree. The legislature deleted a $342,000 item from the governor's budget proposal that was intended for a review panel created by the decree to monitor compliance. Judge John Bartels, who had presided over compliance with the Willowbrook consent decree since the death of Judge Judd, ordered Governor Carey to come up with the funds in accordance with his agreement in the consent decree. That order was quickly dissolved by the United States Court of Appeals for the Second Circuit, however.[35] The appellate court reasoned that when a legislature defies a court's order providing distributive justice, a court's only power is to resort to a traditional corrective justice remedy: "In the face of constitutional violations at a state institution, a federal court can order the state either to take the steps necessary to rectify the violations or to close the institution. Thus, a state cannot avoid the obligation of correcting the constitutional violations of its institutions simply by pleading fiscal inability. . . . But that remedy leaves the question of the expenditure of state funds in the hands of citizens of the state, not in the hands of federal judges."[36]

In practice, however, there is no corrective justice remedy in such circumstances. It is simply impossible for a court to order the inmates of Willowbrook turned out on the streets as a method of trying to secure compliance by the representative branches of government with its order requiring that constitutional violations be remedied.

It is possible, of course, that New York will comply with the remainder of the consent decree by continuing to deinstitutionalize the inmates of Willowbrook. It is also possible that the New York legislature, having determined that the courts will retreat in the face of its refusal to fund a portion of the consent decree, will refuse to fund the rest of the decree. Most likely, some compliance with the rest of the consent decree will continue, the date when Willowbrook is reduced to 250 inmates to be postponed several years beyond the April 30, 1981, date required in the consent decree.

Legislative revolt against judicially required distributive justice after so many years of compliance and judicial retreat in the face of such a late revolt raises the question of whether such a revolt could have succeeded earlier. It is only possible to speculate, but I believe that it could not have been successful much sooner. By 1980, the horrors revealed at Willowbrook in the 1974 trial had receded in memory. Conditions at Willowbrook had improved immensely, and a tour of the institution in 1980 could no longer have produced the effect that such a tour had on Carey when he was newly elected to be governor of New York. The power of the federal court to bring about a consent decree with great distributive justice implications stemmed from the enormity of the corrective justice violations at Willowbrook. The elapse of time and the mitigation of those violations, however, diminished the power of the federal courts to enforce the remedies required by the decree.

The eventual fate of the Willowbrook consent decree suggests that the protection from harm theory is not a panacea; it is nevertheless probably the best rationale the courts have devised for providing distributive justice to inmates of institutions. Among those persuaded of the value of Judge Judd's approach was Judge Johnson. When a case was presented to him challenging conditions in Alabama prisons, Johnson at first indicated an interest in holding that prisoners have a right to rehabilitation, a variation on the right to treatment. By the time he decided the case in 1976, however, Johnson had adapted the protection-from-harm theory to prisons: "The evidence in these cases establishes that prison conditions are so debilitating that they necessarily deprive inmates of any opportunity to rehabilitate themselves or even maintain skills already possessed."[37]

The conditions that inspired Johnson's decision included punishment cells in Alabama measuring four feet by eight feet where as many as six inmates at a time were confined, "with no beds, no lights, no running water, and a hole in the floor for a toilet which could only be flushed from outside."[38]

Such barbarism did not deter Governor George Wallace from accusing Johnson of usurping the powers of the other branches of government and of wanting to confine prisoners in hotel-like comfort. In condemning the decision, Wallace said he would like to see Johnson get a "barbed-wire enema."

Johnson replied publicly, though less rudely, defending judicial intervention:

> The prisoner who lives in constant fear of his life and safety because of inadequate staffing and overcrowded conditions, will not have his rights protected merely by an award of damages for the past injury sustained by him.... The courts have been left with two alternatives. They could throw up their hands in frustration and claim that, although the litigants have established a violation of constitutional or statutory rights, the courts have no satisfactory relief to grant them. This would, in addition to constituting judicial abdication, make a mockery of the Bill of Rights. Utilizing their equitable powers, the Federal Courts have pursued the only reasonable and constitutionally acceptable alternative—fashioning relief to fit the necessities of the particular case.[39]

Perhaps because the attack on Johnson was led by Wallace, by then a discredited political leader, the courts were not intimidated. Subsequent decisions on prisoners' rights followed Johnson's reasoning. In 1977, for example, federal District Judge Raymond Pettine declared the Rhode Island prison system unconstitutional:

> The evidence is overwhelming that the totality of conditions of confinement in Maximum and Medium do not provide the "tolerable living environment" ... that the Eighth and Fourteenth Amendments require for state prison inmates.... the lack of sanitation, lighting, heating and ventilation, and the noise, idleness, fear and violence and the absence or inadequacy of programs of classification, education, physical exercise, vocational training or other constructive activity create a total environment where debilitation is inevitable.[40]

At this writing, the entire prison system or the major prison in sixteen states, the District of Columbia, Puerto Rico, and the Virgin Islands have been declared unconstitutional by courts because they violate the Eighth Amendment's prohibition of cruel and unusual punishment.[41] Most of these decisions adopt the theory that conditions that debilitate prisoners violate the Eighth Amendment. In another twelve states, challenges to the constitutionality of the prisons invoking the right not to be debilitated are now before courts.[42] Efforts to establish this right are also central to scores of cases in the last few years challenging conditions of confinement in local jails.

Ironically, though such a right was established first in a case involving the retarded, it is now questionable whether the Eighth Amendment would still be held to apply to them. In a 1977 case, the United States Supreme Court held that a school child had no right to invoke the Eighth Amendment's prohibition of cruel and unusual punishment in challenging corporal punishment. The Court seemed to suggest that the Eighth Amendment controls only the punishment that may be imposed on those convicted of crimes.[43] And in a 1979 case, the Court held that the Eighth Amendment is not violated by "double-bunking" jail inmates awaiting trial in tiny cells designed for one or by frequent humiliating body cavity searches.[44]

Despite these Supreme Court decisions, lower courts continue to require drastic changes in the conditions in all sorts of asylums. Up until now, the Burger Court's signals to turn back have proved ineffective. With a few exceptions, litigators have stopped bringing right-to-treatment cases. On the other hand, influenced by the views of the former inmates' movement, many recent cases assert a right to refuse treatment. This right was judicially recognized as early as 1971 in a case brought on behalf of a Christian Scientist,

Miriam Winters, who claimed that the New York mental hospital where she was confined violated her religious beliefs when it forcibly injected her with drugs.[45] In subsequent cases, courts have protected inmates of institutions against the use as disciplinary measures of psychosurgery[46] or apomorphine (which induces vomiting) or of anectine (which creates a terrifying sensation of asphyxiation)[47] or other physically intrusive forms of behavior modification. In a 1979 decision, a federal court prohibited forcible treatment with psychoactive drugs at a Boston State Hospital because, "given a nonemergency, it is an unreasonable invasion of privacy and an affront to basic concepts of human dignity to permit forced injection of a mind-altering drug."[48] At this writing, that decision is being reviewed by the United States Supreme Court.

By the end of the 1970s, it was clear that litigators for inmates of asylums had three principal goals: first, deinstitutionalization; second, mitigating intrusion on the autonomy of the confined; and third, mitigating practices that debilitate the confined. Measured against these goals, which were partially obscured at the start of the decade by the right-to-treatment theory, what has litigation accomplished?

Ostensibly, deinstitutionalization has proceeded very far in mental hospitals. Their population declined from a high of about 650,000 in the mid-1960s to about 225,000 at the beginning of the 1980s. Although litigation is often pointed to as a cause, it actually played only a minor part. Three other causes were more important: the transfer of elderly patients from public mental hospitals to private nursing homes, a practice permitting the states to shift costs to the federal government (which has paid the lion's share of the nation's nursing home bill since the enactment of Medicaid in 1965); the widespread use of long-lasting psychoactive drugs (e.g., Prolixin), permitting institutions to medicate out-patients more readily, thereby reducing the duration of confinement, and the rising costs of confinement. The part played by litigation was largely in driving up the costs of institutional care, in a way vindicating the "noble lie" tactic. But though litigation provided the mentally ill with distributive justice while confined, it has been ineffectual in providing them with distributive justice after release from confinement. Lacking services in the community, many former patients are confined again. Such mental patients are not actually deinstitutionalized; rather they go in and out—as many Americans as ever are confined in mental hospitals each year. The decline in the population of these institutions reflects only shorter stays.

The population of institutions for the retarded has also declined, from about 300,000 in the mid 1960s to about 180,000 at the beginning of the 1980s. Litigation has been the main engine of deinstitutionalization of the retarded, who had been even more hidden from public view than other institutional inmates, previously confined in the worst conditions of all. Corrective litigation has been instrumental in securing distributive justice through political as well as judicial action, reallocating state resources to provide care not only in institutions but, more important, in the community. As a result, few of the retarded freed from institutions as a consequence of litigation are reconfined. The development of a theory of corrective justice that permitted courts to dispense distributive justice for the retarded outside asylums accounts for the difference between their situation and the situation of the mentally ill.

The population of prisons and jails rose from about 400,000 in the mid-1960s to about 525,000 by the end of the 1970s. This is attributable to the growth in the crime rate and in public concern about crime and to declining faith in probation and parole. Litigation challenging conditions has had no discernible impact on the number confined in prisons and jails, not even in slowing the growth in their population. To the extent that litigation has had distributive justice consequences, the states have spent additional funds within the prisons to comply with court decisions requiring improved conditions of confinement.

The greatest shift in population has taken place in nursing homes. They quadrupled in population from about 350,000 in the mid-1960s to about 1,300,000 by the beginning of the 1980s. The most important cause was the enactment of Medicaid; other factors include the increased number of the aged in the population and the transfer of former mental patients to private nursing homes. Litigation played no part because the courts generally refuse to apply constitutional standards to private institutions. Nursing homes, therefore, are immune to constitutional litigation even when they get most of their funds from the government.

Litigation to establish a right to refuse treatment has mitigated intrusions on the autonomy of the confined. Extreme intrusions—psychosurgery and the most painful forms of behavior modification—have either been stopped outright or hedged with restrictions. Lesser intrusions, such as forced medication with psychoactive drugs, are under attack and courts are beginning to force institutions to modify their practices.

Litigation has had a demonstrable effect in mitigating conditions that debilitate the confined. As compared to the goals of those bringing the cases, however, much remains to be done. In a few institutions, horrifying conditions have been eliminated. In many more, courts have ordered changes but have had limited success in securing compliance. Nursing homes, where as many people are now confined as in all other asylums combined, have not been affected.

In sum, therefore, litigation has been only modestly successful in achieving its goals and least of all in bringing about deinstitutionalization. There seems little prospect that it will be more successful in the foreseeable future. Except in the case of the retarded—the weakest of the weak and the group for whom judicial intervention was most urgently needed—the headway made through litigation has been limited to that part of deinstitutionalization which provides corrective justice, that is, freeing the confined. Distributive justice has been secured through litigation where it is necessary to provide corrective justice, as in mitigating horrible conditions of confinement within asylums. In instances in which distributive justice has been achieved through litigation to provide services outside the asylum, courts were persuaded that was the only way to provide corrective justice to the retarded for their debilitation inside the asylum.

12

Stopping Executions without Abolishing Capital Punishment

"May it please your honors, and you gentlemen of the jury. I am for the prisoners at the bar, and shall apologize for it only in the words of the Marquis Beccaria: If I can but be the instrument of preserving one life, his blessing and tears of transport shall be a sufficient consolation to me for the contempt of all mankind."[1]

With these words, John Adams opened his statement to the jury in defending the British soldiers on trial in 1770 for the Boston Massacre. Adams's statement invoking Beccaria, known as the father of the movement against capital punishment, seems an appropriate starting point for an account of the movement to end capital punishment through litigation. Although few lawyers in Adams's time emulated him, much later on litigation became central in the movement against the death penalty, and during the past quarter of a century it has dominated the movement.

In Adams's time, some American counterparts of the Enlightenment philosophers took up the cry against the death penalty. A group of them convened at the home of Benjamin Franklin in Philadelphia in 1787 (where the United States Constitution was then being drafted) to listen to Dr. Benjamin Rush read a paper calling for an end to all public punishments, including the death penalty.[2] Although Rush was widely criticized for opposing the death penalty, he intensified the attack. In 1788, he wrote an essay he described as "the boldest attack I have ever made upon a public opinion, or a general practice,"[3] and in subsequent years he published several more crusading essays. He also joined with prominent Philadelphia Quakers in founding an organization to oppose public physical punishments that helped to persuade the Pennsylvania legislature in 1794 to abolish the death penalty for all crimes except first-degree murder. Virginia did the same in 1796 and Ohio in 1815. Other states continued for another twenty or thirty years to execute horse thieves, pickpockets, burglars, and, in some places, even children who demonstrated disrespect to their parents.

Gradual elimination of capital punishment to punish crimes other than murder, and in some states rape or robbery, reflected growing acceptance during the first half of the nineteenth century of the form of punishment advocated by Rush and the Quakers: confinement in prisons. Michigan abolished capital punishment in 1846, making it the first state to do without such a penalty. Rhode Island, Wisconsin, Maine, Iowa, and Colorado followed suit at intervals during the nineteenth century, though the latter two reinstated the penalty a few years after abolishing it. No reliable figures are available on the number of executions carried out before the last decade of the century. Probably the number did not decline during the course of the century because growth in population and in the number of first-degree murders more than matched the gradual restriction in the range of capital crimes.

In the 1890s, there were 1,214 legal executions nation-wide, 154 under state authority, 1,060 under local authority. These were outnumbered by lynchings, some 1,540 dur-ing the decade, reflecting the intense racism of the period. Approximately the same number of legal executions took place in each subsequent decade through the 1940s except during the 1930s when the number peaked at 1,667. Dur-ing the early decades of this century, there was a sharp shift from executions under local authority to executions under state authority and a drastic decline in the number of lynch-ings—five were recorded during the 1940s. During the 1950s, the number of legal executions declined to 717, and there were two recorded lynchings.[4]

By the end of the 1950s, although the death penalty had been abolished in nine states and the number of executions was falling quickly, no sustained movement against it had appeared. No significant national organization made abo-lition a high priority. Periodic campaigns against the death penalty reflected opposition to particular executions, usually out of a belief that those sentenced to die were innocent or out of political sympathy for them. The execution of five anarchists for the Haymarket bombing in Chicago in 1886; the execution of Sacco and Vanzetti and the Scottsboro trial, both in the 1920s; the execution of the Rosenbergs in 1953; and the execution of Caryl Chessman in 1960 after eleven years on death row, all aroused relatively brief crusades.

Lawyers took prominent parts in efforts to abolish the death penalty. They were, of course, directly engaged in legal maneuvers to block executions. In addition, several became crusaders, notably, Clarence Darrow, who from the early 1890s on, volunteered his services to aid defendants accused of capital crimes. As a legendary hero of the bar, Darrow inspired other lawyers to aid defendants facing execution.

Systematic litigation to block executions probably began with the formation in the late 1950s of the New York Committee to Abolish Capital Punishment. Operating on a shoestring out of offices donated by the New York Society for Ethical Culture, the committee recruited a handful of lawyers to intervene in death cases. Led by the committee's volunteer general counsel, Norman Redlich, then a professor and subsequently dean at New York University School of Law, they pressed appeals, raised issues not considered by trial courts that might require new hearings, and petitioned the governor of New York to grant clemency. They had no strategy for ending capital punishment through litigation, only a passion to prevent executions. Their efforts differed from what went before, however, because they took on the burden of trying to stop all executions in a state and because they were not principally motivated by sympathy for the particular defendants facing execution.

Before the 1960s, the NAACP Legal Defense Fund and the ACLU took part in opposition to executions only when they believed the defendants were innocent or were denied fair trials. On such grounds, the ACLU was active in the Sacco and Vanzetti and Scottsboro cases, and the Legal Defense Fund fought against execution of several young black men charged with the 1950 rape of a white woman in Groveland, Florida. By the beginning of the 1960s, however, the Southern California branch of the ACLU, influenced by the Chessman case, took a stand against the death penalty itself, and one of its volunteer lawyers, Gerald Gottlieb, published a pathbreaking law review article arguing that the constitutional prohibition of cruel and unusual punishment barred all executions.[5] At about the same time, lawyers active in the Florida ACLU, led by Tobias Simon, who continued to play a role in death penalty cases until his death in 1982, began to intervene in cases in which blacks were sentenced to death for raping white women. Simon and his colleagues were the principal lawyers for the civil rights movement in Florida. Their role in capital cases was an extension of this effort, reflecting their view that the death penalty was discriminatorily applied because same-race rapes (a rape of a white by a white, a black by a black) almost never resulted in death sentences.

The ACLU, prodded by its California, Florida, and New York branches—the latter influenced by the New York Committee to Abolish Capital Punishment—adopted the position in 1965 that the death penalty itself is unconstitutional. By that time, the Legal Defense Fund had already decided to fight capital punishment per se and was well under way in organizing a campaign to conduct the fight. Tobias Simon and other ACLU lawyers who were attempting to block executions looked to the LDF for support. Given the heavy commitment the ACLU was making to defend conscientious objectors to the war in Vietnam and demonstrators against the war, it was content to leave the main burden of opposing the death penalty to the LDF. Besides, the importance of the argument that the death penalty was applied in a racially discriminatory manner helped to make it seem proper that the LDF should lead the fight against it.

The LDF's primacy in the campaign helped to ensure that the means for combating the death penalty would be litigation. Exclusively a tax-deductible organization, it did not engage in legislative lobbying. (By this time, the LDF had long been independent of its parent organization, the NAACP. The NAACP could engage in lobbying but never committed itself strongly to oppose capital punishment.) Even if the LDF's tax status had permitted it to lobby, it lacked local branches, like those of the ACLU or NAACP, that could work in their state legislatures. The litigation resources the LDF invested in the campaign, on the other hand, were considerable. The work of several talented staff lawyers was supplemented by the volunteer efforts of a young law professor, Anthony Amsterdam, who guided the campaign. His work against the death penalty and his efforts in other civil liberties and civil rights cases were so outstanding that they quickly earned him a reputation as the nation's outstanding cause litigator. The LDF's work was also relatively well financed because the organization succeeded in persuading the Ford Foundation to support its defense of the rights of the poor—including prisoners condemned to death—more generously than any previous litigation program had ever been supported.

Yet in the mid-1960s, it seemed possible that a state legislative campaign might be effective. The climate was more favorable than at any time before or since. Though no group mounted a nationwide legislative campaign, Oregon abolished the death penalty by a 60–40 vote in a popular referendum in 1964, and in 1965 the New York, Iowa, Vermont, and West Virginia legislatures abolished or virtually abolished it. In 1966, a nationwide poll showed that only 42 percent of Americans favored capital punishment for convicted murderers, 47 percent opposed it, and 11 percent were undecided.[6] Public disenchantment with the death penalty was also reflected in the dwindling number of executions: forty-seven in 1962, twenty-one in 1963, fifteen in 1964, and seven in 1965. (There was only one in 1966 and two in 1967 before they ended entirely for a decade, but these further declines were largely attributable to the LDF's litigation campaign.) If the ACLU, which was not restricted by its tax status and which possessed the nationwide structure to undertake a lobbying campaign, had taken the lead in

1965 in efforts to oppose capital punishment, the campaign might well have been as heavily legislative as litigative. And if resources comparable to those the LDF invested in litigation had been made available for a state legislative campaign, a good many states might have been persuaded to repeal their death sentence laws.

Initially, the Legal Defense Fund's assumption of responsibility for challenging the death penalty rested on its view that the penalty was applied in a racially discriminatory manner. It set out to prove this point starting where the discrimination was most glaring: in interracial rape cases. In 1961, the United States Supreme Court reversed the conviction of a black man who had been sentenced to death in Alabama for burglary with intent to commit rape, on the ground that he had been denied counsel at his arraignment.[7] LDF lawyers had represented him before the Supreme Court, and they attempted to use his retrial a couple of years later to challenge the death sentence as racially discriminatory. That plan became moot, however, when retrial resulted in a life sentence.

The challenge to the death penalty for rape as racially discriminatory began in earnest in 1965, when the LDF employed volunteer law students recruited by the Law Students Civil Rights Research Council—formed the previous year as a part of the legal profession's response to the civil rights movement—to collect data about sentencing in rape cases in twelve southern states. The information was fed to a prominent criminologist, Marvin Wolfgang, for analysis. Armed with the results, Wolfgang testified at a habeas corpus hearing in a federal court in Little Rock, Arkansas, in August 1966 on behalf of William L. Maxwell, who was scheduled to be executed for raping a white woman five years earlier. Wolfgang testified that none of the variables that might determine sentencing in rape cases—place of offense, nature of entry, plea, type of counsel, duration of trial, seriousness of injury, type of prior relationship between defendant and victim, defendant's previous record, victim or defendant having dependent children, defendant's marital status, defendant's or victim's age, display of a weapon—could explain racial disparities in punishment.

Despite this uncontradicted testimony, the courts ruled against Maxwell and the LDF. The statistics did not prove that the sentence given to Maxwell reflected racial discrimination by the jury that sentenced him. As the Supreme Court was to insist on proof of discriminatory intent a few years later in cases such as *Milliken, Valtierra, Washington* v. *Davis, Arlington Heights*, and *Mobile* v. *Boulden*, so the courts considering Maxwell's case insisted that his LDF lawyers demonstrate discriminatory intent by the jury. Accepting the LDF's argument would have had implications that the Court found disturbing, as Circuit Judge (later Supreme Court Justice) Harry Blackmun made clear in his opinion for the United States Court of Appeals for the Eighth Circuit:

> At oral argument we asked Professor Amsterdam, counsel for Maxwell, whether (apart from any Eighth Amendment argument) his statistical approach would not mean that it would be constitutionally impossible for a negro defendant in Arkansas ever to receive the death penalty upon conviction of a crime of rape of a white woman. The answer given us was in the affirmative, that is, that it would be constitutionally impossible. At the same time it was conceded, in contrast, that it would be possible for a white man to receive the death penalty upon his conviction for rape. When counsel was asked whether this would not be discriminatory, the reply was that once the negro situation was remedied the white situation "would take care of itself."
>
> The legal logic and the rightness of this totally escapes us.[8]

An unspoken concern may have weighed even more heavily. Suppose the courts accepted the contention that death sentences for rape should be voided because the statistics suggested racial discrimination. Might not comparable statistical evidence be presented that would throw into question other sentences for other crimes? Should it follow that all sentences meted out to racial minorities must be voided if statistics tended to show discrimination? Although accepted principles of corrective justice should have made the courts scrutinize exactingly practices that had such clearly discriminatory and drastic consequences for a racial minority, any court would shy away from reaching a conclusion with such far-reaching and unpredictable implications.

In 1968, the same year that the Eighth Circuit Court of Appeals decided *Maxwell*, the Supreme Court handed down a decision that, at the time, many believed would virtually end executions. In *Witherspoon* v. *Illinois*,[9] the Court held that jurors with conscientious scruples against the death penalty could not be excluded automatically from juries in death cases. Only jurors whose views were such that they would refuse to consider a death verdict could be excluded automatically. With popular sentiment against the death penalty still high, though not as high as three or four years earlier, it appeared that opponents of capital punishment would get to serve on juries in substantial numbers and would prevent juries from returning death sentences. It has turned out that the predictions of *Witherspoon*'s effects were greatly exaggerated. State legislatures and state courts quickly evolved ways to circumvent *Witherspoon*, and prosecutors have come close to nullifying it by finding other grounds to exclude jurors who express scruples against the death penalty. When prosecutors can find no way to eliminate such jurors for cause, they invoke their peremptory challenges to eliminate them. Juries composed after *Witherspoon*, therefore, have been nearly as free from opponents of the death penalty as before that decision.

The LDF, which participated in *Witherspoon* as amicus curiae, was not lulled into relaxing its efforts. It convened lawyers from around the country to develop new strategies for challenging the death penalty and distributed widely a "Last Aid Kit" to guide lawyers for the condemned. It also brought several additional cases to the Supreme Court, among them an appeal from the Eighth Circuit's decision in *Maxwell*. The Supreme Court refused to consider the question of racial disparity in death sentences for rape, however, limiting review to two critical procedural questions that affected the majority of death row inmates: standardless sentencing by juries and sentencing by the jury at the same proceeding as the determination of guilt (the latter required defendants to choose whether to stake everything on acquittal or to diminish the chances of a death sentence by admitting guilt, demonstrating remorse, and so forth).

In the course of oral argument, Justice Stewart questioned the attorney for Arkansas whether jurors with scruples against the death penalty had been excluded when that state tried and sentenced Maxwell. They had been. Although that question was not formally before the Court, Stewart's question raised the possibility that the Court would vacate Maxwell's death sentence in light of its recent ruling in *Witherspoon*. For Maxwell's attorney, Anthony Amsterdam, the state's acknowledgement that the *Witherspoon* standard had been violated provided a near certain way to save the life of his immediate client. But Amsterdam was not only Maxwell's attorney. He was—and is—the leader of the LDF's campaign to stop all executions. A decision resting solely on that ground would not have added to *Witherspoon* in helping to save the lives of other prisoners on death row. Amsterdam was faced with a classic example of a conflict that periodically confronts litigators for causes: a conflict between his responsibility to his immediate client, Maxwell, and the interests of his other clients in the nationwide campaign against the death penalty. Similar conflicts arose in several other death penalty cases. In *Maxwell*, Amsterdam solved the dilemma created by Stewart's question ingeniously, as an erstwhile LDF colleague, Michael Meltsner, recorded:

> "Maxwell has been on death row since 1962. He has twice come within a few days of death. The last time to be saved only by a stay issued by Mr. Justice White of this Court." What many lower courts have done with *Witherspoon* is to vacate the death sentence but order a new penalty trial to determine whether the defendant should live or die. "It would be inhumanity second only to killing this man" not to resolve now "whether the State of Arkansas has any right to try him for his life under the unconstitutional procedures that we are challenging."[10]

This argument provided the Supreme Court with a rationale for vacating Maxwell's sentence in accordance with *Witherspoon* and, simultaneously, in Maxwell's interest, a rationale for reaching the other issues before the Court which affected other death row prisoners Amsterdam and the LDF were also trying to protect. Despite Amsterdam's plea, however, the Court eventually vacated Maxwell's death sentence solely on the ground that the jury had not been composed in accordance with the *Witherspoon* standard.[11] Maxwell received the corrective justice that was his due, but the LDF was frustrated in its effort to use his case to advance its larger political goal.

In 1971, the Supreme Court again considered standardless sentencing and imposition of the death sentence by a jury in the same proceeding as it determined guilt. Neither procedure is invalid constitutionally,[12] the Court decided, imperiling the moratorium on executions that was by then four years old. With the main procedural objections to sentencing practices in death cases disposed of, it appeared that executions could be stopped no longer through litigation unless the Supreme Court could be persuaded that the death penalty per se violates the Eighth Amendment's prohibition of cruel and unusual punishment.

To provide breathing room for consideration of this question in the courts, Senator Philip Hart (D. Mich.) and Representative Emanuel Celler (D. N. Y.) introduced legislation in Congress to provide a two-year national moratorium on executions.[13] Because public opinion had shifted steadily in favor of the death penalty since the high tide of abolitionist sentiment in the mid-1960s, however, Hart–Celler had little chance of enactment, its prospects dimmed further by doubts as to the power of Congress to impose such restrictions on the states. A few weeks after it was introduced, the legislation turned out not to be needed at that moment because the Supreme Court agreed to determine whether death is cruel and unusual punishment. Grounds were now provided for staying all pending executions until the Supreme Court's decision.

The Supreme Court agreed to review four cases: *Aikens* v. *California* and *Furman* v. *Georgia*, involving the death penalty for murder; *Branch* v. *Texas* and *Jackson* v. *Georgia*, involving the death penalty for rape. The victims were white, all the condemned men black.

Aikens was especially gruesome. In separate incidents, Aikens had raped and robbed two women and then murdered them. One woman was five months pregnant when she was murdered. Aikens's lawyer, Anthony Amsterdam, could only describe the crimes to the Supreme Court as "unmitigated atrocities" and "ghastly . . . attended by aggravating features that must necessarily arouse the deepest human instincts of loathing and repugnance."[14] After making this concession, he went on to argue that "the issue before this Court cannot turn upon those features. This is so because if the state may constitutionally punish petitioner's crimes with death, it may also use death to punish murder unattended by the same features. . . . [W]e can conceive no Eighth Amendment principle which, allowing death punishment in the particular circumstances of this case, could confine it to them."[15]

Although the argument turned out not to be persuasive to the Supreme Court—and, indeed, might raise eyebrows in almost any company—it had to be made for Aikens. Differentiating among murderers would have ensured the execution of an Aikens. The circumstances of his crime made it impossible to save his life unless the Supreme Court ventured far into the realm of political justice by abolishing the death penalty entirely. Given the Supreme Court's refusal up to then to require the procedural reforms sought in previous cases, differentiation among murderers would allow the execution of a significant number of the several hundred prisoners then on death row, that is, all those like Aikens who committed particularly loathsome murders.

The argument served Aikens well, but in retrospect it appears that it might have done a disservice to Furman. He had been surprised in the act of committing a burglary and, when he attempted to escape, tripped, causing his gun to discharge, killing his pursuer on the other side of a closed door. Although the killing was accidental, the state law under which Furman was convicted provided the death penalty because it took place during commission of a felony. Furman's life would certainly be spared if the Court permitted execution only of murderers whose crimes were especially gruesome like Aikens's. This was no reason for Aikens's lawyer to avoid an argument attempting to tie the fate of murderers like Aikens to the fate of murderers like Furman. With the advantage of hindsight, however, the potential conflict in the interests of the two men makes this argument on behalf of Aikens troubling because Furman was also represented by Amsterdam, who could hardly argue for Furman the opposite of what he argued for Aikens at the same time. The potential conflict between cause and client that Amsterdam resolved so successfully in *Maxwell* might have caused greater trouble in *Aikens* and *Furman*.

Amsterdam's central argument in his brief on behalf of Aikens proved more persuasive and extricated him from the difficulty produced by representing both Aikens and Furman. "The penalty of death," he contended, "is a cruel and unusual punishment because it affronts the basic standards of decency and contemporary society." The evidence was "the extreme rarity of actual infliction of the death penalty in the United States and the world today."[16] (Of course, the Amsterdam-led LDF campaign was responsible for the transition from rarity to cessation of executions during the previous several years, but as the precipitous decline before the start of that campaign demonstrated, this was a valid argument.) Yet there was an obvious response. Amsterdam confronted it head-on, putting forward the best case *against* judicial invalidation of the death penalty:

> Quite perceptibly, an extreme difficulty must attend any process of constitutional adjudication by which this Court subjects legislation to the test of "enlightened public opinion," and adjudges the validity of a legislature's product according to society's "standards of decency." For both in constitutional contemplation and in fact, it is the legislature, not the Court, which responds to public opinion and immediately reflects the society's standards of decency. If the question asked by the Eighth Amendment really be whether our democratic society can tolerate the existence of any particular penal law that is on the

books, the Eighth Amendment's answer will always be that it can—and for the simple reason that the law is on the books of a democratic society. The conclusion therefore seems to be required that the Eighth Amendment is *not* a judicially enforceable restriction on legislation.[17]

To get out of this bind and to persuade the Supreme Court that the Eighth Amendment is judicially enforceable and that it should invalidate the death penalty, Amsterdam worked a variation on the discrete and insular minority argument:

> [But t]he question is, rather: will contemporary standards of decency allow the general application of the law's penalty *in fact?* The distinction which we draw here lies between what public conscience will allow the law to *say* and what it will allow the law to *do.* . . . The real danger concerning cruel and inhuman laws is that they will be enacted in a form such that they can be applied sparsely and spottily to unhappy minorities whose numbers are so few, whose plight so invisible, and whose persons so unpopular, that society can readily bear to see them suffer torments which would not for a moment be accepted as penalties of general application to the populace.[18]

In other words, evolving standards of decency seem to be a matter for a representative body to determine, but the representative process cannot work in the case of capital punishment because of the nature of the class of persons affected and because the sufferings are so effectively shielded from scrutiny. Accordingly, judicial intervention is warranted.

Amsterdam's reasoning, echoing Kant's categorial imperative, persuaded a majority of the Court that capital punishment—as then administered everywhere in the United States—was unconstitutional.[19] He appeared to have found a way to make the Court believe that it should dispense political justice for so despised a minority as prisoners sentenced to death. Only Justices Brennan and Marshall, however, held that the penalty per se violated the Eighth Amendment, but they were joined by Justices Douglas, Stewart, and White in forming a majority that held that the laws were unconstitutional under which all five hundred or so prisoners then on death rows had been sentenced. As Stewart put it, "The Eighth and Fourteenth Amendments cannot tolerate the infliction of a sentence of death under legal systems that permit this unique penalty to be so wantonly and so freakishly imposed."[20]

Some opponents of capital punishment (this writer among them) contended at the time that the 1972 decision effectively ended capital punishment in the United States. This assessment reflected a combination of wishful thinking and a desire to deter the states from enacting new death laws by persuading them that it would be a waste of time. The latter consideration reflected a tactical judgment that is open to question. Some legislators may have been encouraged to reap the political benefits of support for the death penalty while overcoming any compunctions by telling themselves that the courts would block all executions. Judicial resolution of difficult questions usually stimulates legislative attention to issues previously swept under the rug; sometimes, however, it encourages legislative irresponsibility. Some of those who consciously overstated the significance of the Supreme Court's decision were aware of the risks but calculated—perhaps correctly, perhaps not—that the benefits to their (our) cause would outweigh the harms.

Few state legislators were persuaded that they would be wasting their time. Those intent on enacting new laws had no need to go further for guidance than Chief Justice Burger's dissenting opinion for the Supreme Court's four-member minority. It instructed them that "Legislative bodies may seek to bring their laws into compliance with the Court's ruling by providing standards for juries and judges to follow in determining the sentence in capital cases or by more narrowly defining the crimes for which the penalty is to be imposed[21]. . . . Real change could clearly be brought about if legislatures provided mandatory death sentences in such a way as to deny juries the opportunity to bring in a verdict on a lesser charge."[22]

Within two years, Arizona, Arkansas, California, Connecticut, Florida, Georgia, Idaho, Illinois, Indiana, Louisiana, Montana, Nebraska, Nevada, New Mexico, Ohio, Oklahoma, Rhode Island, Tennessee, Texas, Utah, and Wyoming enacted new death laws. If the Supreme Court's 1972 decisions really had been intended to abolish capital punishment, this was legislative defiance on a more massive scale than took place even after *Brown* v. *Board of Education*. Some legislatures followed Burger's advice to provide standards for death sentences while others opted for his suggestion that the death sentence should be mandatory for certain crimes.

In an attempt to resist the enactment of still more such laws, the ACLU entered the battle against capital punishment in 1974 for the first time in a significant way by appointing a coordinator of state legislative efforts. By this time, however, nearly a decade after public antipathy to the death penalty peaked in the mid-1960s, it was extremely difficult to prevail in state legislative battles. Litigation, which the Legal Defense Fund continued to manage nationwide, continued to be the best method of stopping executions. With the constitutionality of the new laws in doubt as a result of the Supreme Court's 1972 decisions, the LDF succeeded in extending the moratorium on executions pending review of mandatory death sentences and sentencing standards by the Supreme Court.

Review took place in 1976. The Court invalidated mandatory death sentences[23] while upholding several laws providing standards for imposing the death penalty.[24] There was no longer any possibility of maintaining the absolute moratorium on executions then nine years old. The end came more swiftly than most engaged in the battle anticipated, however, when Gary M. Gilmore was executed in Utah in January 1977, just six months after the Supreme Court decision.

The Gilmore story is widely known and has been recorded in exhaustive detail.[25] It achieved such notoriety because Gilmore was the first American legally executed in nearly a decade. It also inspired controversy over the role of litigators serving the abolitionist cause against the wishes of a man loudly professing his antagonism to their attempts to block his execution.

Gilmore was not the first to take such a stand. The handful of men executed in the 1960s before the moratorium included several who resisted efforts by lawyers to interfere. "I want to ride the lightning," Frederick Charles Wood insisted in 1963 when the New York Committee to Abolish Capital Punishment attempted to stop his execution. Wood wrote to Martin Garbus, the lawyer designated by the committee to try to save his life: "I do not welcome intrusion into this stinking case of mine—I have no desire to live out the rest of my life in confinement. You must (or should) understand that capital punishment is, in the final analysis, more merciful than a tortured existence of a lifetime in prison or in an asylum. I should know, sir, as I've done 31 years of suffering in these noble institutions. So . . . please cease and desist."[26]

Garbus did not cease and desist, though he confesses, "That decision has troubled me more than any other I've made concerning a client." He adds, however, "I think we were right."[27] His efforts were unavailing. After a final joke ("Gentlemen, you are about to see the effects of electricity upon Wood"), Wood was electrocuted, the next to last person put to death under New York's capital punishment law before it was repealed in 1965.

James Donald French was executed in Oklahoma in 1966. The only victim of capital punishment nationwide that year, he also had rejected legal assistance. So did José Louis Monge, who was executed in Colorado in 1967, the last man legally executed in the United States before Gilmore in 1977. During the moratorium decade, the most publicized such case involved Robert Lee Massie, who denounced LDF lawyers for blocking his execution in a 1971 article in *Esquire*. "Rotting away in prison for the rest of my days and deteriorating mentally, perhaps even going completely insane," he wrote, "is not a very pleasing incentive for continuing to cling to this life."[28] (Massie subsequently changed his mind and welcomed LDF representation.)

Like Wood and Massie, Gilmore was of above average intelligence and articulated his reasons for wanting the execution to go forward persuasively. On December 29, 1976, three weeks before he was executed by firing squad, he published a letter in a Utah newspaper:

> An open letter from Gary Gilmore to all and any who still seek to oppose by whatever means my death by legal execution. Particularly: ACLU, NAACP. I invite you to finally butt out of my life.
>
> Butt out of my death.
>
> Shirley Pedler [the director of the Utah ACLU], Gees, baby, lay off. I wouldn't dare to be so presumptuous as to presume I could impose any unwanted thing on your life. . . . Get out of my life Shirley. NAACP, I'm a white man. Don't want no uncle tom blacks buttin in. Your contention is that if I am executed then a whole bunch of black dudes will

be executed. Well that's so apparently stupid I won't even argue with that kind of silly illogic.

But you know as well as I do that they'll kill a white man these days a lot quicker than they'll kill a black man. Y'all ain't really disadvantaged lak ya used to be. As for those of you who would question my sanity, well, I question yours.

from my heart
Gary Gilmore[29]

Responding to Gilmore a few days later on behalf of the ACLU, I wrote:

Capital punishment is barbarous. Whether or not Mr. Gilmore says he wants to die, the state enacted the death penalty, the state sentenced him to death, and the state would organize the firing squad and carry out the execution. Our quarrel is with the state, not with Gary Mark Gilmore.... I find it very difficult to disregard Mr. Gilmore's wishes. It's his life. He has been told by the state of Utah he can submit to a firing squad right now or he can appeal his case while he stays in prison with the death sentence hanging over him. The state should never have forced him to make that choice. To defer to the choice Mr. Gilmore has made is to acknowledge the right of the state to engage in savagery and to coerce Mr. Gilmore into becoming an accomplice in a legal homicide.[30]

However one evaluates these arguments, there is no escaping that the ACLU—which litigated against Gilmore's wishes in an unsuccessful effort to prevent his execution—used his case to try to achieve its own purpose of stopping executions, concerned that his execution would make others easier. Even when it was plain that he would be executed, the ACLU kept up the fight, in part because there was a remote chance that the execution could be stopped and in part because of the belief that the more difficulty

Utah had in executing Gilmore, the less likely it was that others would be executed. Gilmore's plainly expressed interests were subordinated to those of the ACLU even though it purported to act in his interests. The ACLU accepted that Gilmore acted rationally—here it differed from the LDF, which intervened on behalf of members of Gilmore's family who claimed that he was insane—but arrogated to itself a right to contravene the wishes of its "client." Like Garbus, who says he thinks he was right to disregard Wood's wishes, I think my ACLU colleagues and I were right in disregarding Gilmore's wishes—but misgivings persist.

Curiously, Gilmore was probably right, at least at the time, in contending that "they'll kill a white man these days a lot quicker than they'll kill a black man." If so, however, it was because public officials in the postmoratorium period attempted to disprove what had been shown several years earlier in LDF litigation, at least in proceeding with the first few executions following the moratorium. That seems the likeliest explanation of the choice of John Spenkelink as the next person to be executed after Gilmore.

Spenkelink was executed in Florida in May 1979. A drifter, he had killed a fellow drifter with whom he had traveled across the country, an older, larger, and stronger man who had forcibly sodomized him. At his trial, Spenkelink claimed that he acted in self-defense, but a jury disbelieved him. The circumstances of the killing made it seem to the jury that he killed in revenge rather than self-defense. But the circumstances would almost certainly have resulted in the commutation of his sentence by the state clemency board except that Spenkelink was white. Since most death row inmates in Florida are black, the white man first in line for execution had to be executed, no matter the circumstances of his crime. Otherwise, it would be difficult for the clemency board to justify its refusal to commute the sentence of the blacks on death row when their turn came for execution.

When I visited Spenkelink a month before he was executed, he seemed puzzled by the failure of the courts to consider seriously his latest claim: that race discrimination had been practiced against him because the death sentence for murder was disproportionately meted out to whites or blacks who killed whites. Statistics on death sentences strongly supported his contention, and it came as a great surprise to him when it was suggested that a court would be reluctant to vacate his death sentence on such grounds for fear of casting doubt on all disproportionate sentences for crimes in which whites were the victims. In the six years he spent on death row before his execution, Spenkelink became preoccupied with the processes of the law, a fascination with its intricacies apparently helping to sustain him. In the process, he acquired great faith in the law. I could not bring myself to tell him that I thought the state would feel obliged to execute him to diminish any public outcry when it started executing blacks.

Four months later, another white was executed, this time in Nevada. Like Gary Gilmore, Jesse Bishop publicly castigated lawyers from the LDF and ACLU for trying to prevent his execution. Indeed, Bishop secured a bit of revenge against them by a last-minute "confession" that he had killed eighteen men in addition to the man whose killing brought about his execution. He offered no details that might have allowed verification. True or not, however, published reports of his boast reinforced popular sentiment in favor of his execution, hurting the campaign against the death penalty, his apparent intent.

After the execution of Jesse Bishop, a year and a half passed before another legal execution took place. Steven Judy, who was executed in Indiana in March 1981, like the other three men since the Supreme Court upheld the constitutionality of capital punishment nearly five years previously, was white and, like two of the others, refused to take part in legal efforts to block his execution. This left John Spenkelink as the one man to be legally executed in the United States since 1967 who resisted efforts to put him to death. The execution of Judy attracted less attention than the execution of Bishop, which attracted less attention than the execution of Gilmore. For litigators intent on preventing executions in the 1980s, the task is as formidable as it was at the start of their campaign. In a fifteen-year span their efforts limited the number of executions in the United States to four, three of whom resisted efforts by lawyers to save their lives. Perhaps comparable expenditure of effort on a legislative campaign would have achieved comparable results, though it seems unlikely. Many more persons probably would have been executed during the second half of the 1960s and during the 1970s except for the litigation campaign. On the other hand, if death penalty laws had been repealed legislatively when the climate was best in the mid-1960s, it is possible that they would not have been reenacted when the climate worsened. It is even possible that public sentiment would not have turned so sharply were it not that the courts were blamed for frustrating the public will by blocking executions.

These speculations do not gainsay the value of litigation in stopping executions. They suggest, however, that ending capital punishment, which involves political justice, is a separate and distinct goal from stopping executions. The courts are willing to stop executions on such traditional corrective justice grounds as the failure to follow proper procedures. On the other hand, the courts seem unwilling or unable to assert the authority to forbid legislatures from maintaining the death penalty.

The lesson of the 1960s and 1970s seems to be that opponents of the death penalty can succeed only by mounting substantial campaigns simultaneously in the courts and in the legislatures. Abolishing capital punishment legislatively cannot succeed, of course, unless the climate again becomes as favorable as in the mid-1960s. For the time being, therefore, their best hope is to stop executions by litigation. At some point, executions temporarily blocked by litigation will resume. If opponents of the death penalty do not devote themselves to legislative effort if and when the opportune moment arrives, however, they may fail in achieving both goals. The corrective justice issues involved in capital punishment are so plentiful, as demonstrated in the last decade and a half, that litigation can stop executions for a long time, but not forever. But the class in whose behalf they are invoked does not have the characteristics that make it likely that the courts will stake their prestige and authority on providing them with political justice.

13

Protecting the Environment:
The Wrong Way

In 1962, the Consolidated Edison Company of New York (Con Ed) announced a plan to build a power plant at majestic Storm King Mountain on the Hudson River. The plant was to provide stored power to Con Ed's customers in the New York City metropolitan area during periods of peak use when the rest of the system could not cope with demand. A few years earlier, the construction of a power plant on such a scenic site might have been lamented, denounced, and, perhaps, opposed in testimony before a regulatory or legislative body, but it probably would not have been challenged in court. In the 1960s, however, litigation seemed the way to deal with every question. Inspired by the publication of Rachel Carson's *The Silent Spring*[1] the same year Con Ed announced its plan for a power plant at Storm King, a new environmental movement came into existence. Its constituency was different from the old-line conservation movement, and it was ready to use different methods.

Old-line conservationists were largely an odd mixture of the wealthy, concerned primarily with protecting the scenic beauty of the environs of their estates and resorts, and of ardent naturalists who were devoted to life in the wilderness, disdaining the comforts of industrial civilization. Their methods were public education and private lobbying. Contemporary environmentalists are predominantly middle class, and most venture into wilderness areas infrequently, if at all. Many, active in other causes in which public disputes have been dealt with through litigation, turn to the courts almost reflexively.

Con Ed's proposed power plant at Storm King helped to attract many new adherents to the infant environmental movement, among them some residents of the area around Storm King, primarily with homes on the opposite bank of the Hudson River to whom the power plant would be most visible. Many residents of the town of Cornwall, New York, where Storm King is located, favored construction of the plant because it would reduce their taxes. Consumers of electric power, whose interests were potentially involved because they would pay for the building and use the power stored, played no significant role in the dispute.

The battle to preserve Storm King Mountain was fought under the leadership of an ad hoc organization, the Scenic Hudson Preservation Conference, one of the first of many organizations formed to do the work of the new movement. It obtained support from such old-line conservation groups as the Sierra Club, the Audubon Society, and the Izaak Walton League and secured the volunteer services of a number of New York City lawyers associated with firms that ordinarily represent corporate interests. In the mid-1960s, hundreds of lawyers from such firms were volunteering their services to defend civil rights in the South, thereby paving the way for some of their colleagues to volunteer their services for causes such as this.

The volunteer lawyers concentrated first on getting the Federal Power Commission (FPC) to deny Con Ed permission to construct the plant at Storm King. The FPC's statutory mandate, dating back to 1920, is to see that "the project adopted . . . shall be such as in the judgment of the Commission will be best adapted to a comprehensive plan for improving or developing a waterway . . . for the use or benefit of interstate commerce, for the improvement or utilization of water-power development . . . and for other beneficial public uses, including recreational uses."[2] Scenic Hudson did not succeed, and the FPC issued a license for the construction of a plant in 1964. When new evidence of danger to fish life in the Hudson was presented to the commission, the FPC declined to reopen its hearings. Scenic Hudson's lawyers went to federal court and, later in 1965, obtained a ruling from the Second Circuit Court of Appeals remanding the case to the FPC for reconsideration. The federal agency, the court found, had not adequately considered alternative power plans or the potential effect on scenic beauty and fish life or its obligation under federal law to consider a "comprehensive plan" for the river.[3] Confronting the question of whether judicial interference was warranted, the judges said, "This court cannot and should not substitute its judgment for that of the Commission. But we must decide whether the Commission has correctly discharged its duties, including the proper fulfillment of its planning function in deciding the 'licensing of the project would be in the public interest.' The Commission must see to it that the record is complete. The Commission has an affirmative duty to inquire into and consider all relevant facts."[4]

The FPC commenced new hearings in 1966. So many witnesses testified in opposition to the construction of the plant and Con Ed was required to go such great lengths in its effort to rebut their testimony that the record of the hearings eventually took up nineteen thousand pages. But when the testimony was complete, the FPC again issued a license to Con Ed to construct the plant.[5] Once again, Scenic Hudson went to court, but this time the Second Circuit Court of Appeals ruled that the FPC had considered all relevant factors and, in addition, that the licensing of construction complied with the requirements of the newly enacted National Environmental Policy Act.[6] In 1972, the Supreme Court, with Justice Douglas dissenting, declined to review this decision.[7]

Scenic Hudson's lawyers asked the FPC to reconsider because, they said, there was new evidence that the power plant would endanger fish life. The FPC refused.[8] Again, Scenic Hudson went to court, this time persuading the Second Circuit to overrule the FPC, requiring the agency to reopen hearings and to consider the new evidence.[9] This 1974 decision was soon followed by another by the same court based on a 1972 amendment to the Federal Water Pollution Control Act[10] prohibiting Con Ed from dredging in the Hudson River without a permit from the U.S. Army Corps of Engineers.[11] The FPC did not resume hearings on Storm King immediately following the 1974 decisions, preferring to await the results of hearings by the federal Environmental Protection Agency.

While various cases Scenic Hudson had filed were under consideration in the federal courts, the organization also proceeded against the plant at Storm King in the state courts of New York. In 1972, it succeeded in persuading a state judge to invalidate certification of the project by the New York commissioner of environmental conservation on the ground that Con Ed had not complied with state laws requiring reasonable assurance that there would be no danger of salt water contamination, no danger of thermal pollution, that fish would not be killed, and that the Catskill Aqueduct would not be damaged.[12] On appeal, however, this decision was overturned.[13]

In 1979, Con Ed announced that it had shelved its effort to construct a power plant at Storm King until 1995, to all intents and purposes an announcement that the plant would never be built. The company's estimates of the power it would need to meet demand from its customers at the time the plans for the plant were first announced had proved to be far greater than actual demand. In 1980, Con Ed was supplying its customers in the New York metropolitan area with no more than about half the power it had estimated a decade earlier that it would need by 1980. Although a decade and a half of litigation by Scenic Hudson had not succeeded in getting a court to do more than order an administrative agency to look at the project more closely, that proved sufficient to kill the project. The litigation delayed it to death.

Formal burial of Consolidated Edison's plan took place on December 19, 1980. On that day, Charles F. Luce, Con Ed's chairman, signed an agreement with representatives of Scenic Hudson and other environmental groups that required the utility to surrender its license to build at Storm King. It was to donate the river property to the state for use as a park; close other plants along the Hudson River during the fish spawning season; and refrain from proposing construction of other power plants that do not include cooling systems along the Hudson River for twenty-five years. Along with other utilities, Con Ed agreed to donate $12 million to a foundation that would study the impact of power plants on aquatic life; it would spend $2 million annually to monitor power plant impact on aquatic life; and it would construct a hatchery that would stock the Hudson each year with six hundred thousand striped bass fingerlings.[14]

"The precedent is as welcome as the settlement," the *New York Times* editorial proclaimed. "Here is proof that negotiations can produce better results than prolonged litigation," the editorial continued, as if the negotiations that produced the settlement could have come about without prolonged litigation.[15]

Since Con Ed's estimate of the power it would have to supply to its customers was wildly misinformed and the Storm King plant was not needed, the demise of the plant must be regarded as a good thing even by those little concerned with its environmental consequences. But was it proper to invoke the authority of the courts for this particular worthy end?

The controversy over construction of the power plant at Storm King is characteristic of many environmental disputes. They are not only a clash between commercial interests and environmental interests but also a struggle between at least two groups of citizens. Those who are trying to protect the environment are often affluent. The less well-to-do are likely to be more concerned with the jobs to be created by projects that threaten the environment and, sometimes, as with the residents of Cornwall, New York, tempted with tax relief. As in the Storm King dispute, affected consumers ordinarily do not play a significant part.

Environmentalists do not often enjoy financial resources comparable to those of their corporate antagonists or the political clout that is a concomitant of that financial strength, but they suffer no special disadvantage in taking part in the political process. And no provision of the Constitution can be readily construed as protecting the environment. Under the circumstances, therefore, the proper place to resolve disputes over environmental questions would seem to be in the representative branches of government. Litigation—though it may effectively promote worthy ends as at Storm King—seems an appropriate means only in circumstances where the representative branches have explicitly provided that disputes shall be resolved in court.

Some environmentalists contend that the courts have a special responsibility to scrutinize closely claims that the environment is threatened because a livable environment is needed to exercise all other rights. David Sive, a New York City lawyer active in environmental causes who played a leading part in Scenic Hudson's campaign to prevent the construction of the power plant at Storm King, is one who holds this view. He calls the right to a habitable environment the "primary civil right." He has written, "There is a special aspect of environmental rights which render them more basic and fundamental than most other traditional civil rights.... That feature is the irrevocability of their breach."[16] Christopher Stone has proposed that legal guardians should be appointed for objects in the environment because they embody our obligation to treat the world around us respectfully.[17] Laurence Tribe has suggested that we should abandon our "homocentric" ways and confer independent juridical status—such as we give to corporations—to wilderness areas and endangered species.[18] And Joseph L. Sax, professor of law at the University of Michigan and a prominent legal scholar closely identified with the movement to resolve environmental disputes in court, has suggested that the judiciary brings several virtues to the consideration of cases like Storm King. He notes that judges are "outsiders" and therefore not susceptible to the political pressures that ordinarily determine the outcome of public policy disputes. They are generally not selected with any thought to their predisposition on environmental matters; they are free "very substantially from the concerns which inevitably affect a specialized administrator or advisor, particularly the need to maintain some sort of politically balanced position among the constituencies with which he regularly deals." The judicial process, he maintains, provides special opportunities for "private-citizen initiatives." There is no "political screening of cases, but once a complaint is filed, the judicial process moves inexorably forward." A judge "can require bureaucrats and even the biggest industries to respond to his questions and to justify themselves"; the judicial process "demands that controversies be reduced to rather concrete and specific issues rather than be allowed to float around in the generality that so often accompanies public dispute."[19]

These are the virtues the courts bring to any matter they consider. A court would bring similar virtues to disputes over foreign policy or war or taxes. We do not look to judges to resolve these questions, however, because we are committed to a different system with its own virtues, representative democracy. We entrust judges, who are not accountable to the electorate, with decisions in which they apply agreed-upon principles and implement the policy determinations of the representative branches. It is another matter entirely to entrust an unrepresentative body with formulating policies.

Responding to this concern, Sax argues that "to enlarge the ambit of judicial activity in environmental matters is not to restrict or supplant other modes for public debate or the resolution of controversy. Administrative regulation will go on, legislative standards will be set, hearings and investigations will continue. . . . Courts serve only to supplement these activities and to encourage them to be carried forward more adequately in the knowledge that there remains another source of redress and review when they can be shown to be inadequate."[20]

Sax's may be the best argument for judicial intervention in environmental matters. Almost certainly, the Federal Power Commission and other regulatory agencies of the executive branch of government do their job more adequately in the awareness that organizations like Scenic Hudson may call them to account in court. Courts reviewing the decisions made by administrative agencies should not merely rubber-stamp the results but should examine closely the procedures by which they were reached to make certain that the agencies played their legislatively required roles. It also seems likely that legislative consideration of environmental issues is better informed because of the evidence that is presented in court hearings and that it is more deliberate because another forum for redress is available. Yet the fact remains that in a matter like the battle over Storm King, the courts did more than merely "encourage [administrative investigation and legislative consideration] to be carried forward more adequately." By forcing the Federal Power Commission to examine the proposal to build a power plant at Storm King in a manner never dreamed of by the authors of the Federal Power Act of 1920, the courts effectively took upon themselves the function of Congress to rewrite the legislation and the function of the executive branch to implement the legislation. The results were laudable, but the process was, at the very least, questionable.

Of course, the manner in which the courts construed the meaning of the Federal Power Act in the Storm King litigation resembles the manner in which they traditionally construe a passage in the Constitution that is inexplicit, such as the guarantee of due process of law. But there are obvious and enormous differences. A constitutional provision is meant to last for the ages, retaining its vitality through efforts to ensure that its spirit governs its application in circumstances never contemplated by its framers. Legislation, on the other hand, is revised constantly to take into account considerations that seem important at a particular moment. Its vitality in new circumstances is ensured by legislative revision, not judicial extrapolation. A constitutional provision like the guarantee of due process of law embodies a principle which the judiciary is uniquely qualified to apply through the exercise of judgment. Legislation like the Federal Power Act, on the other hand, embodies a policy determination which the representative branches are uniquely qualified to make because they weigh competing political considerations. A constitutional provision like the guarantee of due process of law is usually implemented through the dispensation of corrective justice. Occasionally, as I have argued in parts of this book dealing with inmates of asylums, and the right of women to obtain abortions, its implementation may require ventures into the realm of political justice or distributive justice. Legislation like the Federal Power Act, on the other hand, is exclusively concerned with questions of distributive justice and political justice, and it must be implemented without reference to principles of corrective justice. Finally, expansive reading of a constitutional provision like the guarantee of due process of law seems appropriate in circumstances when its protection is sought by a discrete and insular minority suffering from prejudice and unable to secure redress through the political process. Citizens seeking from the courts an expansive reading of the Federal Power Act hardly suffer from any special disability in obtaining redress through the political process. In tipping the scales in favor of environmentalists by forcing delays such as those that took place at Storm King, the courts serve a segment of the populace with no special claim on their solicitude.

As to the contention that the courts should scrutinize exactingly threats to the environment because environmental rights are primary, it is certainly true that other rights could not be exercised in the absence of a habitable environment. But this hardly makes environmental disputes unique. The resolution of disputes over foreign policy or military policy could lead to the destruction of the human race. No one can exercise other rights if lacking sufficient food to sustain life. Unchecked population growth would threaten the capacity to exercise all rights. And so on. If every interest that must be met to permit the exercise of all other rights were to be dealt with by the judiciary, there would be little left to occupy the other branches of government. Doubts about the wisdom of settling environmental questions in court have not seemed to trouble the organizations active in trying to protect the environment, however. Like other protest movements, environmentalists seem preoccupied with the urgency of their cause and eager to take advantage of any forum in which they might be able to prevail.

No environmental cause has seemed so urgent to so many as the campaign to stop utility companies from generating electric power through nuclear energy. This issue has dominated litigation about environmental matters in recent years. The highest hurdle opponents of nuclear power have had to overcome in using the courts to further their cause, as is true of litigants in other environmental cases, has been in obtaining standing to sue. They must demonstrate, as the Supreme Court said in an environmental lawsuit brought by the Sierra Club, an old-time conservation group that has transformed itself into one of the most litigious of the new environmental organizations, that a "party seeking review must allege facts showing that he himself is adversely affected."[21] A generalized claim that all will suffer from damage to the environment is insufficient to confer standing to sue.

Two Supreme Court decisions have been crucial to the environmentalists in their efforts to deal with the standing issue: *United States* v. *Students Challenging Regulatory Agency Procedures (SCRAP)*[22] and *Duke Power Co.* v. *Carolina Environmental Study Group.*[23] In *SCRAP*, five law students challenged an Interstate Commerce Commission order permitting railroads to collect a rate surcharge. The extra cost would make transportation of recyclable goods prohibitively expensive, the students alleged, thereby increasing pollution. The Supreme Court said the students had standing to sue because they also alleged that a consequence of the increase in pollution would be an adverse effect on their use of outdoor recreational facilities. In *Duke Power*, a group of plaintiffs residing in the vicinity of a nuclear power plant challenged the constitutionality of the Price Anderson Act,[24] which had imposed a ceiling of $560 million on damages that may be recovered by litigants injured in a nuclear power plant accident. The law was essential in permitting the construction of nuclear power plants to go forward because, without a ceiling on liability, they would have been virtually uninsurable. The Supreme Court rebuffed the litigants on all their substantive claims but held that the claim that the act amounted to a government taking of private property without due process—because of the limit on compensation in the event of an accident—was sufficient to confer standing to sue.

SCRAP and *Duke Power* construe the standing concept expansively. These decisions stand out in sharp relief against the Supreme Court's decisions in cases affecting the political process itself, such as *Tatum* v. *Laird*[25] or cases affecting minorities who have been limited in their ability to take part in the political process such as *Warth* v. *Seldin*.[26] In *Tatum* in 1972 (see Chapter 10), an allegation that political surveillance chilled expression was not considered a sufficiently "specific present objective harm" to confer standing on the antiwar activists who brought the suit. In *Warth* in 1977 (see Chapter 4), black residents of Rochester, New York, were denied standing to challenge racially exclusionary practices in the suburbs because they could not point to any residences there in which they could afford to live, that is, the exclusionary practices had been wholly effective. Yet in environmental cases in which the injury was more remote, the Supreme Court found that standing existed. The different results seem defensible only if the Supreme Court thinks that environmental disputes have a better claim on the attention of the judiciary than controversies over political surveillance or racial segregation. The Court has never said anything of the sort directly, but its decision on standing are a measure of the headway that environmentalists have made in persuading the judiciary that the rights they attempt to uphold are "primary."

On the other hand, when the Supreme Court confronts on the merits litigation brought by opponents of nuclear power, it holds that the representative branches of government must resolve the policy issues. This question was considered in 1976 by the United States Court of Appeals for the District of Columbia Circuit, which required the Nuclear Regulatory Commission to review further the licensing of a nuclear power plant to ensure a "thorough ventilation of the issues."[27] In a concurring opinion, Chief Judge Bazelon echoed those who insisted that environmental rights are "primary," writing, "Decisions . . . touching the environment or medicine affect the lives and health of all." For this reason, he wrote, the concerns expressed by environmentalists enjoy "a special claim to judicial protection."[28] But when that Court of Appeals decision was reviewed by the Supreme Court in 1978, Justice Rehnquist wrote for the high Court in *Vermont Yankee Nuclear Power Corp.* v. *Natural Resources Defense Council:*

> Nuclear energy may some day be a cheap, safe source of power or it may not. But Congress has made a choice to at least try nuclear energy, establishing a reasonable review process in which courts are only to play a limited role. The fundamental

policy questions appropriately resolved in Congress and in the state legislatures are not subject to reexamination in the federal courts under the guise of judicial review of agency action. Time may prove wrong the decision to develop nuclear energy, but it is Congress or the states within their appropriate agencies who must eventually make that judgment. In the meantime courts should perform their appointed function.[29]

The decision in *Vermont Yankee* was a significant setback to the efforts of environmentalists to use the courts to vindicate their cause. But it was not a death knell. The Supreme Court's decisions in SCRAP and *Duke Power* ensure that opponents of nuclear power will not be thrown out of court summarily for lack of standing to sue. They will continue to be able to use litigation to delay, if not directly to stop, nuclear power plant construction. Even if the courts routinely uphold regulatory agency decisions because such decisions "are not subject to reexamination in the federal courts under the guise of judicial review of agency action," litigation is not foreclosed. Under *Vermont Yankee*, federal courts may determine whether the record developed by a regulatory agency is adequate. When it is not, a federal court may remand for additional administrative proceedings. Merely contending in court that a record is inadequate brings on judicial proceedings that delay construction of a nuclear power plant. Making that contention successfully adds administrative agency proceedings and, very likely, another round of judicial proceedings, delaying construction a long time. As Storm King made clear, delay is a powerful weapon in the hands of environmentalists. Delay permits time to pass in which it can be determined whether predictions of power needs are realistic; it allows the development of alternate sources of energy; it raises the cost of construction of nuclear power plants, thereby deterring utilities from building them; and it permits political opposition to develop. Many more nuclear power plants would be in operation today were it not for the litigation campaign against them. It may be, as was certainly the case with the stored power plant at Storm King, that stopping construction and operation of nuclear power plants is a very good thing. But even if that is true, from the standpoint of anyone concerned with the appropriate role of the courts in a democratic society, it is at least a questionable use of their powers.

14

Thoughts on Results

The election of Ronald Reagan as the fortieth president of the United States could be attributed to many factors, among them Reagan's own capacity to inspire the confidence of the electorate and a widespread belief that his opponent, Jimmy Carter, had failed as president. The condition of the American economy was a major factor. So was the failure of the Carter administration to resolve the hostage crisis in Iran by the time of the election. Each of these may have loomed larger in the results of the election than popular antagonism to the causes that are discussed in this book. Even so, the Reagan administration appeared to interpret its victory primarily as a mandate to undo what those espousing such causes have achieved through litigation.

The administration, with widespread public approval, began to try to prevent federal judges from promoting school desegregation; it placed in charge of the Equal Employment Opportunities Commission leadership that opposed vigorous enforcement of federal laws promoting equal opportunity; it strenuously opposed the Equal Rights Amendment; it actively supported efforts to overturn *Roe* v. *Wade* by a constitutional amendment and to get the Supreme

Court to reverse itself by a statutory declaration that a fetus is a person entitled to the constitutional protection of the Fourteenth Amendment. In addition, it secured deep cuts in welfare benefits and repudiated the very idea that the poor are entitled to any government assistance. It sought to rid itself of restraints on military intervention in other countries and on the practices of the intelligence agencies. It supported capital punishment and more punitive use of incarceration. It systematically declined to enforce many of the legal restraints on practices of government and industry that adversely affect the environment.

The Reagan administration's attitude toward litigation as a means of promoting such causes was evident in the public utterances of the attorney general on efforts to terminate the federally funded legal services program. The program cost the federal government only about $320 million a year, a pittance by federal budget standards. It probably wastes less than any other federal program. What is objectionable about the legal services program to the Reagan administration is not cost but the fact that it effectively challenges practices of government bureaucracies that ignore the rights of the poor. As governor of California, Reagan did battle with the California Rural Legal Services, widely regarded as one of the outstanding litigation organizations funded by the federal legal services program. As president, he tried to kill the entire program nationally. When Congress refused to go along, he appointed leadership intent on drastically reducing the program's effectiveness.

The Reagan administration's receptivity to proposals to strip the Supreme Court of jurisdiction to hear certain kinds of cases—proposals of dubious constitutionality—underscored its hostility to litigation as a means of promoting the causes considered in this book. The advent of that administration necessarily threw into sharper focus fundamental questions about the reliance on litigation. Might alternative methods produce more enduring results, even if more slowly? Can interest groups progressing through reliance on litigation preserve their gains? Would those espousing causes through litigation be stronger if they were forced to rely on the ordinary processes of influencing representative government? Does cause litigation have a future?

Inevitably, answers must be speculative and require overbroad generalizations. Yet these questions are so central that it may be less irresponsible to hazard answers than to shirk them.

Though I write when many of the gains for the causes discussed are threatened, even with the advantage of hindsight litigation still seems an appropriate way to advance most of these causes. Most gains could not have been achieved at all, much less enduringly, in any other way. Inmates of asylums, for example could not employ the ordinary political processes. Litigation is the only way they can make their cause known other than by rioting. Even riots, which took place with some frequency in American prisons long before the litigation era, produced only sporadic attention to conditions in asylums. It could hardly be otherwise in the case of institutions that, by definition, confine those found unfit to live in ordinary society.

Other interest groups, such as those who challenge restrictions on their right to count equally in voting, might have made their cause known without litigation but it would have been futile. Their grievance was that the ordinary political processes were stacked against them. Because that assertion had merit, they could not prevail by exclusive reliance on the political process. The representative bodies of government rebuffed them because those complaining lacked the appropriate representation. It requires a naive faith in the altruism of elected public officials to expect them to vote themselves out of office to provide fair representation to those who do not count equally. Voting rights secured through litigation are not threatened today because those who won equal representation enjoy the power to resist encroachment on such rights. At this writing, it seems likely that the essential provisions of the Voting Rights Act of 1965 will be preserved and, perhaps, new legislation may make the law even stronger. Even if those trying to repeal the law had succeeded, the principal effect would be to prevent those whose votes do not yet count equally, such as blacks in Mobile, Alabama, effectively disenfranchised by at-large voting (see Chapter 5), from securing electoral equality. Disenfranchisement, such as occurred in the South at the end of the nineteenth century, seems inconceivable, a testament to the results blacks have achieved through litigation.

Nationwide, schools may be de facto as segregated as before *Brown* (though not in the states directly affected by *Brown*). But racial minorities, as a consequence of litigation, are no longer invisible. The rest of America is aware of them and they are aware of themselves. They will not disappear again. Today, it may be that concentration of energies and resources on the ordinary political processes is in the best interests of racial minorities. It may even be that it was in their best interests to devote more energy and resources to the ordinary political processes in the years when the Supreme Court was leading the nation toward racial equality. But the enduring result of litigation is that racial minorities are now able to participate effectively—though not yet equally—in the ordinary political processes.

Women might have achieved more enduring results through ordinary political processes—as by ratification of the Equal Rights Amendment—had they managed to persuade more women that they had common interests that should be advanced in this way. The failure to do this seems to have more to do with the way feminists have articulated their goals than with the particular methods they have chosen to advance those goals. The energies and resources the women's movement has devoted to ordinary political processes are far greater than those devoted to litigation; therefore, litigation cannot be said to have diverted critical efforts from the drive to ratify the ERA. Nor does litigation seem to blame for the women's backlash. The abortion question aside, there has been no discernible backlash against gains for women's equality secured through litigation. By contrast, the political resistance to the ERA itself has been very great.

The most that can be said about interference with ratification of the ERA by litigation is that the case for the ERA would have been stronger except for the progress the women's movement made through litigation. This adopts a "worse is better" theory of social change. In practice, worse is usually worse.

Of all the gains made through litigation by the interest groups we have considered, the right of a woman to obtain an abortion seems the most vulnerable at this writing. Had criminal sanctions against abortion been repealed legislatively, as happened in New York and a few other states before *Roe v. Wade*, would the results be more enduring? Perhaps. That part of the antiabortion movement which is primarily hostile to a congeries of changes in public policy brought about by court decisions might not then have focused on abortion. In that respect, the antiabortion movement would be considerably weaker. That leaves the question of whether criminal sanctions against abortion could have been repealed legislatively in many states other than those that acted before *Roe v. Wade*. Even with hindsight, it is difficult to say, but it appears unlikely. The right-to-life backlash against abortion had already emerged as a powerful force by the time

Roe v. *Wade* was decided in 1973. The Supreme Court decision provided right to life with impetus, but it was already strong enough to prevent most states from repealing abortion laws legislatively. When repeal took place in New York in 1970, it appeared that women generally were united, or would unite, in seeking equality and in seeking the right to obtain abortions. That impression was soon dissipated. The year that the Supreme Court decided *Roe* v. *Wade* was the last in which a significant number of states ratified the Equal Rights Amendment. By the end of 1973, the deep divisions among women were becoming apparent. Just as the Equal Rights Amendment made little headway in state legislatures from 1974 on, so little headway could have been made in state legislatures in repealing antiabortion laws once these divisions surfaced. Indeed, states like New York that repealed antiabortion laws at the beginning of the 1970s might have reenacted them in the mid-1970s if the Supreme Court had not held them unconstitutional. The judicially established right of women to choose abortions may not survive, but because women who attempt to exercise this right are, as a group, politically powerless, alternate ways of securing this right probably could not have secured it more enduringly.

Welfare recipients advanced their cause modestly through litigation. Those gains they made, such as the right of recent arrivals in a state to obtain public assistance, could not have been won through the ordinary political processes. The only other way they might have been won would have been through social upheaval. The possibility of such an upheaval does not seem to have been forestalled by litigation because litigation probably did not have a palliative effect on the poor. To the contrary, some of those who had promoted litigation saw it as a means of precipitating a crisis that would lead to upheaval and thus to effective change. That strategy failed, and litigation itself proved too puny to implement the grand scheme of establishing a constitutionally guaranteed right to live. The incapacity of the courts to take on such a task should have been evident at the outset, though it was not because of the courts-can-do-anything atmosphere of the 1960s. The rights that welfare recipients secured through litigation during the late 1960s and the early 1970s are not seriously threatened, but those rights offered little protection against the cutbacks in benefits implemented by the Reagan administration.

Litigation was one of many ways in which opponents of the war in Vietnam tried to further their cause, but direct legal challenges to the war had no discernible impact. To the extent that the war powers legislation is an outgrowth of the litigation against the war, it has had negligible impact on American military policy since then. The United States sent military advisers to El Salvador in 1981 just as it sent military advisers to Vietnam two decades ago. The wisdom and propriety of American military intervention in El Salvador were extensively debated, but the war powers legislation was rarely mentioned in the public press, and the provisions of the legislation that grew out of antiwar litigation—so far, at any rate—have been of no consequence. Litigation commenced under the war powers legislation to try to impede American military intervention in El Salvador seemed unlikely to succeed. Few were even aware of that litigation; it had no discernible impact on the public debate over El Salvador. By comparison with the energies and resources invested in political aspects of the antiwar effort, those devoted to challenging the Vietnam war in court were meager. Even so, many talented lawyers took part in the litigation campaign, and federal courts spent a significant amount of time considering the cases filed. All that now seems a waste. War, it is clear, cannot be directly affected by litigation.

Litigation is a more potent weapon against practices of the national security state that indirectly bear on the nation's propensity for getting into wars. Court cases are particularly effective in challenging government practices that restrict the democratic process in the name of national security. Even though the national mood in the early 1980s seemed more tolerant of government secrecy and political surveillance than when much of the litigation against such practices was commenced in the 1970s, the results achieved through litigation may well prove enduring. In the early days of the Reagan administration, there were press accounts of proposals by federal officials to reinstitute CIA spying on Americans. Those reports provoked an outcry and, almost immediately, the proposals were repudiated by senior spokesmen for the new administration. The leadership of the FBI, the target of much of the litigation of the 1970s challenging political surveillance, appeared disinclined to revert to the past practices that discredited the bureau when they were exposed through litigation. It would be polyannaish to predict that the federal government will abstain from political surveillance in the future, but awareness of the embarrassment caused by litigation will impede those who want to resume the most abusive practices.

Litigation challenging secrecy caused less embarrassment. Accordingly, the Reagan administration has instituted new measures against those who reveal secrets. Congress may give its approval to more far-reaching measures. Yet, despite the relative lack of success of litigation in protecting those disclosing government secrets, going to court still seems the best way to protect them in the future. At the very least, litigation prevents the government from quickly penalizing whistle-blowers and allows the possibility that their revelations will turn the tide of public opinion in their favor before penalties can be imposed. That happened in the case of Daniel Ellsberg, who disclosed the Pentagon Papers, and it could well happen again.

The long-term consequence of environmental litigation may be the most difficult of all to estimate. On the one hand, litigation to protect the environment was effective in stopping or stalling many projects of government and industry that would have destroyed natural resources. On the other hand, the Reagan administration enjoyed great public support for its contention that the American economy has been stifled by overregulation. Much of the regulation that the administration seemed determined to eliminate is a direct or indirect consequence of litigation. It could be that the antiregulatory tide will sweep away all the gains environmentalists made through litigation. Or it could be that litigation is still an effective weapon for impeding projects that would do great damage to the environment. Only time will tell.

Whatever the long-term effect on the protection of natural resources, environmental litigation has probably stripped the courts of some of the prestige they won in championing the causes of disadvantaged minorities. No matter how bitterly the courts are detested for particular decisions that have favored minorities, most Americans respect, though often grudgingly, an institution that is sensitive to the grievances of the disadvantaged, especially when the courts are as resolute as they were in the decade and a half after *Brown*. Court decisions or court-imposed delays affecting the environment do not inspire such respect. They are cheered by those who favor an outcome achieved through litigation and damned by those on the other side. When an antienvironmental mood takes hold in the country, as at present, it bodes ill for the prestige of the judiciary perceived as intervening in matters beyond its ken.

Environmental litigation was not a factor in 1968, when presidential candidate Richard Nixon sensed growing public antipathy to judicial power, largely brought on at that time by Warren Court decisions like *Miranda* v. *Arizona*[1] that freed criminals on "technical" grounds at a time when Americans were deeply concerned with rising crime rates. The Court seemed to some to have so far dissipated its prestige in criminal due process cases as to permit a takeover by the executive branch. Nixon pledged to appoint "strict constructionists" to serve on the Supreme Court. Franklin Roosevelt had had no opportunity to appoint any member of the Supreme Court during his first term as president and felt compelled to threaten to pack the Court to change its direction. Circumstances permitted Nixon to appoint four members to the Court in his own first term. As Nixon made plain, he chose the persons he did because he thought their judicial philosophies comported with his own. It appeared that the Supreme Court's ventures in distributive and political justice on behalf of discrete and insular minorities were at an end. Organizations engaged in cause litigation such as the American Civil Liberties Union became more concerned with preserving victories they had won in the decade and a half of the Warren Court era than with trying to extend the bounds of judicial decision making.

The momentum built by the Warren Court proved stronger than was at first understood by most cause litigators. In 1971, the Burger Court held that apparently neutral criteria for employment that had the effect of discriminating by race were impermissible;[2] in 1972, the Burger Court held that all death penalty laws then in effect were unconstitutional;[3] in 1973, the Burger Court held that criminal sanctions against medical abortions were unconstitutional;[4] and in 1975, the Burger Court held that nondangerous persons could not be confined custodially in mental hospitals against their will.[5]

Those and other Burger Court decisions extended the era of judicial activism that began with the Warren Court's decision in *Brown v. Board of Education.*

It would be misleading to suggest that the Burger Court has been as receptive as its predecessor to those seeking to advance causes through the courts. Indeed, many of its decisions have reflected hostility to such efforts. The Burger Court has handed down a number of decisions that changed the ground rules for federal court practice in a manner that seemed intended to discourage cause litigation. These decisions invoke technical principles of comity,[6] justiciability,[7] and standing[8] so as to complicate enormously the litigation process. Litigators on behalf of causes have complained bitterly that such decisions have the effect of closing the doors of the federal courts to victims of abuses by government. Not that the Burger Court has voted no on the principles but that it has increasingly kept challenges themselves from coming before it for decisions on principle.

Although these decisions by the Burger Court set back cause litigation, they were not deathblows. An important reason is that the cause litigation bar is larger, better financed, more sophisticated, and more resourceful in the era of the Burger Court than it was earlier. By bringing into existence the robust public interest law bar that exists today, the Warren Court's decisions helped to maintain their own momentum. The Burger Court is confronted by numerous organizations and lawyers with a stake in advancing causes through litigation. Any decision that creates procedural difficulties for cause litigators is now the target for sustained attack until, often, a way is found to circumvent or overcome it. Cause litigators do not always succeed, but by the sheer volume of their efforts they find ways to limit the damage to their work by a Supreme Court predominantly unreceptive to their use of litigation. They also prevail frequently in lower court cases that never reach the Supreme Court. In this respect, as in others, the continuing vitality of cause litigation in obtaining political justice and distributive justice is part of the legacy of the Warren Court's decision in *Brown v. Board of Education.*

No doubt, an important factor in Richard Nixon's failure to end judicial policy making was Watergate. Not only did it strip Nixon and Nixonism of moral authority, but it bolstered the prestige of the judiciary. "Iron" John Sirica was widely admired—though not by civil libertarians—for his conduct of the trial of the Watergate burglars. And the Supreme Court was admired for delivering the *coup de grace* to Nixon by forcing him to yield the White House tapes. Although Nixon made noises about resisting a court order to turn over the tapes, he discovered that the authority of the Supreme Court was too great to permit him to defy it. In submitting to its authority, of course, Nixon reinforced that authority.

The Reagan administration attack has been different and appears more serious. It has not focused on the Supreme Court itself. Warren Burger, as the embodiment of the Court, appears too much in tune with the Reagan administration to present a target such as Earl Warren presented to Nixon. Rather, the Reagan administration attack focuses directly on the causes that have made headway through litigation.

Reagan has not embodied the forces that have launched the attacks to the same extent as Nixon did embody the attack on the court itself. Watergate thus discredited Nixon's attack. The attack on the right of women to obtain abortions, however, has been led by such members of Congress as Senator Jesse Helms and Representative Henry Hyde, the attack on the Voting Rights Act by Senator Strom Thurmond, the attack on the idea that the poor are entitled to government assistance by Budget Director David Stockman, the attack on environmental protection by Secretary of the Interior James Watt. And so on. Reagan has presided over these attacks, but he has not led them. Because the leadership has been diversified, the attacks are more formidable and difficulties they face have not discredited that leadership.

Most important, the movements that advocate the causes under attack have become far more dispirited than at the time of Nixon's attack on the Court. The Court of final appeal is perceived to be basically insensitive to their goals, unresponsive to their advocacy. They are thus attacked by all three governmental branches, the executive, the legislative, and the judicial. Some, like the welfare rights movement, are more than dispirited; they are dead. Even the liveliest movements discussed here, the women's rights movement and the environmental protection movement, are in difficulty. These two movements were in their infancy when Nixon launched his attack on the Supreme Court; the gains they made through litigation were still to come. Today they are both reeling under attack from countermovements. Antifeminists have the upper hand in battling feminists, and those engaged in energy production have the upper hand over environmentalists.

Yet despite the present unhappy circumstances, it does not yet seem time to bring down the curtain on the litigation era that started with *Brown* v. *Board of Education* in 1954. Some of the private organizations that sponsor cause litigation, such as the American Civil Liberties Union, the NAACP Legal Defense Fund, and the environmental litigation groups, are in good health even though the causes they espouse are in difficulty. Organizationally, these groups thrive on adversity. Financial contributions to them increase because their supporters are alarmed. And the present weakness of the causes they espouse is more pronounced in the executive branch and in the halls of the representative branches of government than in the courts. Litigation may not be an effective instrument for advancing such causes during the next few years, but it may be the most effective instrument for preserving what those causes have achieved up to now. Cause litigation has a future, it seems plain, though that future may never again include such heady victories as during its golden era, the two decades from *Brown* to the mid-1970s.

15

Conclusion: Further Thoughts on Legitimacy

Ultimately, it is necessary to return to the question: Is it legitimate for courts to employ their authority to make public policy? I have argued that judicial policy making is legitimate (1) when compelling principles of corrective justice dictate ventures into the realms of distributive justice and political justice and (2) when such ventures unclog political processes that prevent the representative branches of government from functioning representatively, or (3) when such ventures help disadvantaged minorities compete fairly in our pluralist democracy, and that it is not legitimate in other circumstances. It is time to make explicit a further element of the argument that, so far, has only been implicit.

As has been noted previously, the most heated controversies and the most persistent doubts about the legitimacy of judicial policy making arise from judicial dispensation of distributive justice or political justice to aid disadvantaged minorities. Court orders requiring a state to pay the cost of abortions for poor women or to pay for group homes for the retarded or to hire a certain proportion of firemen from among minority applicants are examples of such judicial action. In part, of course, negative public response reflects the very prejudice against those minorities that warrants judicial solicitude for them. Doubts about special judicial assistance to such minorities may also rest on more defensible grounds because it is neither possible to discover in the actual language of the Constitution nor otherwise to fix precisely the criteria that entitle a particular minority to benefit from such judicial solicitude. Nor is it possible to ascertain exactly when a minority ceases to be disadvantaged and climbs onto the plateau of American politics where it may compete fairly. Assuming that courts should dispense distributive justice or political justice in the interests of disadvantaged minorities—however it is determined that they deserve such assistance—it is not easy to say what limits courts should impose on themselves. Yet despite the difficulties in charting the exact routes that judges should follow, it seems to me that one aspect of any venture in judicial policy making confirms their legitimacy. It is that the representative branches retain the power to nullify policy making by the judiciary.

Judges, it seems to me apparent from the way litigation works in shaping public policy, lack the power to dispense distributive justice or political justice except to the extent that the executive and legislative branches of government go along. If the elected representatives of the people refuse to go along, a judge possesses no power with which to compel their compliance except to condemn them as lawless. Such condemnation is of moment only when the acts of the judiciary confer the prestige on judges that gives it force. Lacking prestige because of *Dred Scott*, the Supreme Court's decision was flouted by President Lincoln and the Civil War Congress, and Chief Justice Taney could not secure compliance with his orders in *Merryman*. For similar reasons, the

1937 Supreme Court switched in time to save the nine from Roosevelt's court-packing plan. Its prestige reconstructed by a decade and a half of attention to individual rights, the 1952 Supreme Court forced Truman to give up seizure of the steel mills while a war was under way. Prestigious as never before because of *Brown*, Earl Warren and his brethren compelled a reluctant President Eisenhower to send troops to Little Rock. Although the circumstances are not ordinarily so dramatic, throughout American history the capacity of the courts to enforce their decisions has depended on the degree to which they personify justice. It is the source of their authority to shape public policy.

Another way of saying the same thing is that the legitimacy of judicial policy-making power is validated by inherent judicial powerlessness. The other branches of government can enforce their will by their control of the "strength or the wealth of the society," as Alexander Hamilton put it, but the courts "can take no active resolution whatever." When judges purport to dispense distributive justice, they act as though they control the wealth of the society. When they purport to dispense political justice, they act as though they control the strength of the society. Lacking control over the sword or the purse, however, courts lack the power to enforce such judgments except to the degree that the other branches of government defer to them.

More than a century ago, Walter Bagehot wrote in his classic work *The English Constitution* that one of the functions of the House of Commons is "an informing function—a function which though in its present form quite modern is singularly analogous to a medieval function. In old times one office of the House of Commons was to inform the Sovereign what was wrong. It laid before the Crown the grievances and complaints of particular interests. Since the publication of the Parliamentary debates a corresponding office of Parliament is to lay these same grievances, these same complaints, before the nation, which is the present sovereign. The nation needs it quite as much as the king ever needed it."[1] Obviously, this informing function is performed in the United States by Congress, particularly through the hearings conducted by specialized committees. But we are a vastly more heterogeneous society than the Victorian England which was the focus of Bagehot's thinking, and it has become necessary for us to develop additional mechanisms to serve the informing function. Pluralism does not work unless all those with sufficient interests in common to make up its elements are able to inform others of their interests.

Perceived as a process that requires representative ratification to have effect, judicial policy making is such an institutional mechanism. Although such a function for the judiciary may not have been contemplated by the framers of the Constitution, in the last thirty years litigation has been the most important way of informing the nation of the grievances of disadvantaged minorities. Bagehot wrote of the English nation, "It only comprehends what is familiar to it—what comes into its own experience, what squares with its own thoughts. 'I never heard of such a thing in my life,' the middle-class Englishman says, and he thinks he so refutes an argument."[2] The same could be said of a middle-class American. Without the dramatic intervention of so dignified an institution as a court, which puts its own prestige and authority on the line, most middle-class Americans would not be informed about such grievances. They would not have known about the plight of blacks under segregation except for *Brown*. They would not have known about the plight of the retarded except for cases like Willowbrook. Were it not for cases like *McRae*, they would not have been aware of the situation of poor teenagers who require abortions.

For judicial attempts to exercise policy-making authority to succeed, judges and litigators must persuade others either that the courts traditionally enjoy or that the law confers on them this authority. This is a powerful restraint on the courts. In an extraordinary moment, the period when the courts led the nation in ridding itself of enforced racial segregation, judicial authority was especially great because it had charismatic qualities. Even then, however, actual power remained in the hands of the elected representatives of the people. If President Eisenhower had not dispatched troops to Little Rock, the courts would have been powerless to desegregate Central High School. When those representatives respect the authority of the unelected branch of government, in effect, they ratify judicial judgments, as Eisenhower did despite his evident unhappiness with the course he followed. It is that process of ratification, which does not take place when the judiciary lacks prestige, that confirms the legitimacy of ventures beyond the realm of corrective justice.

To argue that representative ratification confers legitimacy on judicial policy making implies a corollary: refusal to ratify is also legitimate. This is not necessarily to say that it is right. I believe, for example, in the rightness of the Supreme Court's decision in *Griggs*, prohibiting any employment practice that operates to exclude blacks and cannot be shown to be related to job performance (see Chapter 5). Yet *Griggs* clearly goes beyond the realm of corrective justice because it requires the hiring of blacks in circumstances in which there is no showing of intent to discriminate and racially neutral criteria for employment may be determined in good faith. Were it not that a compelling principle of corrective justice is involved, that is, providing equal employment opportunity, the Supreme Court's decision would be illegitimate. Were it not that a discrete and insular minority suffering from prejudice is involved, that is, blacks, the Court's order would be, nevertheless, illegitimate even though the decision is based on a compelling principle of corrective justice. (If Duke Power Company's employment criteria have the unintended discriminatory effect of favoring applicants born in North Carolina over applicants born elsewhere, the corrective justice principle of equal opportunity should not be sufficient to invalidate those criteria. Those born in the forty-nine states other than North Carolina do not constitute a disadvantaged minority.) Yet, though *Griggs* seems right, it treads on territory that a representative democracy ordinarily reserves to elected officials. The people's representatives confirm the legitimacy of *Griggs* by ratifying it, either expressly or *sub silentio*. Though I believe they would be wrong not to ratify *Griggs*, this approach compels me to accept the right of elected representatives to do such a wrong. Those like me who believe in the rightness of *Griggs* are required by this approach to persuade others, not that the decision is right—though that would be desirable—but that it is right for the courts to decide *Griggs* as they did.

Judicial dispensation of distributive justice in *Griggs*, therefore, does not usurp the power of the representative branches of government. Rather, it places the question dealt with in *Griggs* on the agenda of the representative branches. The minority in whose interest the decision was rendered could take care of itself if it competed fairly on the plateau of American politics. But it does not compete fairly. Bagehot pointed out that, lacking a mechanism to make it hear the complaints of minorities, "a free nation never hears any side save its own. The newspapers only repeat the side their purchasers like: the favorable arguments are set out, elaborated, illustrated; the adverse arguments maimed, misstated, confused. The worst judge, they say, is a deaf judge; the most dull government is a free government on matters its ruling classes will not hear."[3] In Bagehot's view, it is "the second function of Parliament in point of importance, that to some extent it makes us hear what other wise we should not."[4] In my view, it is the first function of contemporary American courts in point of importance that to some extent they make us hear what otherwise we should not. Having heard, we may reject. But we have little claim to being a democratic society if we deny the minorities through the courts the opportunity to be heard.

In suggesting that it is legitimate—which does not make it right—for the representative branches of government to reject what minorities claim as their due by nullifying judicial ventures in distributive justice or political justice, I do not mean to imply that nullification is also legitimate in the realm of corrective justice. Lincoln acted legitimately when he refused to obey Justice Taney's venture in political justice in *Dred Scott* but illegitimately when he ignored Justice Taney's corrective justice order in *Merryman*. The latter was illegitimate even though Lincoln's refusal to respect the order in *Merryman* may be attributable to Taney's loss of prestige in *Dred Scott*. A century later, those southern political leaders who defied the Supreme Court's decision in *Brown* acted illegitimately. Although *Brown* had enormous distributive justice and political justice implications, of itself, it was a judicial exercise in corrective justice. The Supreme Court ordered an end to intentional discrimination by race, a traditional and lawful judicial responsibility, even though it was a responsibility the courts had long evaded.

Examined in this way, judicial policy making cannot be said to thwart representative policy making; rather, it is an aspect of representative policy making, contributing to it in ways that have proved essential in making American democracy work. Our review of the way litigation is employed in promoting racial equality, in attempting to make the votes of all count equally, in promoting sexual equality, in helping women control their own reproductive capacity, in attempting to transform public assistance to the poor from charity to a right, in attempting to stop a war, in challenging government secrecy and government information gathering, in attempting to free the inmates of asylums and improve conditions in asylums, in attempting to abolish the death penalty, and in attempting to protect the environment makes it plain that what may be said by a judge in deciding a court case is never the last word on a question of public policy. In every instance, litigation operates as part of a public policy debate. Frequently, it launches the debate, as *Brown* launched the public debate over racial equality and as litigation challenging conditions in asylums like Partlow and Willowbrook launched the public debate over how the state should deal with the retarded.

For participants in public policy litigation, there are many lessons that follow from this view of the process. Interest groups attempting to advance their causes may lack the capacity to influence their elected representatives and, so, turn to litigators instead of employing the ordinary political processes. Yet in bringing litigation, their capacity to influence public officeholders may grow. On the other hand, inattention to what takes place in the representative branches of government while litigation is underway makes it more difficult to prevail in court and makes it less likely that a favorable decision will secure compliance. Litigators serving interest groups in advancing causes do not serve their clients effectively if they limit themselves to persuading judges; they must also persuade the public. Arguments and evidence presented in court may serve that purpose if they are publicized. Even arguments that do not prevail in court may secure public attention to a grievance that a disadvantaged minority cannot place on the public agenda in any other way.

The cause litigator's duty to persuade does not end with a loss in court. By going to court on behalf of interest groups such as poor women seeking abortions, or prisoners sentenced to death, or the mentally retarded, litigators establish themselves as spokesmen for their clients' causes. In the case of such minorities, though their members have powerful interests in common, they lack the means for bringing forward spokesmen from their own number or otherwise finding spokesmen for their causes. Lawyers espousing such causes under the auspices of organizations practicing public interest law fill a vacuum by establishing themselves as spokesmen. When the United States Supreme Court held in *General Electric Company* v. *Gilbert*[5] that the federal law against sex discrimination in employment does not require that disabilities arising from pregnancy should be compensated as disabilities attributable to other causes are, women's rights activists turned to Congress for a remedy (see Chapter 6). Their principal spokesmen were litigators who had lost *Gilbert*. When the Supreme Court held that standardless death sentences and imposition of the death sentence by a jury in the same proceeding as it determined guilt were constitutional, Congress was asked to impose a moratorium on executions until the Supreme Court reviewed the argument that capital punishment itself is unconstitutional (see Chapter 10). The principal spokesmen for death row inmates were litigators who had lost *McGautha* v. *California*,[6] the case in which the procedural objections to the administration of the death penalty were rejected.

The litigators who lost *Gilbert* prevailed on Congress to provide a remedy; the litigators who lost *McGautha* did not. But in both instances, as in many others, the availability of effective spokesmen to carry on the fight in other arenas is an outgrowth of litigation. The difficulties the clients in these cases encounter in being heard in the ordinary political process are manifest in their lack of other spokes-men. The importance of litigation in enabling them to be heard is manifest in the emergence of their lawyers as their spokesmen in the political forum as in court. It seems clear, therefore, that cause litigators unprepared to carry on the struggle in the political forum do not fully serve the needs of their clients. The disadvantaged resort to litigation as a way of entering the political process; win or lose in court, their struggle is not at an end. If they obtain distributive justice or political justice from the courts, representative ratification is required to ensure that they actually benefit. If they lose in court, they still have a chance of prevailing elsewhere if they make themselves heard through litigation and, thereby, if they persuade the representative branches of government.

Judges presiding over public policy litigation are gener-ally acutely aware of these constraints on their powers. If they do not persuade others that it is proper for them to decide as they do the questions on which they pronounce judgments, they sacrifice their capacity to personify justice. Again, this does not mean that they must persuade others that their decisions are right; only that, as a matter of tradi-tion or of law, they are entitled to hand down such decisions. Yet this is often a Herculean task and the stakes are enormous. The prestige of the courts rests on the way judges meet this responsibility, and their authority to secure compliance with all their decisions, even those dispensing corrective justice, derives from their prestige.

It is, of course, tempting to many judges to maintain their authority by avoiding far-reaching decisions. But this is not the way they establish their prestige. As *Brown* indicates, the farthest reaching decisions may do the most to enhance judicial prestige. For judges concerned with maintaining their authority, the task is to make certain that their deci-sions are firmly grounded in principles of corrective justice.

When they venture into distributive justice or political justice, they have a duty to make it plain why the ordinary political processes will not suffice or why the beneficiaries of their decisions must rely on the courts to advance their causes. Inattentive to their need to persuade, or unable to persuade, judges run the risk that their decisions will be nullified, perhaps as quickly as Justice William O. Douglas's brethren on the Supreme Court nullified his action enjoining the bombing of Cambodia (see Chapter 9).

The common responsibility of all those engaged in public policy litigation is to persuade. Because they circumvent the ordinary political processes, they must be all the more persuasive. Even if they cannot persuade others of the rightness of their causes or of the results they achieve through litigation they must persuade the participants in the ordinary political process that they are right to proceed along a different path. If public policy litigation is legitimate because of its informing function, it follows that those who do not use it to inform sap it of legitimacy.

Notes

Introduction

1. Alexis de Tocqueville, *Democracy in America* (London: Oxford University Press, 1946), p. 83.

2. Raoul Berger, *Government by Judiciary* (Cambridge, Mass.: Harvard University Press, 1977), p. 408.

3. William French Smith, Address to the Federal Legal Council in Reston, Virginia, October 29, 1981, as quoted in *New York Times*, October 30, 1981.

4. Charles Fried, "Curbing the Judiciary," *New York Times*, November 10, 1981.

5. Anthony Lewis, "Earl Warren," in *The Warren Court: A Critical Analysis*, ed. by Richard H. Sayler, Barry B. Boyer, and Robert E. Gooding, Jr. (New York: Chelsea House, 1980), p. 7.

6. Learned Hand, *The Bill of Rights* (Cambridge, Mass.: Harvard University Press, 1962), p. 73.

7. United States v. Nixon, 418 U.S. 683 (1974).

8. Powell v. McCormack, 395 U.S. 786 (1969).

9. Roe v. Wade, 410 U.S. 113 (1973).

10. Califano v. McRae, 433 U.S. 916 (1977).

11. Harris v. McRae, 48 U.S. L.W. 4941 (1980).

12. Goldwater v. Carter, 617 F.2d 697 (1979).

Chapter 1 Making Pluralism Work

1. U.S. 483 (1954).

2. Israel Zangwill, *The Melting Pot* (New York: Macmillan, 1909), p. 17.

3. 60 U.S. 393 (1857).

4. Robert Paul Wolff, *A Critique of Pure Tolerance* (Boston: Beacon Press, 1965), p. 45.

5. Max Weber, *Economy and Society* (New York: Bedminster Press, 1968), 1:215 et seq.

Chapter 2 Thoughts on Legitimacy

1. *Federalist Papers*, No. 78

2. Aristotle, *Nicomachean Ethics*, Book V, Chapter 7.

3. Ibid.

4. Ibid.

5. Ibid. Chapter 6.

6. Baker v. Carr, 369 U.S. 186.

7. Korematsu v. United States, 323 U.S. 214 (1944).

8. 60 U.S. 393 (1857).

9. 17 Fed. Cas. 144 (1861).

10. 304 U.S. 144 (1938).

11. Kovacs v. Cooper, 336 U.S. 77 (1949).

12. *Federalist Papers*, No. 78.

13. Jones v. Opelika, 319 U.S. 103 (1943).

14. John Hart Ely, *Democracy and District* (Cambridge, Mass.: Harvard University Press, 1980), p. 88.

15. Eugene Rostow, *The Sovereign Prerogative*, 1962), p. 165.

16. Geoffrey Hazard, "Social Justice through Civil Justice," *University of Chicago Law Review* 36 (1969): 699.

17. 394 U.S. 618 (1969).

18. 397 U.S. 471 (1970).

19. New York State Association for Retarded Children, Inc. v. Rockefeller, 393 F. Supp. 715 (consent decree approved) (E.D. N.Y., 1975).

Chapter 3 Racial Equality: Assuming Leadership

1. 347 U.S. 483 (1954).

2. *New York Times*, May 18, 1954.

3. *Washington Post and Times-Herald*, May 18, 1954.

4. *San Francisco Chronicle*, May 18, 1954.

5. *Minneapolis Tribune*, May 18, 1954.

6. *St. Louis Post-Dispatch*, May 18, 1954.

7. *Hartford Courant*, May 18, 1954.

8. *Chattanooga Times*, May 18, 1954.

9. *Pittsburgh Courier*, May 18, 1954.

10. *Chicago Defender*, May 18, 1954.

11. *Atlanta Daily World,* May 18, 1954.

12. *Boston Chronicle,* May 18, 1954.

13. *New York Times,* May 18, 1954.

14. Ibid.

15. Ibid.

16. Ibid.

17. Executive Order 9981, July 26, 1948.

18. Brown v. Board of Education, October Term 1952, Supreme Court of the United States, Brief for the United States as Amicus Curiae, December 1952, p. 6.

19. Ibid.

20. Ibid., p. 4.

21. Friedman, ed., *Argument: The Oral Argument before the Supreme Court in Brown v. Board of Education of Topeka, 1952–5* (New York: Chelsea House, 1969), p. 279.

22. Ibid., p. 135.

23. Ibid.

24. 60 U.S. (19 How.) 393 (1857).

25. 347 U.S. 483.

26. Bolling v. Sharpe, 347 U.S. 497 (1954).

27. Id. at 500.

28. Id.

29. Brown v. Board of Education.

30. Id., 347 U.S. 483.

31. Jack Harrison Pollack, *Earl Warren: The Judge Who Changed America* (Englewood Cliffs, N.J.: Prentice-Hall, 1979), p. 174.

32. Richard Kluger, *Simple Justice* (New York: Knopf, 1975), p. 707.

33. Ibid.

34. Pollack, *Earl Warren,* p. 176.

35. Kluger, *Simple Justice,* pp. 708–9.

36. Bolling v. Sharpe at 497.

37. Plessy v. Ferguson, 163 U.S. 537 (1896).

38. See Edmund Wilson, *Patriotic Gore* (New York: Farrar, Straus, Giroux, 1965), pp. 535–37.

39. Louis A. Martinet to Albion W. Tourgeé, October 5, 1891, in Otto H. Olsen, *The Thin Disguise* (New York: Humanities Press, 1967), p. 57.

40. State v. Hicks, 44 La. Ann. 770 (1892).

41. Albion W. Tourgeé to Louis A. Martinet, October 31, 1893, in Olsen, *Thin Disguise,* pp. 78–80.

42. Plessy v. Ferguson at 537.

43. Id. at 552.

44. Id. at 551.

45. Id. at 559.

46. Id. at 559.

47. *New York Tribune,* May 19, 1896.

48. Ibid., March 7, 1857.

49. See Olsen, *Thin Disguise,* p. 25.

50. *New York Journal,* May 20, 1896.

51. Langston Hughes, *Fight for Freedom* (New York: Norton, 1962), p. 22.

52. 245 U.S. 60 (1917).

53. Id. at 82.

54. Nathan Margold, "Preliminary Report to the Joint Committee Supervising the Expenditure of the 1930 Appropriation of the American Fund for Public Service to the NAACP" (unpublished and undated, probably 1931), p. 1.

55. Ibid., p. 3.

56. Ibid.

57. Ibid.

58. Ibid., p. 93.

59. Ibid., pp. 93–94.

60. W.E.B. DuBois, "Does the Negro Need Separate Schools," *Journal of Negro Education* 4 (1935): 328.

61. Ibid.

62. Ibid.

63. Pearson v. Murray, 169 Md. 478 (1936).

64. Missouri Ex Rel. Gaines v. Canada, 305 U.S. 337 (1938).

65. Id. at 350.

66. Sipuel v. *University of Oklahoma,* 332 U.S. 631 (1948).

67. *Sweatt v. Painter,* 339 U.S. 629 (1950).

68. *McLaurin v. Oklahoma State Regents,* 339 U.S. 687 (1950).

69. *Sweatt v. Painter and McLaurin v. Oklahoma State Regents,* Memorandum for the United States as Amicus Curiae, 1950.

70. Henderson v. United States, 339 U.S. 816 (1950), Memorandum for the United States as Amicus Curiae.

71. *Sweatt* v. *Painter* at 633–34.

72. *McLaurin* v. *Oklahoma State Regents* at 641.

73. *Jackson Daily News*, May 18, 1954.

74. W. E. B. DuBois, *National Guardian*, May 31, 1954.

75. *Just Schools: A Special Report Commemorating the 25th Anniversary of the Brown Decision* (Chapel Hill: Institute for Southern Studies, 1979), p. 54.

76. W. E. B. DuBois, "Two Hundred Years of Segregated Schools," February 1955, reprinted in Philip S. Foner, *W. E. B. DuBois Speaks* (New York: Pathfinder, 1970), p. 283.

77. Martin Luther King, Jr., *Stride toward Freedom*, (New York: Harper & Bros., 1959), p. 197.

78. Ibid., p. 156.

79. *Browder* v. *Gayle*, 142 F. Supp. 707 (N.D. Ala. 1956), 712.

80. Id. at 352 U.S. 903 (1956) per curiam.

81. Max Weber, *Economy and Society* (New York: Bedminster Press, 1968), p. 245.

Chapter 4 Racial Equality: Relinquishing Leadership

1. *Brown* v. *Board of Education*, 349 U.S. 294 (1955).

2. Id. at 301.

3. Robert Carter, "The Warren Court and Desegregation," 1969, reprinted in Derrick A. Bell, Jr., *Race and Racism and American Law*, (Boston: Little Brown, 1973), p. 457.

4. *Ex Parte Merryman*, 17 Fed. Cas. 144 (1861).

5. Alexander Bickel, *The Least Dangerous Branch*, (Indianapolis: Bobbs-Merrill, 1962), p. 255.

6. Emmett John Hughes, *The Ordeal of Power* (New York: 1962), Dell, p. 211.

7. *New York Times*, July 18, 1957.

8. Hughes, *Ordeal of Power*, p. 212.

9. 358 U.S. 1 (1958).

10. Id. at 19.

11. Bickel, *The Least Dangerous Branch*, p. 267.

12. United States Commission on Civil Rights, *Fulfilling the Letter and Spirit of the Laws: Desegregation of the Nation's Schools*, 1976.

13. 377 U.S. 218 (1964).

14. 382 U.S. 103 (1965).

15. 391 U.S. 430 (1968).

16. 396 U.S. 19 (1969).

17. 402 U.S. 1 (1971).

18. Id. at 24.

19. Bob Woodward and Scott Armstrong, *The Brethren* (New York: Simon and Schuster, 1979), p. 112.

20. See, for example, President Nixon's Message to Congress, March 17, 1972.

21. See, for example, H.R. Joint Resolution 620, 92d Cong., 1st sess. (1971).

22. 413 U.S. 189 (1973).

23. Id. at 201–2.

24. 418 U.S. 717 (1974).

25. Id. at 752.

26. See *Columbus Board of Education* v. *Penick*, 443 U.S. 449 (1979); *Dayton Board of Education* v. *Brinkman*, 443 U.S. 526 (1979).

27. James S. Coleman, et al., *Equality of Educational Opportunity* (Washington, D.C.: U.S. Government Printing Office, 1969), p. 326.

28. Christopher Jencks, *Inequality* (New York: Harper Colophon, 1978), p. 8.

29. Kenneth B. Clark, "Alternative Public School Systems," in Harvard Education Review, *Equal Education Opportunity* (Cambridge, Mass.: Harvard, 1969), p. 174.

30. *New York Times*, March 16, 1981.

31. See Gary Orfield, *Must We Bus? Segregated Schools and National Policy* (Washington, D.C.: The Brookings Institution, 1978), p. 77.

32. 265 U.S. 60 (1917).

33. Id. at 74.

34. Id. at 81.

35. 271 U.S. 323 (1926).

36. Id. at 330.

37. Id. at 331.

38. See Leon Litwack, *North of Slavery* (Chicago: University of Chicago Press, 1961), p. 168.

39. 334 U.S. 1 (1948).

40. Id. at 18.

41. Quoted in Clement E. Vose, *Caucasians Only* (Berkeley and Los Angeles: University of California Press, 1969), p. 212.

42. Ibid., p. 213.

43. Article I, §26, California Constitution.

44. Reitman v. Mulkey, 387 U.S. 369 (1967).

45. 42 U.S.C. 1982.

46. Jones v. Alfred H. Mayer Co., 392 U.S. 709 (1968).

47. 402 U.S. 137 (1971).

48. Id. at 141.

49. 422 U.S. 490 (1975).

50. Id. at 523.

51. 425 U.S. 284 (1976).

52. Kenneth B. Noble, "Suburbia: Blacks Surveyed," *New York Times*, August 10, 1980.

53. 42 U.S.C. §2000e et seq.

54. 401 U.S. 424 (1971).

55. Id. at 432.

56. Id. at 431.

57. Woodward and Armstrong, *The Brethren*, p. 123.

58. 426 U.S. 229 (1976).

59. 42 U.S.C. 1981.

60. Washington v. Davis, 426 U.S. 229 (1976).

61. 438 U.S. 265 (1978).

62. Id. at 316.

63. 99 S. Ct. 2721 (1979).

64. 48 U.S.L.W. 4979 (June 2, 1980).

65. 97 S. Ct. 1272 (1977).

66. 97 S. Ct. 555 (1977).

Chapter 5 Political Equality: A Lustrous Achievement

1. John Locke, *On Civil Government* (London: Everyman's Library, 1924), p. 118.

2. Article I, Section 3.

3. Article II, Section 1.

4. Article II, Section 1.

5. Article I, Section 3.

6. Article V.

7. Article I, Section 7.

8. Article II, Section 2.

9. Fourteenth Amendment, Section 2. Originally, this provision was in Article I and applied only to "free persons." Their number was to be increased by three-fifths of the number of slaves.

10. Robert B. McKay, *Reapportionment* (New York: Twentieth Century Fund, 1965), pp. 24–25.

11. 328 U.S. 549 (1946).

12. Id. at 552.

13. Id. at 556.

14. United States v. Carolene Products, 304 U.S. 144 (1938), footnote 4.

15. Dyer v. Kazuhisa Abe, 138 F. Supp. 220 (D. Hawaii 1956), *reversed on other grounds*, 256 F. 2d 728 (9th Cir. 1958).

16. 364 U.S. 339 (1960).

17. 369 U.S. 186 (1962).

18. Id. at 226.

19. Id. at 301.

20. Id. at 268.

21. Archibald Cox, *The Role of the Supreme Court in American Government* (New York: Oxford University Press, 1976), p. 100.

22. Raoul Berger, *Government by Judiciary* (Cambridge, Mass.: Harvard University Press, 1977), p. 407.

23. See, for example, William Van Alstyne, "The Right to Vote, and the Understanding of the Thirty-Ninth Congress," *Supreme Court Review* 33 (1965).

24. Jack H. Pollack, *Earl Warren: The Judge Who Changed America* (Englewood Cliffs, N.J.: Prentice-Hall, 1979), p. 207.

25. 344 U.S. 533 (1964).

26. Victor S. Navasky, *Kennedy Justice* (New York: Atheneum, 1971), p. 321.

27. Quoted in Robert G. Dixon, Jr., *Democratic Representation* (New York: Oxford University Press, 1968), p. 212.

28. Reynolds v. Sims, 373 U.S. 533, 577 (1964).

29. Robert B. McKay, *Reapportionment Reappraised* (New York Twentieth Century Fund, 1968), pp. 12–13.

30. See, for example, Avery v. Midland County, 390 U.S. 474 (1968); Hadley v. Junior College, 397 U.S. 50 (1970); Rosenthal v. Board of Education, 479 F.2d 276 2d Cir. (1974).

31. See, for example, Salyer Land Co. v. Tulare Lake Basin Water Storage Co., 410 U.S. 719 (1973).

32. Navasky, *Kennedy Justice*, p. 321.

33. 42 U.S.C. 1973 et seq.

34. United States Commission on Civil Rights, *Political Participation*, 1968), p. 12.

35. See, for example, Hadnott v. Amos, 394 U.S. 358.

36. 403 U.S. 124 (1971).

37. 412 U.S. 755 (1973).

38. Id. at 767.

39. Id. at 769.

40. Id. at 770.

41. Laurence H. Tribe, *American Constitutional Law* (Mineola, N.Y.: Foundation Press, 1978), p. 754.

42. 48 U.S.L.W. 4436 (April 22, 1980).

43. Id. at 4440.

44. Id. at 4446.

45. Id. at 4448.

46. Id. at 4449.

47. Id. at 4452.

48. *New York Times*, December 26, 1980.

Chapter 6 Sexual Equality and the Difficulties of Sisterhood

1. Quoted in Barbara Babcock, Ann Freedman, Eleanor Norton, and Susan Ross, *Sex Discrimination and the Law* (Boston: Little, Brown, 1975), p. 5.

2. Bradwell v. Illinois, 83 U.S. 120 (1873).

3. 404 U.S. 71 (1971).

4. Quoted in Jack Greenberg, *Judicial Process and Social Change* (St. Paul: West Publishing, 1977), p. 373.

5. Reed v. Reed, 404 U.S. 71 (1971).

6. Barbara Brown, Thomas I. Emerson, Gail Falk, and Ann Freedman, "The Equal Rights Amendment: A Constitutional Basis for Equal Rights for Women," *Yale Law Journal* 80 (1971): 871.

7. 411 U.S. 677 (1973).

8. Id. at 686–87.

9. Id. at 692.

10. 416 U.S. 351 (1974).

11. 410 U.S. 113 (1973).

12. 410 U.S. 179 (1973).

13. 417 U.S. 484 (1974).

14. Id. at 496.

15. Id. at 496–97.

16. 429 U.S. 125 (1976).

17. 42 U.S.C. Sec. 2000e et seq.

18. Pub. L. No. 95-555, 92 Stat. 2076 (1978).

19. Id.

20. 429 U.S. 190 (1976).

21. Id. at 197.

22. Id. at 211.

23. Id. at 220–21.

24. 342 F. Supp 1224 (D. Minn. 1972), aff'd., 477 F.2d 1292 (8th Cir. 1973).

25. Id. at 1302.

26. 526 S.W. 2d 766 (Tex. Cir. App. 1975).

27. Califano v. Goldfarb, 97 S. Ct. 1021 (1977); Califano v. Webster, 97 S. Ct. 1192 (1977).

28. Massachusetts v. Feeney, 442 U.S. 256 (1979).

29. 429 U.S. 421.

Chapter 7 Retreating under Fire

1. 410 U.S. 113 (1973).

2. *New York Times*, August 19, 20, 1962.

3. 367 U.S. 497 (1961).

4. Id. at 539.

5. Id. at 541.

6. Lochner v. New York, 198 U.S. 45 (1905).

7. 381 U.S. 479 (1965).

8. Id. at 484–85.

9. Id. at 486–87.

10. Id. at 491.

11. Id. at 524.

12. Id. 526–27.

13. Lawrence Lader, *Abortion* (Indianapolis: Bobbs Merrill, 1966), p. 1.

14. Ibid., p. 2.

15. *New York Times*, March 8, 1966.

16. The New York Civil Liberties Union (of which the author was then director) arranged at the time for private payment of the costs of the transcript.

17. Arlene Carmen and Howard Moody, *Abortion Counseling and Social Change* (New York: Judson Press, 1973).

18. U.S. v. Vuitch, 402 U.S. 62 (1971).

19. *New York Times*, February 17, 1969.

20. Doe v. Bolton, 410 U.S. 179 (1973); Roe v. Wade, 410 U.S. 113 (1973).

21. Roe v. Wade, at 153.

22. Id. at 163.

23. Id.

24. Id. at 174.

25. Petition for rehearing, Roe v. Wade, February 1973.

26. John Hart Ely, "The Wages of Crying Wolf," *Yale Law Journal* 82 (1973): 935–37.

27. Id. at 935.

28. Laurence H. Tribe, "Foreword: Toward a Model of Roles in the Due Process of Law," *Harvard Law Review* 87, 1.

29. Id. at 14.

30. 432 U.S. 438 (1977).

31. 432 U.S. 464 (1977).

32. 432 U.S. 519 (1977).

33. Pub. L. No. 94–439, §209 Stat. 1434 (1976).

34. McRae v. Mathews, 421 F. Supp. 533 (E.D. N.Y. 1976).

35. Califano v. McRae, 433 U.S. 916 (1977).

36. Harris v. McRae, 48 LW 4941 (1980).

37. No. 76 C. 1804 (E.D. N.Y.), January 15, 1980.

38. Id. at 315–16.

39. Id. at 321.

40. Harris v. McRae at 4948.

41. Id. at 4953.

Chapter 8 Ending Poverty: Too Great a Task

1. John Kenneth Galbraith, *The Affluent Society* (Boston: Houghton Mifflin, 1958).

2. Ibid., p. 328.

3. Ibid., p. 325.

4. Ibid., p. 326.

5. Ibid., p. 330.

6. Ibid., p. 331.

7. Ibid.

8. Michael Harrington, *The Other America* (New York: Macmillan, 1963). The page references that follow are to the Penguin Books edition (Baltimore, 1963).

9. Ibid., pp. 170–71.

10. Ibid., p. 181.

11. Frances Fox Piven and Richard Cloward, *Regulating the Poor* (New York: Pantheon, 1971), p. 291.

12. Charles Reich, "Individual Rights and Social Welfare: The Emerging Legal Issues," *Yale Law Journal* 74, (1965): 1256–57.

13. Edward V. Sparer, "Social Welfare Law Testing," *The Practical Lawyer* 12 (1966): 4.

14. Quoted in Robert M. O'Neil, *The Price of Dependency* (New York: Dutton, 1970), p. 287.

15. *Federalist Papers*, No. 78.

16. Daniel P. Moynihan, *The Politics of a Guaranteed Income* (New York: Random House, 1973), p. 330.

17. Richard A. Cloward and Frances Fox Piven, "A Strategy to End Poverty," *The Nation*, May 2, 1966.

18. Frances Fox Piven and Richard Cloward, *Poor People's Movements* (New York: Pantheon, 1977), p. 276.

19. King v. Smith, 392 U.S. 309 (1968).

20. Shapiro v. Thompson, 394 U.S. 618 (1969).

21. Goldberg v. Kelly, 397 U.S. 254 (1970).

22. Parrish v. Civil Service Commission, 66 Cal. 2d 260, 425 P. 2d 223 (1967).

23. Shapiro v. Thompson at 633.

24. Id. at 629.

25. *Brief of Amici Curiae*: The Center on Social Welfare Policy and Law, National Welfare Rights Organization, Associated Catholic Charities, Inc. and Seven Neighborhood Legal Services Offices Now Prosecuting Similar Cases, *Dandridge v. Williams* (1969).

26. Dandridge v. Williams, 397 U.S. 471 (1970).

27. Jefferson v. Hackney, 406 U.S. 535 at 575 (1972).

28. Camara v. Municipal Court, 387 U.S. 523 (1967).

29. Wyman v. James, 400 U.S. 309 (1971).

30. E.g., Department of Agriculture v. Moreno, 418 U.S. 528 (1973); Department of Agriculture v. Murry, 413 U.S. 528 (1973).

31. Edward Sparer, "The Right to Welfare," in Norman Dorsen, ed., *The Rights of Americans* (New York: Pantheon, 1970), p. 82.

32. Daniel P. Moynihan, *The Politics of a Guaranteed Income*, p. 334.

33. Piven and Cloward, *Poor People's Movements*, p. 295.

Chapter 9 Challenging War: A Futile Effort

1. 323 U.S. 214 (1944).

2. Id. at 216.

3. Id. at 218–19.

4. Id. at 219.

5. Id. at 223.

6. Ex parte Milligan, 71 U.S. (4 Wall) 2 (1866).

7. Contrast, for example, Yates v. United States, 354 U.S. 298 (1957) with Dennis v. United States, 341 U.S. 797 (1951).

8. 249 U.S. 47, 52 (1919).

9. United States v. Mitchell, 246 F. Supp. 874, 898 (1965).

10. 354 F. 2d 767 (2d Cir. 1966).

11. 386 U.S. 972 (1967).

12. Id. at 973.

13. Mora v. McNamara, 389 U.S. 934 (1967).

14. Baker v. Carr, 369 U.S. 186 (1962).

15. 343 U.S. 579 (1952).

16. Id. at 587.

17. Article III, Section 2.

18. Massachusetts v. Laird, 327 F. Supp. 378 (D. Mass. 1971), aff'd, 451 F.2d (1st Cir. 1971).

19. Transcript of proceedings in Berk v. Laird, June 5, 1970. Reprinted in Leon Friedman and Burt Neuborne, *Unquestioning Obedience to the President* (New York: Norton, 1972), p. 35.

20. Transcript of proceedings in Orlando v. Laird, June 12, 1970. Reprinted in Friedman and Neuborne, *Unquestioning Obedience*, p. 40.

21. Berk v. Laird, 429 F.2d 302, 306 (2d Cir. 1970).

22. Orlando v. Laird, 317 F. Supp. 1013, 1019, (E.D. N.Y. 1970).

23. Berk v. Laird, 317 F. Supp. 715, 730 (E.D. N.Y. 1970).

24. Orlando v. Laird, 443 F.2d 1039, 1043 (2d Cir. 1971).

25. U.S. Congress, Senate, *Congressional Record*, Cong., sess., 1971, 117, pt.: S. 8322 (daily ed. June 4, 1971).

26. Ibid., p. 8323.

27. U.S. Congress, Senate, *Congressional Record*, Cong., sess., 1971, 117 pt.: S. 9688 (daily ed. June 22, 1971).

28. New York Times Co. v. United States, 403 U.S. 713 (1971).

29. Holtzman v. Schlesinger, 361 F. Supp. 553 (E.D. N.Y. 1973), rev'd, 484 F.2d 1307 (2d Cir. 1973), cert. denied, 416 U.S. 936 (1974).

30. 94 S. Ct. 1 (1973).

31. 94 S. Ct. 8 (1973).

32. 94 S. Ct. 11 (1973).

33. Neuborne and Friedman, *Unquestioning Obedience*, pp. 273–74.

34. S. Rpt. 92–606 (Feb. 9, 1972).

35. 50 U.S.C. 1548(a).

Chapter 10 Challenging the National Security State: A Not-So-Futile Effort

1. Christopher Pyle, "Conus Intelligence: The Army Watches Civilian

Politics," *Washington Monthly*, January, 1970, p. 4.

2. 408 U.S. 1 (1972).

3. Id. at 13–14.

4. Id. at 26.

5. 430 F.2d 326 (2d Cir. 1973).

6. John Shattuck, *Rights of Privacy* (Skokie, Ill.: National Textbook Company, 1977), p. 81.

7. 454 F.2d 1362 (1st Cir. 1972).

8. 524 F.2d 862 (3d Cir. 1975).

9. 5 U.S.C. 552a.

10. 5 U.S.C. 552.

11. Handschu v. Special Division, 349 F. Supp. 766 (S.D. N.Y. 1972).

12. Kendrick v. Chandler, Cir. A. 76-C-449 (W.D. Tenn.)

13. Alliance to End Repression v. James O'Grady, et al., Civ. A. 74-C-3268 (N.D. Ill.); American Civil Liberties Union, et al. v. City of Chicago et al., Civ. A. 75-C3295 (N.D. Ill.).

14. Article I, Section 9.

15. Richardson v. Sokol, 409 F.2d 3 (3d Cir. 1969).

16. Richardson v. United States, 465 F2d 844 (3d Cir. 1972).

17. United States v. Richardson, 418 U.S. 166 (1974).

18. See e.g., Harrington v. Bush, 553 F.2d 190 (D.C. Cir. 1977).

19. United States v. Marchetti, 466 F.2d 1309 (4th Cir. 1972).

20. Victor Marchetti and John Marks, *The CIA and the Cult of Intelligence* (New York: Knopf, 1974).

21. Philip Agee, *Inside the Company: CIA Diary* (Harmondsworth: Penguin, 1974).

22. John Stockwell, *In Search of Enemies* (New York: Norton, 1978).

23. Frank Snepp, *Decent Interval* (New York: Random House, 1978).

24. Snepp v. United States, 48 LW 3527, S. Ct. February 19, 1980.

25. State of the Union Address, January 23, 1980.

26. Bob Woodward and Scott Armstrong, *The Brethren* (New York: Simon and Schuster, 1979).

27. Snepp v. United States at 3528.

28. Id. at 3530.

29. Anthony Lewis, "A Lawless Decision," *New York Times*, February 22, 1980.

30. Snepp v. United States at 3528.

31. Id. at 3527; emphasis added.

32. Haig v. Agee, 49 USLW 4869 (June 29, 1981).

33. Civ. A. 75-1773, D.D.C. 1976.

34. *Final Report of the Select Committee to Study Government Operations with Respect to Intelligence Activities*, United States Senate, 94th Cong., 2d sess., Report No. 94-755, April 23, 1976.

35. See "Comparison of Documents Released in *Halkins v. Helms* with the Final Report of the Senate Select Committee to Study Governmental Operations with Respect to Intelligence Activities" (Washington, D.C.: Center for National Security Studies, August 1979).

36. See e.g., Phillippi v. Central Intelligence Agency, 546 F.2d 1009 (D.C. Cir. 1976); Military Audit Project v. Bush, 418 F. Supp. 876 (D.D.C. 1976); Halperin v. Colby, Civ. A. 75-676 (D. D.C. 1976).

37. John D. Marks, *The Search for the Manchurian Candidate* (New York: New York Times Books, 1979).

38. George Lardner, Jr., "CIA Asking Hill to Cut Back Public Access to Agency's Files," *Washington Post*, February 29, 1980.

Chapter 11 Reforming Asylums: No Other Way

1. Stroud v. Swope, 187 F.2d 850 (9th Cir.) 1951.

2. George Bernard Shaw, preface to Sidney and Beatrice Webb, *English Prisons under Local Government*, 1922.

3. Warren Burger, Address to the American Bar Association, Houston, Texas, February 8, 1981.

4. Morton Birnbaum, "The Right to Treatment," *American Bar Association Journal* 46 (1960): 499.

5. Rouse v. Cameron, 373 F.2d 451 (D.C. Cir. 1966).

6. Id. at 457.

7. American Psychiatric Association Position Statement on the Question of Adequacy of Treatment, *American Journal of Psychiatry* 123 (1967): 1458.

8. Wyatt v. Stickney, 325 F. Supp. 781 (M.D. Ala. 1971).

9. Id. at 785.

10. Wyatt v. Stickney, 344 F. Supp. 373, 375 (1972).

11. Id. at 383–84.

12. Id. at 378.

13. Bruce Ennis, *Prisoners of Psychiatry* (New York: Harcourt, Brace, Jovanovich, 1972), p. 106.

14. Wyatt v. Stickney, Civil Action No. 3195-N M.D. Ala., March 2, 1972.

15. Id. "Motion to Add Persons Needed for Just Adjudication," September 21, 1971.

16. Id., October 25, 1979.

17. David J. Rothman, "Decarcerating Prisoners and Patients," *Civil Liberties Review*, Vol. 1, no. 1 (Fall 1973), p. 21.

18. 422 U.S. 563 (1975).

19. 357 F. Supp. 752 (E.D. N.Y. 1973).

20. Donaldson v. O'Connor, 493 F.2d 507, 518 (1974).

21. Id. at 527.

22. *Madness Network News* 2, no. 4 (September 1974): 16.

23. Bob Woodward and Scott Armstrong, *The Brethren* (New York: Simon & Schuster, 1979), p. 373.

24. O'Connor v. Donaldson at 576 (1975).

25. Id. at 573.

26. American Psychiatric Association Task Force on the Right to Treatment, "The Right to Adequate Care and Treatment for the Mentally Ill and Mentally Retarded," May 8, 1975, p. 5.

27. O'Connor v. Donaldson at 587–89.

28. New York State Association for Retarded Children, Inc. v. Rockefeller, 357 F. Supp. 752, 759 (E.D. N.Y. 1973).

29. Id. at 769.

30. Id.

31. New York State Association for Retarded Children, Inc. v. Carey, 393 F. Supp. 715 at 718 (E.D. N.Y. 1975) (consent decree approved).

32. Id. §V(1).

33. Id. §V(2).

34. New York State Association for Retarded Children, Inc. v. Carey, supra., January 2, 1980.

35. U.S.C.A. 2nd Cir. No 80-7289, 80-7295, June 4, 1980.

36. Id. at 6.

37. Pugh v. Locke, 406 F. Supp. 318 (M.D. Ala. 1976).

38. Id. at 323.

39. Frank M. Johnson, Jr., "Thinking about the Federal Judiciary," *New York Times*, April 9, 1977.

40. Palmigiano v. Garrahy, 448 F. Supp. 956 (D. R.I. 1977).

41. Pugh v. Locke, 406 F. Supp. 318 (M.D. Ala. 1976); Harris v. Cardwell, C.A. No. 75-185 (D. Ariz. 1977); Holt v. Sarver, 309 F. Supp. 362 (E.D. Ark. 1970); Ramos v. Lamm, C.A. No. 77-k-1093 (D. Colo. 1979); Anderson v. Redmon, 429 F. Supp. 1105 (D. Del. 1977); Costello v. Wainwright, 397 F. Supp. 20 (M.D. Fla. 1975); Williams v. Edwards, 547 F. 2d 1206 (5th Cir. 1977) (La.); Johnson v. Levine, 450 F. Supp. 648 (D. Md. 1978) and Nelson v. Collins, 455 F. Supp. 727 (D. Md. 1978); Gates v. Collier, 501 F.2d 1291 (5th Cir. 1974) (Miss.); Burks v. Teasdale, 603 F.2d 59 (8th Cir. 1979) (Mo.); Laaman v. Helgemoe, 437 F. Supp. 269 (D. N.H. 1977); Chapman v. Rhodes, 434 F. Supp. 1007 (S.D. Oh. 1977); Battle v. Anderson, 564 F.2d 388 (10th Cir. 1977) (Okla.); Palmigiano v. Garrahy, 443 F. Supp. 956 (D. R.I. 1977); Trigg v. Blanton, C.A. No. A6047 Fulton Co. Chncry Ct., Nashville, Tenn. (1978); Bustos v. Herschler, C.A. No. C76-143-B (D. Wyo. 1976); Inmates, D.C. Jail v. Jackson, 416 F. Supp. 100, 119 (D. D.C. 1976); Martinez-Rodrigues v. Jimenez, F. Supp. 582 (D. P.R. 1976), Barnes v. Gov't. of the V.I., 415 F. Supp. 1218 (D. V.I. 1976).

42. Georgia, Illinois, Indiana, Kentucky, Massachusetts, Nevada, New Mexico, North Carolina, South Carolina, Texas, Utah, and Washington.

43. Ingraham v. Wright, 97 S. Ct. 1407 (1977).

44. Bell v. Wolfish 441 U.S. 520 (1979).

45. Winters v. Miller, 446 F.2d 65 (2d Cir. 1971) cert, den. 404 U.S. 985 (1971).

46. Kaimowitz v. Mich. Dept. of Mental Hygiene (No. 73-19454-AW Cir. Ct. Wayne City, Mich., July 10, 1973).

47. Knecht v. Gillman, 488 F.2d 1136 (8th Cir. 1973); Mackey v. Procunier, 477 F.2d 877 (9th Cir. 1973).

48. Rogers v. Okin, Civil Action No. 75-1610-T (D. Mass., October 1979).

Chapter 12 Stopping Executions without Abolishing Capital Punishment

1. Quoted in Catherine Drinker Bowen, *John Adams and the American Revolution* (Boston: Little, Brown, 1950), pp. 394–95.

2. Dr. Benjamin Rush, *An Enquiry into the Effects of Public Punishments upon Criminals and upon Society* (Philadelphia: Joseph James, 1787).

3. Quoted in Philip Mackey, *Voices against Death* (New York: Burt Franklin & Co., 1976), p. 1.

4. These statistics are from William J. Bowers, *Executions in America* (Lexington, Mass.: Lexington Books, 1974).

5. Gerald Gottlieb, "Testing the Death Penalty," *Southern California Law Review* 34 (1961): 268.

6. *International Review on Public Opinion* 2, no. 3 (1967): 84. In 1960, the comparable figures were 51 percent in favor, 36 percent opposed, and 13 percent undecided.

7. Hamilton v. Alabama, 368 U.S. 52 (1961).

8. Maxwell v. Bishop, U.S. C.A. 8th Cir. 398 F.2d 138 (1968).

9. 391 U.S. 510 (1968).

10. Michael Meltsner, *Cruel and Unusual* (New York: Random House, 1973), pp. 166–67.

11. Maxwell v. Bishop, 398 U.S. 262 (1970).

12. McGautha v. California, 402 U.S. 183 (1971).

13. S. 1969, H.R. 8414, 92d Cong., 1st sess., (1971).

14. Brief for Petitioner Aikens v. California (1971) in Jack Greenberg, *Judicial Process and Social Change* (St. Paul: West Publishing, 1977), pp. 476–77.

15. Id. at 477.

16. Id. at 478.

17. Id. at 482.

18. Id. at 483.

19. Furman v. Georgia, 408 U.S. 238 (1972).

20. Id. at 310. In labeling death "a unique penalty," Stewart seemed to signal that the Supreme Court would not respond sympathetically to lawsuits challenging lesser sentences as also "freakishly imposed."

21. Id. at 400. Burger confessed, however, that "there is little reason to believe that sentencing standards in any form will substantially alter the discretionary character of the prevailing system of sentencing in capital cases" (Id. at 401).

22. Id. at 401.

23. Woodson v. North Carolina, 428 U.S. 280 (1976); Roberts v. Louisiana, U.S. (1976).

24. Gregg v. Georgia, 428 U.S. 153 (1976); Jurek v. Texas, 428 U.S. 262 (1976); Profitt v. Florida, 428 U.S. 242 (1976).

25. Norman Mailer, *The Executioner's Song* (Boston: Little, Brown, 1979).

26. Martin Garbus, *Ready for the Defense* (New York: Farrar, Straus & Giroux, 1971), pp. 243–44.

27. Ibid., p. 244.

28. Robert Lee Massie, "Death by Degrees," *Esquire* 75 (April 1971): 179.

29. Mailer, *Executioner's Song*, p. 784.

30. Aryeh Neier, "'Butting In' for the Utah Slayer," *New York Times*, January 8, 1977.

Chapter 13 Protecting the Environment: The Wrong Way

1. Rachel Carson, *The Silent Spring* (Boston: Houghton Mifflin, 1962).
2. Federal Power Act 16 U.S.C. 803(a) (1920).
3. Scenic Hudson Preservation Conference v. FPC, 354 F.2d 608 (1965).
4. Id. at 620.
5. 44 FPC 350 (1970).
6. Scenic Hudson v. FPC, 453 F.2d 463 (2d Cir. 1971).
7. 470 U.S. 926 (1972).
8. 51 FPC 1567 (1973).
9. Hudson River Fisherman's Association and Scenic Hudson Preservation Conference v. FPC, 498 F.2d 827 (2d. Cir. 1974).
10. 33 USCA 1344 (1972).
11. Scenic Hudson v. Callaway, 499 F.2d 127 (2d Cir. 1974).
12. Scenic Hudson v. Diamond, 69 Misc. 2d, 330 N.Y.S. 2d 71 (1972).
13. In the Matter of de Rham v. Diamond, 39 A.D. 302 N.Y.S. 2d 771 (1972), *aff'd* 32 N.Y. 2d 33, 343 N.Y.S. 2d 84 (1973).
14. *New York Times*, December 20, 1980.
15. Ibid.
16. David Sive, "Some Thoughts of an Environmental Lawyer in the Wilderness of Environmental Law," *Columbia Law Review* 70 (1970): 643.
17. Christopher Stone, "Should Trees Have Standing?—Toward Legal Rights for Natural Objects," *California Law Review* 45 (1972): 450.
18. Laurence H. Tribe, "Ways Not to Think about Plastic Trees: New Foundations for Environmental Law," *Yale Law Journal* 83 (1974): 1315.
19. Joseph L. Sax, *Defending the Environment* (New York: Knopf, 1971), pp. 108–13.
20. Ibid., p. 113.
21. Sierra Club v. Morton 405 U.S. 727.
22. 412 U.S. 669 (1973).
23. 96 S. Ct. 2620 (1978).
24. 42 U.S.C. 2010 (2970).
25. 408 U.S. 1 (1972).
26. 422 U.S. 79 (1977).
27. Natural Resources Defense Council, Inc. v. United States Nuclear Regulatory Commission, 547 F.2d. 633, 644 (D.C. Cir. 1976).
28. Id. at 657.
29. 98 S. Ct. 1197 (1978).

Chapter 14 Thoughts on Results

1. 384 U.S. 436 (1966).
2. Griggs v. Duke Power Co., 401 U.S. 424 (1971).
3. Furman v. Georgia, 408 U.S. 238 (1972).
4. Roe v. Wade, 410 U.S. 113 (1973).
5. O'Connor v. Donaldson, 422 U.S. 563 (1975).
6. See e.g., Younger v. Harris, 401 U.S. 37 (1971).
7. See e.g., Rizzo v. Goode, 423 U.S. 362 (1976).
8. See e.g., Warth v. Seldin, 422 U.S. 490 (1975).

Chapter 15 Conclusion: Further Thoughts on Legitimacy

1. Walter Bagehot, *The English Constitution* (Garden City, N.Y.: Doubleday & Co., 1958), p. 174.
2. Ibid.
3. Ibid., p. 175.
4. Ibid.
5. 429 U.S. 125 (1976).
6. 402 U.S. 183 (1971).

Index

Stone, Justice Harlan Fiske, 29–32
Stone's footnote (4)
  Colegrove v. Green, 104
  Equal Rights Amendment and, 126
  judicial activism and, 29–32, 126
  judicial policy making and, 32
  representation, population and, 104
  women's rights and, 125
Storm King Mountain, 270–275, 283
Strength of society. *See* Political justice
Substantive due process, Harlan, John
  Marshall, Justice, 142–143
Substitute father regulations, Welfare
  and, 170
Suffrage, Fourteenth Amendment,
  application of, 108
Supreme Court of the United States
  economic theories, legislation and,
    29–30
  grounds of authority, 20
  political context, decisions and,
    107–108
  Reagan administration and,
    286–287
Surveillance
  challenges to, 200
  CIA and, 203
  files, destruction and, 202
  lesson from, 213–214
  litigation, consequences of, 204–205
  political, 198–200
Suspect classification
  Frontiero v. Richardson, 127–128
  gender, sports and, 135
  Kahn v. Shevin, 128–129
  women, abortion and, 149
  women's rights and, 124
Sutton, Percy, 150
*Swan v. Charlotte-Mecklenburg Board of
  Education*, 79–80
Sweatt, 66–67, 99–100
Sweatt, Marion, 65–67
Switch in time that saved nine, 29
Symmetry of the Constitution,
  argument, 112

Taney, Chief Justice Roger
  Brown II, 76
  Dred Scott v. Sandford, 28
  persons, legitimacy of, 152
  prestige and, 305

school desegregation, 45–46
Tatum, Arlo, 198–199
Tatum v. Laird, 198–199, 281
Teenage pregnancy, 159
Texas, voting discrimination, 115
Tietze, Dr. Christopher, 145–146
Timbers, Federal Judge William, 183
Title VII (Omnibus Civil Rights Act),
  93–94, 97–99
  Griggs v. Duke Power Company, 94
  Washington v. Davis, 95
Tourgée, Albion Winegar, 50–56, 58–59
Tradition, authority of, 19–20
Treatment, right to, asylums and,
  219–227
Treatment, right to refuse, 230–231,
  241–242
Tribe, Laurence, 116, 153–154, 276
Truman, Harry, 43–44, 185–186
Twentieth Century Fund, 110–111

Unanimity, importance of, *Brown*, 49
*United States Steelworkers of America v.
  Weber*, 97–98
*United States v. Carolene Products. See
  Carolene Products*
United States v. Vuitch, 147–148, 151

Vann, David, 112
Vermont Yankee, 282–283
Vinson, Chief Justice Fred, 47, 89
Voting, at large, 115–120
Voting rights
  congressional attacks, 296
  corrective justice and, 35
  gains through litigation, 287–288
  legislation and, 122
  litigation and, 114
  representative democracy and, 34
Voting Rights Act, 17–18, 114
Vuitch, Dr. Milan, 147–148

Wallace, George, 81, 239–240
War
  appropriations, congress and,
    190–191
  Berk and, 189–190
  bombing of Cambodia, 193
  Congressional responsibility and,
    194–195
  court authority and, 184–185